THE PAPERBOUND BOOK IN AMERICA

"Books, like ships,

have the toughest armor,

the largest cruising range,

and mount the

most powerful guns."

Franklin D. Roosevelt

From a letter by Franklin D. Roosevelt to W. Warder Norton, December 1, 1942. *The History of the Council on Books in War Time— 1942-1946.*

THE

PAPERBOUND

BOOK

IN AMERICA

The History of Paperbacks and Their European Background

BY FRANK L. SCHICK

R. R. Bowker Company · *New York* · *1958*

Library of Congress Card Number: 58-10097

© 1958 by R. R. Bowker Company

62 West 45th St., New York 36, N. Y.

Price $7.50

Printed and Bound in the
United States of America

To Renée, Tommy and Jamie

PREFACE

It is the purpose of this book to describe the development of American paperbacks as they are found today displayed across the North American Continent in over 100,000 outlets -- drug, department and chain stores, supermarkets and news-stands, as well as in traditional bookstores. Never before in the history of the printed book have so many readers simul-taneously been offered such a variety of books at such a low price. This inundation of paper pulp permits one for the first time to speak of the influence of books in terms of mass exposure.

The average mass-market paperback edition today numbers 200,000 copies. Many favorite titles have been reissued time and again and their sales have reached millions of copies. It has been said for centuries that some books have exerted a great influence upon the thoughts of individuals or certain segments of the population or even resulted in repercussions throughout an entire country, continent or civilization. The influence of these books on the masses has always been indirect, comparable to Andrew Mellon's economic concept of the sieve theory: a limited intellectual elite read, talked and wrote about these books, and their content, modified and popularized, came down to the people via the pulpit, the lectern, the proverbial cracker barrel and later the newspaper, radio and television. The intermediary agents were necessary because of economic barriers and a scarcity of books, leisure time, reading ability and economic resources. The inexpensive paperback appeals directly to the consumer with its prominent covers and promising titles, which may mislead as well as entice. The paperback available at a low price stimulates a quick purchase, and the prospective reader will rarely consult a review or speak with a friend to determine the wisdom of his investment. Literary fare which sells in such quantities is bound to affect the tastes and thoughts of the public. Sales figures, in turn, have a decided effect on publishers. If a title sells well, the publisher will provide more of the same for his customers.

No attempt has been made to present a literary evaluation of popular writing in America, a subject which has been exhaustively treated by Frank L. Mott in 'Golden Multitudes' and James D. Hart in 'The Popular Book.'

The literature on the subject of paperback publishing indicates generally that this development in the publishing trade came upon us rather suddenly, with its roots going back to the nineteenth century. An examination of early types of American printing like almanacs, tracts, sermons and chapbooks reveals that inexpensive paperbound original and reprint publications existed since the beginning of printing in the American colonies. Production techniques changed and the contents of the books were adapted to the times, but the basic format remained surprisingly similar. Methods of distribution and display are new but paperbound books were already sold in the seventeenth century side by side with drugs and sundries. In order to follow the historical development, a great deal of the available literature was read and specimens of all types of paperbound publications were examined, especially the holdings of The University of Michigan, Columbia University and the New York Public Library. The literature bearing directly on the subject is comparatively scant because writers treat the history of books usually from two points of view: the historian of literature is concerned with the content between the covers of books and pays scant attention to their appearance; the historian of the book arts focuses his investigations on the book as a work of artistic merit and is inclined to disregard the cheap, unattractive, inexpensive volumes. Usually librarians and collectors did not find them worthy of their attention and, as they were published to be read rather than reserved, many of them were consumed in the process, which makes them comparatively rare.

The first part covers the history of paperbacks from 1639 to 1939 in survey form and serves as a general introduction to the current phase, which is presented in the second and third parts. The histories of the individual firms are arranged by chapters according to the specialization of their activities as they relate to paperback production and, within each chapter, chronologically according to the dates of the release of the first paperbacks of significance to the contemporary development. This order demonstrates the evolutionary unfolding of a format and the spreading of an idea, rather than the story of a "revolution." This method of presentation has been freely adapted from Robert Proctor's technique (also known as "Proctor's order") as applied to bibliography in his 'Index to Early Printed Books' and 'Catalogue of Fifteenth Century Printed Books.'

The basic information was gathered in a series of interviews and correspondence with the presidents, executive directors and editors-in-chief of the various firms, as well as with some sales managers and distributing agents. The initial interviews were arranged by Dan Lacy, managing director, and Peter S. Jennison, assistant managing director, of the American Book Publishers Council. Without their cooperation, this book would not have been possible. A mail survey conducted with the assistance of Anne J. Richter, Book Editor of the R. R. Bowker Co., in the fall of 1957 brought the information up-to-date.

My sincere appreciation goes to all the men and women of the publishing firms who gave unstintingly of their time to assist in this project. I would particularly like to thank Frederic G. and Daniel Melcher, Chandler B. Grannis, Anne J. Richter and Arthur Hale from the Bowker Company and Professor Ray L. Trautman of the School of Library Service, Columbia University, who generously shared their intimate knowledge of events and personalities in the book industry with me. Freeman Lewis, of Pocket Books, Inc., and William F. Callahan, Jr., of the Dell Publishing Company, were very helpful with their suggestions and read the manuscript. Lewis M. Stark and his assistant, Philomena C. Houlihan, of the Reserve Division of the New York Public Library, made the rich resources at their disposal freely available. The documentation throughout is the acknowledgement of a debt to all those mentioned.

In their present form, the following pages are a considerable expansion and complete revision of the original manuscript which was submitted as a doctoral dissertation to the Department of Library Science of the University of Michigan. The committee consisting of Professors Rudolph H. Gjelsness, Russell E. Bidlack, Robert F. Haugh and Raymond L. Kilgour were generous in providing help and advice. Without the encouragement and assistance of my wife this book on books could not have been completed.

Frank L. Schick

Washington, D. C.

TABLE OF CONTENTS

PART II

AMERICAN PAPERBACKS: THE CURRENT PHASE, 1939-1957

PART III

PUBLISHERS OF PAPERBACKS

LIST OF ILLUSTRATIONS

Appearing between pp. 78-79 and 94-95

xv

Publisher's Note.

In order to differentiate between names of
series and titles of books, a somewhat
unorthodox style has been followed in the
text and footnotes -- putting series names
in double quotes and titles in single quotes.

INTRODUCTION

The story of books has been written a thousand times, yet the approach to the subject in this book is new. Ever since books began, printers, booksellers, publishers have made recurrent efforts to bring book ownership to a greater number of people by means of lower prices, improved production or better publishing methods, and these determined efforts have reached a new climax in the programs of the last twenty years which we have come to call, for the lack of a newer term, "the paperbacks."

A fresh direction has been given to the uses and usefulness of books which has inspired vigorous publishing efforts, opened up vast new avenues of distribution, given new breadth to teaching and extended the possibilities of international exchange of ideas through books.

The invention of printing gave the opportunity to multiply books, paper supplied an easily-used material, and the small-sized editions of an Aldus or an Elzevir could be marketed popularly. The gradual lifting of limitations on printing over the years promoted wider markets, an iron press made for more rapid production, case binding brought the central planning in a publisher's hands; then came wood for paper, mechanized type setting and speedy binding machines.

The potential for mass production of handy-sized books was finally matched with the new machinery for merchandise distribution which had been developed for other products, the chain store, the newsstand and outlets in transportation terminals. The books produced for these outlets were bound in paper because its use squeezed out a further paring of costs, and thus has brought into being a new area of book publishing. As yet the extent of its effect on writing, publishing and especially on popular education cannot be fully estimated.

Dr. Schick knew the paperbacks of Europe in his early days and the American Armed Services Editions as a GI. After V-E day his experiences with books resulted in his becoming a Division Librarian. His continuing interest in paperbound books led to the choice of this subject for a doctoral dissertation at the University of Michigan's Department of Library Science.

This material, now completely revised, rearranged and brought up-to-date by additional research, has provided this important study, showing where the movement stands today, and giving an historical background which traces the continuous development of the paperbound book from the beginning of printing in America to the present.

Frederic G. Melcher

Part 1

THE HISTORY

OF PAPERBACKS

IN EUROPE

AND AMERICA

CHAPTER 1

THE EMERGENCE OF THE INEXPENSIVE BOOK
IN GREAT BRITAIN

Early Reprints

The history of paperbacks is closely related to the development of the inexpensive book and the cheap reprint in particular. Paperbacks, as we know them today, are primarily a twentieth-century phenomenon. Their special type of binding became possible only after certain technical discoveries had been made and commercially exploited. Their number and variety could not exist without modern methods of mass distribution.

The purpose of all book production, whether written by hand or produced by some mechanical process ranging from inscriptions on the walls of caves to the newest photomechanical methods, has always been to record thought. The problem of generations was to produce writing in quantity. Ancient Rome handled it by mass production of copies based on the economy of cheap slave labor. During the Middle Ages, multiplication of manuscripts was either accomplished in monasteries, where fewer economic problems existed, or by individual scribes, a more costly procedure. The patient work of the artisan entrepreneurs and the monks is responsible for the beauty of medieval manuscripts, as well as for the frequent misreadings and progressive corruption of texts by compounding old mistakes with new ones.

After the invention of printing with movable type, book production followed two patterns: original printing from manuscripts and printing of new editions, either identical in text or revised, abbreviated, or changed in some other way. Reprints and new editions have always served the purpose of filling an existing or estimated demand for a book and, by supplying the same text at a lower price in a less expensive binding, to open up new avenues of sale. The development of reprint publications is so diffused and interwoven with regular book production that it cannot easily be divorced from it. Reprints have always been the backbone of inexpensive paperback editions, and even today the original paperback is rather the exception than the rule.

One of the first printers to supply good, inexpensive materials was Aldus Manutius, who established a printing office in Venice in 1490. He was a scholar and his ambition was to make the ancient classics available to the learned men of his day in correct versions and legible type. He did not publish for the wealthy collector but rather for the scholar who traveled from university to university and who could not afford to buy books unless they were cheap. In order to produce handy volumes which would be convenient for packing into the traveling scholar's saddlebag, he reduced the size of the large tomes characteristic of the incunabula period. He devised a sturdy, unadorned cover, designed smaller faces in Greek and Roman type, and later also introduced the italic. He was the first to replace wooden book coverboards with cardboard.

Other outstanding printers between the fifteenth and seventeenth centuries who brought inexpensive and textually accurate books into the hands of the public were William Caxton, Gryphius of Lyons, Simon de Colines, the Estienne family, whose members worked in Paris and Geneva, and the Plantin-Moretus family, which settled in Antwerp. In the seventeenth century, the House of Elzevir continued the tradition of providing accurate texts for the scholars and the reading public at low cost.

The Development of Book Binding in Great Britain

The development of binding practices in Great Britain is being considered because British influence in America in most cultural and technological advances, and particularly in the manufacture of books, has been continuous from colonial days to the present time.

During the first century of English printing the artisan printer was the central figure in the chain of events which led from the manuscript to the completed and bound book. Unless a book was bound to order according to a customer's specifications, the printer decided what kind of binding to use, often varying it according to the type of book (for instance, prayer-books for ladies of the Court were frequently bound in velvet or silk). The most commonly used material for cheaper bindings was parchment, consisting of sheepskin specially dressed with alum[2] Vellum, a special type of parchment made of calfskin, was also well liked but more expensive. Around the middle of the sixteenth century, morocco, processed from goatskin, became a favorite covering material. Since this leather had to be imported it was used only for more expensive bindings. At that time sheepskin came into use for cheaper bindings and replaced the more expensive calfskin by the eighteenth century. Generally speaking, leather of some kind or other was the accepted covering material for full and half bindings from the fifteenth to the eighteenth century, with wooden boards being used as a base at first and replaced by paste and mill boards between the sixteenth and seventeenth centuries. The close association between printing and binding can be seen by the composition of early boards consisting of spoiled sheets of print glued together.

At the beginning of the seventeenth century, the publisher or bookseller started to displace the printer "as the dominant partner in the business of making and selling books."[3] This shift in the manufacture of books had a lasting effect on bindings. The displacement of the printer is characteristic of the growing importance of the salesman over the artisan; he employed the printer and sometimes, for volumes which he was to exhibit in his own bookshop, also the binder. As Steinberg [4] points out, the imprint indicates the divergence of printer, publisher and bookseller, as it appears until the end of the seventeenth century in a combination of the printer and bookseller, such as: Printed by . . . for . . . and are to be sold . . . Using again the imprint as the logical explanation for the ascendency of the publisher he points to examples which indicate that bookshops were frequently owned by publishers and that when one name was omitted it was usually that of the printer. Until 1770, the publisher issued most of his books

> either in loose quires, or stitched, or at most in a plain paper wrapper, which ordinarily was a mere sheet-covering, making no pretension to 'sit the book's figure,' but being a reach-me-down of the most casual kind[5]

The printed sheets were intended to be bound, which, in the eighteenth century, meant "bound in leather."

The evolution of binding styles other than leather took place between 1750 and 1820. The rough brown paper wrappers of the beginning of the century were provided with printed labels which have been traced to 1765. By 1802 they were so popular that books issued unlabelled had become the exceptions. Labels gave a certain degree of permanence to wrappered bindings as they permitted identification of the shelved book. They provided increasingly more information, and titles were often printed directly on the wrappers or the paper covering the boards of heavier books. Stiffened wrappers were used with increasing frequency and after 1802 unstiffened wrappers were found only occasionally.[6] The transition from paper wrappers to books bound in boards presents a gradual change in the publishers' attempt to make the temporary binding more permanent. Publishing had become a separate profession, frequently divorced from bookselling; the sale of books in sheetform to booksellers for retail distribution was falling into disuse; wholesale sheet buyers and book distributors appeared as middlemen and had the sheets bound or boarded.

These developments suggested edition binding to the publishers. The search for cheap and durable covers culminated in the use of cloth bindings, which were first tried between 1821 and 1825 and had found general acceptance and widespread use by 1840. Around 1830, the casing-in method was used successfully and rapidly spread to all commercial binderies. Shortly afterwards, goldblocking on cloth and printing from type with colored inks on cloths became generally accepted techniques.

The Unbound or Paperbound Book to 1840

How far the unbound or paperbound book goes back in history is hard to tell, since, as far as could be ascertained, few previous studies have been made on this topic. Some individual specimens were uncovered in various libraries and have been described in the trade literature. Since this question deals with "ephemera," to which little attention has been paid, comparatively few items remain. The available evidence concerning printed wrappers (which form only a part of the wider classification, including unprinted wrappers) was discussed by William A. Jackson, who provides the following definitions:

> In the earlier and truer form the wrapper is an entity by itself, printed at a different time and even on a different press or by another shop or process, and is unconnected physically with the book or pamphlet which it encloses except by the stitching or glue with which it is attached. It is usually printed on paper, but paper generally of a thicker sort than the book to be enclosed, and occasionally on paper pasted down on some stiffening material, either a heavier paper or pasteboard.[7]

This type of wrapper may be called the unintegrated type and corresponds to the one in common use today. The other, integrated type of wrapper is "printed on the recto of the first leaf of the first quire and on the verso of the last leaf of the last quire, with the other sides either blank or containing no material which is continuous with matter which is an integral part of the book . . ."[8] Both of these types of wrappers go back to the fifteenth century and establish therefore evidence for "incunabula paperbacks."

The earliest known copy of the unintegrated wrapper is 'Von Ordnung der Gesundheit' by Hans Schönsperger produced in 1482, which shows a woodcut imitation of a blind-tooled leather binding of the time, a curious parallel to the first movable types which imitated the manuscript writing of the period.[9] (Plate 1) Jackson cites several other known copies from the incunabula period, as well as several from the sixteenth century. If the few specimens which were found can be used as guide to total production, there seems to be a decline of this type of wrapper in the seventeenth, followed by a marked increase in the eighteenth century. These wrappers cover an amazing variety of subjects and an early eighteenth century American production even serves as an example of an attempt at sensational advertising; the wrapper title, 'The Trial and Execution of the Bloody Brother', is different from the title on the title page which reads: 'Some Account of the Trial of Samuel Goodere, Esq.', Boston, (Kneeland and Green), 1741.

Integrated wrappers also originated in the incunabula period, the earliest ones being traced to 1493 and 1494; these are Italian and precede the Aldine 'Catullus' of 1502, which is an exact prototype, though not a very interesting one, of the integrated wrapper . . . In it there is printed on the first and last pages the three names 'CATVL- LVS./TIBVLLVS./PROPERTIVS./' It is not quite clear what was Aldus's purpose in printing what is in effect a half-title at both the beginning and end of his book.[10]

Known English integrated wrappers go back to the late sixteenth century and were far more popular during the seventeenth century, possibly for reasons of economy and simpler handling in production, the earliest copy known to Jackson is Francis Seager's 'The Schoole of Vertue,' R. Jones, 1953. "Printed wrappers on reinforced or thicker paper and the newly popular 'wrap-arounds' evidently superseded integrated wrappers during the eighteenth century . . ."[11]

Type of Publications Appearing in Paperbound Form

During the sixteenth and seventeenth centuries, the time of the Reformation, the Civil War and the Restoration, the expression of opinions frowned upon by Church or State was carried out by illegal printers and distributed by enthusiastic reformers willing to run the risk of disseminating them among the people. The publication of tracts became an outlet for repressed feelings and during the Civil War reached an unparalleled peak. The incomplete Thomason collection of these tracts in the British Museum Library is only a pale reflection of the profusion of this type of literature. The most famous tract was, and still is today, Milton's Areopagitica, which he called "a Speech for the Liberty of Unlicensed Printing." He published it in 1644 under his own name, but without that of the printer or bookseller. This extralegal publishing had to adopt the cheapest way of binding and printing. They were small (approximately 5½" x 7"), unbound paper pamphlets without covers and with a printed title page which had a simple ornamental border.

Other cheap publications which appeared in England during the sixteenth century and continued to the beginning of the nineteenth century were chapbooks. They were small pamphlets of popular, sensational, juvenile, moral or educational character, originally distributed by chapmen or hawkers, not by booksellers. The earliest ones were printed in black

letter and illustrated with woodcuts. Some were finely printed.
The popular ones sold for a penny and did not appear much
before 1700. [12]

Chapbooks consisted usually of a sheet of paper folded in
octavo, making a pamphlet of 24 pages. Many of the chapbooks
were meant for children and enjoyed great popularity among
the younger generation. They contained legends, jests, ballads
and songs; for the adults there were religious, supernatural,
romantic, biographical and criminal stories. They were primarily meant for the poorer classes of the population and
rapidly declined after 1800, when they were replaced by other
forms of popular literature, namely, part-issues and periodicals
which included serialized novels.

The practice of reprinting fiction in serial form in periodicals dates from the beginning of the eighteenth century. The
tax law of 1712 provided for taxation of periodical publications
of one or two folio leaves, but made no provisions for a tax on
publications of three folio leaves. [13] In order to evade the tax
and fill the superfluous space, the reprinting of fiction was
found to be a good solution. Daniel Defoe's 'Robinson Crusoe'
appeared in 1719 and 1720 in 'The Original London Post,' making it the first novel ever to be serialized.

Issuing or reprinting whole books in several parts became
popular in the eighteenth century, though the first publication
which could be called a part-issue really appeared much earlier;
'Poor Robin's Intelligence' came out in a series of unnumbered
folio leaves, appearing weekly from March, 1676, to November,
1677, and was followed by several more 'Poor Robin' series.

During the nineteenth century a very large amount of
literature was issued in parts, ranging from poetry to household management, and from excellent fiction to the innumerable
cheap adventure stories (or "bloods") which are comparable to
today's "crime comics." The most important part-issues were
best-selling novels, beginning with "The Posthumous Papers of
the Pickwick Club," which made its unknown author famous,
and including many Victorian writers besides Dickens -- Thackeray, Ainsworth, Lever and Surtees. At a shilling a copy, they
truly reached a mass audience and competed heavily with the
circulating libraries and the magazines.

The part-issues came out in monthly, fortnightly or weekly
installments; the last part contained the title page and pre-

liminary material and the complete novel could be bound either in cases supplied by the publisher or according to the customer's taste. The wrappers of the part-issues were usually of colored paper, often the choice of color being an identification for the author.

Around the middle of the century the magazines began to feel threatened by the part-issues and reduced their price to a shilling. As they offered more than just a part of a novel, they enjoyed great popularity and by 1880 the part-issue boom had died down. These publications were replaced by reprint series, with serialization of novels being strictly limited to magazines and newspapers.

Inexpensive Books: 1840--1935

From about 1840 on, the complete mechanization of the binding trade progressed rapidly, making it possible to produce more inexpensive books and reprints. John Bell was one of the earliest publishers to bring out cheap reprints in uniform editions at a uniform price. His successful series of true literary merit, which he called "British Poets," appeared in over 100 volumes between 1777 and 1782. Others who attempted to emulate his example did not succeed until the invention of wood pulp permitted the production of books at a lower price than ever before. Cheap "libraries," usually bound in paper board, were stimulated by the development of railroad travel and the leisure time which this type of transportation enforced on travelers. The books were uniformly bound and priced, and hundreds of titles came out in rapid succession. Archibald Constable saw the unlimited possibilities of this new format and spoke of "literature for the millions." [14] His vision paid off handsomely when he issued his 'Miscellany' between 1827 and 1835. Other publishers were attracted by these new possibilities. John Murray released his "Family Library," between 1829 and 1834, Colburn and Bentley their "Novels," from 1831 to 1854. These series were primarily educational, but other publishers felt that they could compete better if they were to stress the recreational aspects. The first series of this type was Simms and McIntyre's "Parlour Library" which issued some 300 titles between 1847 and 1863. [15] Competition and the number of titles reprinted increased rapidly. George Routledge made a bid for the travellers' attention with the

1300 volumes of his "Railway Library" between 1848 and 1898. Both series sold at one shilling a copy and were displayed in railroad bookstalls. Competitive series like the "Travellers' Library," "Run and Read Library," and many others appeared in rapid succession. Publishers changed names of series, opened new and closed out old ones with the greatest of ease, giving the whole operation a casual and impermanent character. Most of these books were "novels of varying merit and they ranged downwards in price from 1s 6d to 6d. They had little elegance of format, and many of them dealt only in the more expendable kind of fiction." [16] The profusion of titles and the large editions forced a reduction in price of regular trade publications, particularly of popular novels.

The series most comparable to today's American paperbacks were the yellowbacks -- cheap editions, usually but not always reprints of popular novels, bound in strawboard covered with glazed paper, usually but not always of yellow color. The idea to publish books of "boarded fiction, covered with glazed colored paper, bearing on their front an illustration relevant to the contents, and with picture, incidental ornament, titling and advertisement material produced by more than one printing" [17] have been traced by Sadleir in two instances to the 1840's and referred to as "prophetic yellowbacks." After this beginning, cheap editions developed in the "Parlour Library," an adaptation of an earlier series of monthly volumes called "The Parlour Novelist" which was a paper wrappered publication. Both series were published by Simms & McIntyre. The "Parlour Library" was an immediate success because never before had the public been offered novels so cheap, yet so handy. Imitators followed and the style format of the typical yellowback was evolved and reached its golden age between 1855 and 1870. From 1853 on, the standard yellowback size was 6 5/8" x 4 1/8" or thereabouts. How popular these books were is illustrated by the fact that Routledge published 'The Life and Enterprises of R. W. Elliston' in 1857 bound in yellow cloth, imitating the yellowback look to the last detail, but priced several times as high. The cycle seems closed when the expensive book imitates the cheap one in content and appearance.

By 1870, the yellowbacks had deteriorated as a true type; more sensational and sporting novels invaded the field, followed by thrillers and detective stories. Cover engravings disappeared and some series were cloth covered. By 1880, they had been replaced by the clothbound reprint series.

Among the outstanding accomplishments of the 1880's should be mentioned Routledge's "National Library" which started in 1886 and appeared in a three-pence paperbound and six-pence clothbound edition. This series was well received and the average sale of each title was around 30,000 copies. It can be looked upon as a transition to the many clothbound series specializing in classical literature of the English language and translation of other works of western civilization. The great impetus for these series was the adoption of the British Copyright Act of 1842, which stipulated that copyright expires seven years after the author's death or forty-two years after the original publication date. Among these series are Nelson's "New Century Library," which was later called Nelson's "Classics," Collins's "Pocket Classics," and Dent's "Everyman's Library." Their success was immediate and has been lasting. By the middle of 1955 Nelson had passed 50 million copies, Collins had sold over 25 million copies of about 300 titles and Dent, with almost 1000 volumes of "Everyman's Library," had reached a total sale of nearly 41 million. [18]

During the first quarter of the twentieth century in England there were a number of cheap editions on the market which were not distributed by the regular bookstores.

Woolworth alone sold many millions of copies of the Readers Library, and such publishers as Collins, Hodder & Stoughton and Hutchinson had innumerable series of books, some paperbound in magazine style, others in mutation cloth boards, which sold from sixpence upward to two shillings, but in the main these books were devoted to crime, light romance, books based on successful films and books on the Wild West; without exception they had pictorial covers. [19]

Sir Allen Lane, publisher of Penguin Books, tried for a more sophisticated type of publication than the series mentioned above. Immediately preceding him, between 1925 and 1935, several unsuccessful attempts at starting paper editions of good literature had been made.

Benn's . . . 9d series of short original novels had failed owing to the lack of sufficiently good material,

and Gollancz's Mundan's series priced at 3s had
some extremely good titles, but never seemed to get
off to a good start, . . . probably on account of their
price. [20]

With the publication of Penguin Books in 1935, a new
trend in paperback publishing had begun in Great Britain,
followed a few years later, in 1939, by the appearance of
American Pocket Books, setting off the present wave of paperbacks which are the main concern of this study.

Penguin Books

Sir Allen Lane, publisher of Penguin Books, entered the
publishing field at the age of sixteen, when he began to work for
his uncle, John Lane of the Bodley Head. He formed his own
opinions about what kind of books people want to read and why
they do or do not buy them. He found to his surprise that many
of his friends had not read books which he himself considered
excellent reading and he analyzed the lack of interest as being
due to two causes: for one thing, many books were priced too
high for the prospective buyer, and secondly, many bookstores
were so drab and forbidding that people who were not book
collectors or not too familiar with books shied away from entering them. He reasoned that if book buying were made as casual
as the purchase of a package of cigarettes, and if the price
were low, books could be put within easy reach of almost
anyone. The big problem was what kind of book would be the
most suitable for such a project.

When he visited the United States in 1930, Sir Allen, then
twenty-eight years old, purchased with his limited resources
the rights to the 'Peter Arno Parade.' As the Bodley Head did
not care to publish it, he decided to bring it out himself under
the Bodley Head imprint, using their distribution system but
assuming all risks and paying a percentage fee for the services rendered. He also published another American book under
the same conditions and it sold sufficiently well to encourage
him to go ahead. His idea was

first to select books that were both first-rate entertainment and also really good quality, to build up a

really representative list of good modern literature; secondly to keep the standard consistently high, so that the Penguin should, in time, stand as a hall-mark of excellence. [21]

To bring down the price in order to compete with the trashy "bloods" he decided on paperbacks in attractive makeup. To widen the market he looked for other than the regular trade outlets. He chose reprints as well as originals to offer his readers, and after he had become convinced that such a formula would be successful, Penguin Books, London, was born on July 30, 1935. Ten titles were selected, a dummy book made up, and Allen Lane traveled across Great Britain to sell his idea. These titles were:

André Maurois, 'Ariel'
Ernest Hemingway, 'A Farewell to Arms'
Eric Linklater, 'Poet's Pub'
Susan Ertz, 'Madame Claire'
Dorothy L. Sayers, 'The Unpleasantness at the Bellona Club'
Beverley Nichols, 'Twenty-five'
E. H. Young, 'William'
Mary Webb, 'Gone to Earth'
Compton Mackenzie, 'Carnival' [22]

The booksellers were not at all enthusiastic and the trade predicted a great failure. While the presses were printing the first editions of 20,000 copies, with the break-even point calculated at 17,500, Lane approached Woolworth's. The bookstores had liked the Penguin list but not the format and price. Woolworth's liked the format and price but not the titles. Just before turning down the offer, the bookbuyer for Woolworth's had a visit from his wife and on the spur of the moment consulted with her on the titles; this changed his mind and he placed an order which resulted in successful sales. Penguin Books were here to stay; they sold well and in October, 1935, the second group of ten titles came off the press, still from the Bodley Head, but independent of the publishing house. On January 1, 1936, a new firm was established: Penguin Books, Ltd., with a capital of one hundred pounds sterling, the three Lane brothers, Allen, Richard and John, as directors and with their own distributing system. In 1937, the Bodley Head went into voluntary liquidation, and Penguin moved to new quarters at Harmondsworth, Middlesex, with a list of over 100 titles.

Devoted at first to the reprinting of fiction, Penguin Books began in 1937 to experiment with the possibility of offering their readers serious nonfiction titles. Two new series were begun: (1) The "Pelicans", featuring at first reprints and later original publications of an educational nature covering subjects like archaeology, philosophy, architecture, psychology and science, and (2) "Penguin Specials" which were stressing new titles on political and contemporary topics, reflecting the growing tension of the impending war. Authors included names such as H. G. Wells, Sir Norman Angell, Wickham Steed, Hugh Dalton, Lord Wavell and Harold Laski.

> Among the more spectacular achievements of the firm during recent years has been the publication of the Penguin Millions, that is the simultaneous issue, on one day, of a million books by a single author . . .

> The first of the Penguin Millions was a set of Bernard Shaw's plays, produced in honour of his ninetieth birthday in 1946. There was another million of Wells's novels which, intended for his eightieth birthday which he did not live to see, served as a memorial at his death. Other authors whose works were produced a million at a time were Agatha Christie and Evelyn Waugh, and Penguin Books observed the twenty-first anniversary of D. H. Lawrence's death by the simultaneous publication of ten volumes of his works.[23]

In 1939, the "King Penguins" were started. This series of about seventy-five titles deals with various aspects of the arts. The books are beautifully illustrated, bound in decorated boards, and range in subject from 'Bayeux Tapestry' to 'Woodcuts of Albrecht Dürer "Modern Painters" is an art series, each volume containing sixteen colored and sixteen black and white illustrations and an essay by a prominent critic on the works of each artist. The thought behind this series was to rival the famous German "Insel Bücher" which they vaguely resemble. The art lover may also choose from eleven Penguin Prints, ranging from Turner to Picasso.

"Penguin Classics," started in 1946, presents good new English translations of outstanding literary works; these include titles by Aesop, Homer, and Tacitus, Chaucer, Dante, and Cervantes, Voltaire and Rousseau, Ibsen, Tolstoy, and Zola, as well as other famous authors of all times and countries.

In 1956, after twenty-one years of publication, the complete catalog of Penguin Books contained nearly 2400 titles of which over one thousand were kept in print. Over the last few years an average of 250 titles appeared annually. As of 1957 about 1200 titles of the total production were "Penguins," almost 400 "Pelicans," 170 "Penguin Specials," and there were about eighty "King Penguins," sixty-five "Penguin Classics," forty "Penguin Poets," thirty "Penguin Shakespeares," thirty "Penguin Music Scores," and twenty "Penguin Modern Painters." On the practical side, the "Penguin Handbooks" present about thirty titles ranging from 'Beekeeping' and 'Tree Fruit Growing' to 'The Intelligent Parent's Manual.' "Penguin Reference Books" include foreign language dictionaries and special dictionaries of biology, music, psychology, etc. "The Things We See" series consists of titles like 'Houses,' 'Gardens,' 'Pottery and Glass,', and there are "Penguin Guides," "The Buildings of England," and "Music Scores."

Almost 250 titles for children appear in various series, like "Baby Puffin Books," "Puffin Story Books," the "Puffin Picture Books," the "Puffin Cut-Out Books" and, for the very young, the "Porpoise Books." There are also five books on puzzles and quizzes.

The most ambitious publication is the 'Pelican History of Art,' which, when completed, will consist of forty-eight cloth bound volumes. The six volumes published so far are richly illustrated and cost $8.50 per volume. In commemoration of Penguin's twenty-first anniversary 'The Penguin Atlas of the World' was released. It had been in preparation for many years and is an outstanding publication in production and design at the price of $2.50 a copy.

Penguin also publishes a number of periodicals on various topics, all of which have the appearance of paperbacks rather than magazines, but are published as continuations, usually bimonthly or quarterly. Several, like 'Penguin New Writing,' 'Penguin Russian,' 'Penguin Parade,' have been discontinued. 'New Biology,' started in July, 1945, and 'Penguin Science News,' begun in June, 1946, are still appearing.

Penguin's relationship with hardcover publishers is unique. In 1948, the firm concluded an arrangement with a group of publishers granting Penguin first option on reprint rights, and Penguin has sold reprint rights of its paperback originals repeatedly to regular trade houses. Since 1951, Sir Allen has written,

> we have produced cloth bound editions of some of our original titles which hitherto had appeared only in our normal paper covers. We knew that because there was no other edition available libraries were binding our ordinary standard productions so that they would stand up to a longer life on the shelves, but owing to the fact that our normal paper is not a very strong one it was only a compromise and for that reason, during the last few years we have been in the habit of printing 1,000 or perhaps 2,000 copies of our original run of 50,000 on a better paper and binding these in a cloth case. It is an extremely small portion in relation to our total production and I don't think that it is likely to increase to any considerable size. We have found from experience that it is very much better to publish the cloth and paper edition simultaneously as then the would-be purchaser has the choice before him, whereas if the cloth edition comes out later he has often already purchased the paperbound edition and doesn't like the thought of having to duplicate his purchase. [24]

This simultaneous publishing plan is a recent and special development and, according to Sir Allen, is not comparable to Ballantine's simultaneous releases.

Penguins are usually printed in editions of 50,000 to 65,000 copies and reprints made for as few as 30,000. The format has remained unchanged over the years at 7 1/8" x 4 3/8". The sedate Penguin covers contrast distinctly with most American varieties. (Plate 2.) Gilbert Highet's remark about their make-up is carried prominently on Penguin promotion materials and reads as follows: "Not one of the Penguin books has a cover which emphasizes the fact that human beings are mammals. On the contrary, they treat us as intellectuals." Until 1950 Penguins avoided, with very few exceptions, any kind of pictorial cover. The covers depended entirely on typographical patterns, lettering and color for their appeal, orange being used for fiction, green for detective stories, dark blue for biographies, red for plays, light blue for "Pelicans," etc.

Panels were laid out horizontally but more recently have been changed to stress vertical lines which permit the use of simple line drawings. Descriptive sentences have also been occasionally added and some covers have become fairly elaborate though they are still executed with the typically sedate and tasteful "Penguin look" which is quite different from some of the luridness of American inexpensive series and the modern design of the higher priced ones. Penguins are still sewn and not "perfect bound". The quality of the covering paper has been improved over the years and great attention been paid to type design and layout. Sixty-five books with the Penguin imprint have been chosen for awards for the best designed British books by the National Book League.

Penguin promotion relies on circulars, lists, showcards and other display material which is provided in generous quantities to stores handling their books. Advertising in newspapers or periodicals is rarely used because the expense for 250 titles a year would be prohibitive. Exhibits, both in the British Isles and abroad, have also proven very successful and the books are reviewed in the press and over the radio. Over 5 million copies of Penguin Books were sold in the British Isles in 1956 and approximately the same number abroad. (In 1947 2.09 million books were sold abroad, in 1950 2.56 and in 1953 3.67).

Penguin has subsidiary companies in the U.S.A. (since 1950), Australia (since 1947) and Canada. There are Penguin agencies in several European and South American countries and the books are sold in almost all countries around the world. [25]

The phenomenal success of Penguin's truly globe-circling activities, setting the pace for the entire American paperback industry, makes one search for its secret. A partial answer may be found in Sir Allen's personality, intuition, subtle sense of humor and family tradition. When asked about the choice of books for publication he admitted that it started with personal preference, later reinforced by his editorial board. In finding people with special knowledge whose tastes ran along his own general lines, he was especially successful. The first editor of the "Pelican" series was Krishna Menon, later Indian Ambassador to the United Nations. Kurt Enoch and Victor Weybright, who are presently heading the New American Library, worked for Sir Allen and Ian Ballantine, president of Ballantine Books, was his first American branch manager. Among others are Nikolaus Pevsner, art editor of Penguin Books, former Slade Professor of Fine Art at Cambridge, Sir Kenneth Clark, editor of "Modern Painters," former Slade Professor at Oxford and E.V. Rieu, editor of "Penguin Classics," who received an Honorary Litt. D. for his Penguin translation of 'The Odyssey.' In his venture Sir Allen is carrying on the family tradition of publishing--one of his uncles, John Lane, was a publisher of yellowbacks, the nineteenth-century forerunners of the Penguins.

Post-War British Paperbacks

In the fall of 1957, over thirty British publishers were engaged in bringing out paperbacks. In a survey completed during this year the majority indicated that they had entered the paperback market since January 1946.[26] The increasing competition among publishers and the many choices offered to the public has resulted in a decrease in the size of first printings. The prices of all series is uniformly 2s, 2s6d and occasionally 3s6d. Discounts are generally 33 1/3 percent.

Most British paperbacks are quite different from Penguin Books and resemble more closely the American mass market lines. They are usually reprints while three out of five Penguins are originals and they all carry picture covers, somewhat more sedate but usually less well designed than their American counterparts.

During 1956 the average monthly title production came to about ten and the following series released eight or more titles: "Digit Books," "Panther Books," "Penguin Books," "Pan Books," "Corgi Books," "Ward Locke Paper Novels," "Fontana Books," "Hodder Pocket Books." Some of the series, as in the United States, are released by regular trade publishers like Collins, Fontana Books, Hodder & Stoughton, Macmillan's (St. Martin's Library"). These are, however, also frequently distributed through general paperback channels, as the distribution system is not as sharply defined as in the United States. The largest selling lines are Penguin, Pan, Fontana, Corgi and Hodder, with Penguin being the strongest British export series. "Corgi Books," a wholly-owned subsidiary of Bantam Books, carries on an independent publishing policy adapted to the British market. The "Seraph Books" of the Society for the Promotion of Christian Knowledge specialize in religious titles. Western series like "Ten Gallon Westerns," released by Foulsham and "Sombrero Westerns" (Frederick Muller) are popular. "Four Square Books," issued by Landsborough Publications Ltd., are backed by the Four Square Tobacco Company. The author lists contain many American names like Rex Stout, James T. Adams, Leslie Charteris, William MacLeod Raine, Irwin Shaw, Luke Short, Zane Grey.

About two thirds of all titles are entertainment literature of the lightest variety; the remainder are contributions of varying seriousness and literary merit; about half of these are supplied by Penguin, the others by five to six other firms, among them prominently "Signet" and "Mentor Books,." This series, distributed through Frederick Muller, originates in America with the New American Library which emerged from the first American Penguin branch, thus closing the circle of Anglo-American paperbound publishing relations.

A closer examination of recent British titles leads to the conclusion that on both sides of the Atlantic we are rapidly moving towards some midway meeting ground whereby we are adjusting to their somewhat higher, and they to our lower, reading standards. It may be hoped that we will jointly make strides to present more of the best by providing in each country more opportunity for promising writers in hardbound publishing after which their books could be more cheaply and intensively made available.

[1] Wilhelm H. Lange, 'Das Buch im Wandel der Zeiten' (Wiesbaden: F. Steiner, 1951), p. 149.

[2] Marjorie Plant, 'The English Book Trade. An Economic History of the Making and Sale of Books' (London: G. Allen & Unwin Ltd., 1939), p. 208.

[3] George P. Winship, "The Literature of Printing," 'The Dolphin, No. 3, A History of the Printed Book' (New York: Limited Editions Club), p. 485.

[4] Sigfrid H. Steinberg, 'Five Hundred Years of Printing' (Harmondsworth: Penguin Books, Ltd., 1955), p. 142.

[5] Michael Sadleir, 'The Evolution of Publishers' Binding Styles, 1770-1900' (London: Constable & Co., 1930), pp. 8-9.

[6] Ibid., p. 12.

[7] William A. Jackson, "Printed Wrappers of the Fifteenth to the Eighteenth Centuries," 'Harvard Library Bulletin', VI:3, Autumn 1952, p. 313.

[8] Ibid., p. 314.

[9] Illustrations of such leather bindings can be found in: Ernst Kyriss, 'Verzierte Gotische Einbände im Alten Deutschen Sprachgebiet,' 1. Tafelband (Stuttgart: Max Hettler Verlag, 1953), p. 45 (Tafel 12) and p. 77 (Tafel 44).

[10] Jackson, op. cit., p. 318.

[11] Ibid., p. 321.

[12] Harry B. Weiss, 'A Book about Chapbooks' (Trenton, N. J.: privately printed, 1942), p. 6.

[13] Graham Pollard, "Serial Fiction," 'New Paths in Book Collecting, Essays by Various Hands,' edited by John Carter (London: Constable & Co., 1934), p. 254.

[14] Steinberg, op. cit., p. 248.

[15] Hans Schmoller, "Reprints: Aldine and After," 'Penrose Annual,' 1953 (London: Lund Humphrie & Co., 1953), XLVII, p. 36.

[16] Sir William E. Williams, 'The Penguin Story' (Harmondsworth, Middlesex: Penguin Books, Ltd., 1956), p. 9.

[17] Michael Sadleir, "Yellow-backs," 'New Paths in Book Collecting, Essays by Various Hands,' John Carter, ed. (London: Constable & Co., 1934), p. 129.

[18] Steinberg, op. cit., p. 256.

[19] Letter from Sir Allen Lane, May 7, 1954.

[20] Ibid.

[21] Lynton Lamb, "Penguin Books -- Style and Mass Production," 'The Penrose Annual, 1952' (London: Lund-Humphries & Co. Ltd., 1952), XLVI, p. 40, quoting Sir Allen Lane.

[22] 'Penguins, A Retrospect, 1935-1951' (Harmondsworth: Penguin Books Ltd., 1952, p. 1.

[23] Ibid., p. 12.

[24] Letter from Sir Allen Lane, May 7, 1954.

[25] Sir William E. Williams, 'The Penguin Story' (Harmondsworth: Penguin Books, Ltd., 1956).

[26] W. Balleny, "British Paperback Survey," 'Publishers Circular and Booksellers Record,' CLXXI: 4742 (May 18, 1957), pp. 598-99.

CHAPTER 2

EUROPEAN CONTINENTAL PUBLICATIONS WITH
EMPHASIS ON GERMAN PAPERBACKS

European Publications in General

The pattern of continental publishing differs considerably
from country to country because production as well as distribution, and sales follow methods which evolved over the first
three centuries of printing with little outside influence. The
continental impact on American paperback publishing was and
still is comparatively limited, though the American book trade
has been particularly familiar with West European productions
which have been imported since colonial days. Edition binding,
the wholesale quantity binding to the order and at the expense
of the publisher and distributor, as opposed to individual binding executed for the retail bookseller or the purchaser, was
made feasible through the use of cloth, the most common
material used for binding of books as published in the English-
speaking countries since the second quarter of the nineteenth
century.[1] This practice reserved the paperback field in Great
Britain and the United States primarily for reprints and shorter
publications of the pamphlet type.

The development of edition binding as it occurred in the
British Isles and America has no exact parallel in Europe. The
countries of the Romance language group, consisting of France,
Belgium, Italy, Spain and Portugal, publish most of their trade
books on good paper but in paper covers. Usually they bind
only encyclopedias, dictionaries, and other typical reference
books, and collected works or limited editions. Countries of
the Germanic language group, including Germany, Denmark,
Sweden, Norway, the Netherlands, Switzerland and Austria,
have a considerably higher percentage of clothbound books than
those of the Romance language group, but probably not as high
as found in the United States and Great Britain. There exist

no statistics on the percentage of paper versus clothbound
books, or even exact figures on book production in various
countries. 'The Library of Congress Information Bulletin' of
October 25, 1954 gives some data but admits that they can be
"added or compared only with an attitude of unconcern for
elements of statistical validity."[2] Inspection of the large storage
facilities of the book importing firm of Stechert-Hafner, Inc. in
New York made it obvious that the largest percentage of paperbound books comes from France, Italy and Spain.

> Before cloth binding became general, books were
> issued by publishers in temporary covers intended
> to keep them clean and intact until they reached the
> hands of their eventual purchasers. The practice per-
> sists in France to this day. There, even expensive
> limited editions on the finest paper are still issued
> in paper covers.
> The idea was that gentlemen preferred to have
> their books bound by their own binder in the general
> style of similar books in their libraries. Books were,
> therefore, issued either in paper wrappers or in paper-
> covered boards. Very cheap books and pamphlets
> were issued without any covering, just stitched to-
> gether.[3]

Paperbacks in France, Italy and Spain

The most remarkable fact about publishing in cheap paperback format on the continent is the scarcity of references made
in connection with this development in France, Italy and Spain,
where all interest in the subject seems to exhaust itself in
the study of fine bindings. A French bibliophile and book
dealer of repute, Jean-Albert Michaux, wrote in reply to a
request for assistance in search for source material that
he was unable to locate a study on the subject but that the
"livre broché" has apparently always existed in France and
that a large number of paperbound books can be found since the
end of the eighteenth century.

The publishing pattern of France, Italy and Spain makes it
difficult to distinguish between the regular trade edition and
the inexpensive reprint or cheap fiction designed for mass
consumption. The term "livres brochés," referring to paperbound books, came into use, according to the 'Grande Encyclo-

pédie', in the second half of the eighteenth century for a book
from 120 to 150 pages which did not receive the recognition
of a binding. Until the end of the eighteenth century, the book
in France had been an artistic product and had followed a continuous and logical evolution like other manifestations of the
arts.[4] In the nineteenth century, book publishing everywhere
was becoming increasingly industrialized but while mechanization and case bindings made rapid strides in Great Britain,
the United States and Germany, the French were slow in
adapting cloth-covered casings and continued to bring out their
books in paper covers regardless of size of edition.[5] In the
first decade of the nineteenth century, French publishers
began to abandon the practice of selling books bound or wrapped
in plain covers obviously intended for permanent binding; instead they used vividly colored paper covers with printed labels.
According to Michaux, this trend had a marked upswing with
the publication of the "éditions romantiques," around 1820, by
Béranger, Nodier, Paul-Louis Courier, Victor Hugo, Balzac,
Lamartine, Vigny, Mérimée, Chateaubriand, Stendhal, Sainte-
Beuve, G. de Nerval. During the post-Napoleonic era great
aristocratic wealth was reduced and the level of general
education broadened. As a result, an increasing demand for
good, popular literature in inexpensive form was felt which
Jean-Baptiste Alexandre Paulin was one of the first to recognize. He responded by releasing books in part-issues over a
long period of time at a low price per issue and with a great
deal of publicity. That this idea suggested itself to him is not
surprising since he had already successfully published two
magazines, 'Le National' and 'L'Illustration'. The first book
published in this fashion was his edition of 'Gil Blas de Santil-
lane' by Alain René Lesage. [6] Other publishers were quick to
follow his example, among them Dubochet who released 'Don
Quichotte' and Hetzel who brought out the novels of Charles
Nodier in this format in 1844.

Michaux mentions that many of the "éditions romantiques"
were specimens of fine printing, excellently done with designs
covering the front and back cover as well as the spine of the
paperbounds but he complains that few well-preserved specimens remain due to the binders' practice in this period of
discarding the covers. Among the best known series he
mentions the yellow covers of the "Bibliothèque Charpentier",
Hachette's "Bibliothèque des Gares" and Hetzel with his Jules

Verne titles. Some of these popular books came out in large editions and Brun gives as an example 'Paul et Virginie' by Jacques Henri Bernadin de Saint-Pierre, which was brought out in part-issues in an edition of 30,000 copies by Curmer in 1838.

During the second half of the nineteenth and the first half of the twentieth century regular trade and cheaper reprint editions were released by the same publishers. French original trade books are printed in comparatively small impressions and reissued time and again, often decades later, from the same plates. To distinguish trade books from cheaper reprints would amount to an examination of quality of paper and price rather than make-up, styles and titles, except that the cheap editions show more illustrations and gaudier covers. While in Anglo-American practice reprints are frequently issued in series, the French release many of their original editions in this way. Of reprint series, "La Renaissance du Livre" and "Le Livre de Demain" had become well known before World War II.

At the outbreak of the war, cased bindings were just beginning to become an economic proposition for most publishers as a result of modernization of binderies and were more widely used in France. Shortages brought about by the war stopped this movement and paper bindings remained the general practice.

> The price had to be the starting point and the limiting
> factor in each publishing venture. It was inevitable that
> on the continent of Europe the principle of the pocket-
> book should be copied by publishers from the pattern of
> England and also of America. For the first time in
> Europe books were marketed as branded articles, like
> chocolate and cigarettes. The format and cover were
> standardized and a uniform price was fixed . . . France
> . . . has made some progress toward the livre de
> poche.[7]

The trend towards the English and American type of paperback in the 1950's is exemplified by several types of series. The books published by Gallimard are mostly reprints, with four-color covers, they are bound with glue and have colored edges on all three sides. The "Livre de Poche" series resembles the cheap type of American paperbacks and specializes in popular fiction in glossy covers with gaudy illustrations. Larousse brings out reprints of classical works in sedate paper covers in its "Classiques Larousse," and the Presses Universitaires de France publish original nonfiction titles in their "que sais-je?" series, which appear in attractive covers of typical French design and typography. Hachette releases several pocket book lines, among them a new series of historical reprints such as General de Gaulle's 'War Memoirs,' Stefan Zweig's 'Marie-Antoinette' and Regine Pernoud's 'Jeanne d'Arc'. On the other hand, by 1956 more and more French trade books were being brought out in hard covers, which had previously been reserved for children's books, school books, classics and book club selections.

Publishing trends in Spain, Italy and Portugal are similar to those of France. Progress in mechanization of binding techniques has been very slow and expensive books are still frequently bound in leather. Practically all others are marketed in paper covers and are unbound, and the few casebound have usually been deficient in techniques and taste. In the last few years, some attempts at improvement of bindings have been made as modern machinery was obtained. The blurring of lines between original and reprint editions is similar to the French situation. Cover art for the cheap reprints is louder and in worse taste and the paper usually of inferior quality.

Italy has been famous for beautifully produced and illustrated books since the incunabula period. Since World War II a somewhat higher percentage of original editions has been clothbound because the "materials and processes used for printed paper cover, the varnished jacket, and the cellophane which often covers the whole, reach a cost even greater than that paid to a binder for a 'case'."[8] Many carefully designed books, printed on good paper and well illustrated, are presented in simple paper covers in order to keep the price down. Reprints appear exclusively in paper and in the last few years have shown a very artistic use of cover art. The "Biblioteca Moderna Mondadori" and the pocket-sized publications of Giulio Einaudi are very popular and the latter present "a remarkably good appearance through powerful grouping and a clever use of color. This series provides an interesting example of how excellent results may be procured with modest means."[9]

Early German Paperbacks

Germany, with the longest history of book production, combined many aspects of the guild tradition with cartel arrangements. The outstanding and distinguishing trade practices were the widely visited book fairs at Frankfurt and Leipzig, and the rigidity in the production and distribution of books, which resulted in a strict separation of original and subsequent publishing. Inexpensive printing and reprinting became an important activity as early as the fifteenth and sixteenth centuries, comprising more than half of the total book production. Inexpensively printed materials consisted of "Flugschriften and Broschüren" -- broadsides and tracts, pamphlets and the counterpart of American and British chapbooks -- sold at fairs and in "Kneipen" (a combination inn and taproom). Religious conflicts like the Reformation movement were fought out in tracts; Luther used them from the beginning to state his ideas and spread them among the masses.

Books were generally expensive and produced in small editions until the beginning of the nineteenth century. Original publishers controlled the trade rather rigidly and did not encourage additional printings. "Reprint" publishers had to rely on hucksters for the sale of their wares which were mainly "Volksbücher" (popular books), a crude form of literature indulging in courtly romances, love stories and often more gory literary fare. During the eighteenth century reprint publishers were increasingly trying to enter into the domain of original publishers. The struggle over the method of distribution of books by the barter system, which has been popular among the printer-booksellers of Germany since the end of the sixteenth century, using the book fairs as a meeting ground for their exchange transactions, came to a climax in the 1760's and 1770's when the successful publishers organized and finally had legislation enacted prohibiting reprinters from participating in the Leipzig book fair. The other publishers organized in protest and from that time on reprinting was concentrated in the southern parts of Germany, Austria and Bohemia. The leaders of the reprint group were Varrentrapp in Frankfurt and Trattner in Vienna. Prices of books were reduced and many authors either published their works themselves of founded cooperative publishing enterprises and learned societies, many of which were short-lived. [10,11]

Due to the division of Germany into various independent states, no uniform law concerning reprints could be adopted until the copyright law of 1901 was enacted, though Austria, Prussia and other limited jurisdictions within the German Reich had laws regarding reprints from the 1820's on. As the

line between original and reprint publishing was so much
more closely defined than in the countries of the Romance
language group, the German examples of reprint series came
more readily to the attention of British and American publishers and their influence on the inexpensive reprint trade in
Great Britain and the United States was greater.

Nineteenth Century Popular Editions

The first German publisher to go into cheap book production
in a large way with editions of German classical literature and
serious nonfiction in "Volksausgaben" (popular editions) was J.G.
Göschen in 1817, followed by Karl J. Meyer in 1826. These
books provided in cheap, paper or board covered editions
material which was in demand due to the interest in popular
education brought about by the writings, among others, of
Rousseau, Lessing, Herder, Goethe and Schiller.[12]
Göschen aimed to spread good and serious literature at
low prices, whether reprints or originals, while Meyer
concentrated on the reprint field. He was one of the first to
introduce the concept of the series and issued in 1827 the same
book in four different editions. The regular book trade was
opposed to his methods, but he did well and found numerous
imitators, among them the brothers Frankh in Stuttgart. From
this time on there was a fairly rapid spread of inexpensive,
popular literature (Schicksals and Schauerliteratur). These
cheap romances and horror stories were distributed as series
(Bossange in Leipzig), or appeared as part-issues (Groschen-
lieferungen) or as cheap magazines (Pfennig Magazine). The
rapid expansion resulted in a flooding of the market similar
to that in the United States in the 1830's and 1840's, but occurred in Germany a decade earlier.
The serious paperback was not displaced by these developments. Karl Preskauer continued the drive for good literature
in form of travel and popular libraries and founded in 1841
the Berliner Volksbücherei and the Verein zur Verbreitung
guter und wohlfeiler Volksschriften (Society for the Diffusion
of Good and Inexpensive Popular Literature) in Zwickau. From
1850 on the movement for good, inexpensive literature for the
masses increased rapidly. The Social Democratic party got
into the field of cheap paperback book production for purposes
of popular education and the spreading of class ideologies under

the leadership of LaSalle and Bebel and the formation of the Arbeiterbildungsvereine (workmen's education societies). Various religious organizations were opposed to the spread of good literature and political information in this fashion, as they saw in this activity a threat to their efforts to distribute religious material in the form of tracts and inexpensive editions of the Bible. (The Casteinische Bibelanstalt has been distributing such materials since 1701).

As a result of these divergent moves, paperback publishing increased greatly in the nineteenth and twentieth centuries. Among the most notable firms following the patterns of Meyer and Göschen were the Bernhard Tauchnitz Verlag (founded 1837) and the Philipp Reclam Verlag (1867).

Tauchnitz Verlag

The Tauchnitz Verlag and its publications remained unique in their inception and execution. Christian Bernhard Tauchnitz got interested in publishing through the efforts of his uncle, Karl Tauchnitz, who had made a name for himself by bringing out good and inexpensive editions of Greek and Roman classics and by being the first German publisher to use stereotyping. At the age of twenty-one Christian B. Tauchnitz founded his firm and began his famous collection of British authors (Tauchnitz Edition) in 1841, bringing out reprints of British and, later, American authors also in paperbacks, but restricting sales and distribution exclusively to non-English speaking countries. Tauchnitz, and later his son, Christian Carl Bernhard, made frequent trips to England and established personal connections with Dickens, Disraëli, Carlyle, Thackeray and many other famous authors of the period, all of whom were happy to have their works appear in "Tauchnitz Editions." (Plate 3.) Often these continental reprints came out shortly after the original editions, and at times even simultaneously.

By 1937, the year of the firm's centenary, 5290 titles had been issued, all reprints with the exception of a few memorial editions which were also sold in Great Britain and the United States. "Editorially, the series was a brilliant achievement. . . (and) the books were marvels of careful proofreading."

Two other Tauchnitz series, "German Authors" and "France Classique," did not enjoy the same success. The first was a series of English translations of German authors, meant for export to Great Britain, and the second a counterpart to the English edition of French authors. They were published from 1845 to 1859 but failed to meet the competition of the British and Belgian reprint trade.[14]

Reclam Verlag

In 1828 a young man by the name of Anton Philipp Reclam established a book store in Leipzig. His family had been in the book trade and publishing business for a long time and he eventually gave up his store and went into full time publishing. During the 1840's he issued a number of liberal political tracts against the authoritarian regime of Metternich in Austria as inexpensive, papercovered pamphlets. He also brought out a humor magazine and an almanac and, between 1844 and 1847, sixty-one volumes of a cheap reprint series of popular literature ("Wohlfeile Unterhaltungsbibliothek für die Gebildete Lesewelt") which consisted of little booklets providing recreational reading material, occasionally with slight erotic overtones. He published Latin and Greek classics for school use, Bibles, dictionaries and music.

Philipp Reclam was a cautious man and carefully evolved a plan for inexpensive reprints directed at a wide market. He was able to lower the price of his publications through the use of stereotyping, which had first been tried on a large scale by Tauchnitz, and through the purchase of a printing plant for the production of his own publications. In 1858 he went into paperback publishing with a complete edition of the Wigand translation of Shakespeare's dramatic works in twelve little volumes. This translation had first been published in 1836 and was subsequently brought out by several firms without much success. Reclam reduced the price by almost 50 percent over the previous reprints by using paper covers and printing large editions. Between 1858 and 1865 Reclam sold only the entire set, but later each play came out separately. Issued in twenty-five little volumes, the series was a great success.

Then in 1867, after a new German copyright law had gone into effect which put a book in the public domain thirty years after the author's death, the "Universal-Bibliothek" was founded. Many other firms, even old houses like Grote and Brockhaus, went into the field of reprinting classical literature inexpensively after 1867. Joseph Meyer attempted to sell the

"Groschen Bibliothek Deutscher Klassiker" between 1848 and 1854. Thus, Reclam's idea was not entirely new (even the name had been used before) but there were several novel features, which, as in the twentieth century cases of Penguins and Pocket Books, were a fortunate combination for success. The format was attractive, the paper better than that of most other similar publications. There were no subscriptions sold and every dealer could order as many copies of a single or a group of titles as he pleased. Every volume was a complete unabridged work, no anthologies were published, the print was small but legible, and advertising was kept at a minimum, in order to keep the price low enough for everyone to be able to afford to build a library to his taste. The average edition was 2,000 copies. During the first ten years eighty titles appeared annually. After forty years, 5,000 titles had appeared; and after seventy-five years, 8,000. An interesting experiment in distribution was the installation of vending machines for Reclam Books in 1912. By 1917 close to 2,000 machines were in operation and sold between 1913 and 1940 about twelve million copies. Depending on location, the machines were serviced by the publisher or by near-by bookstores. They were discontinued after 1940 and the idea never did catch on in the machine-conscious United States, although some American firms have sporadically experimented with them and such vending machines are occasionally still in use.

Over the years, substantial changes were made in editorial policy, but basically the success of Reclam was due to offering good literature at the lowest possible price. The post World War II period in Germany found the firm again in operation. Covers were redesigned and modernized. Since 1956 heavier boards have been used for covers, resembling the more expensive American paperback series like "Anchor Books", but using no illustrations.

Other German firms attempted similar lines, even imitating the format and features of the cover, but they did not compare either in size or public esteem. The most outstanding were Hendel's "Bibliothek der Gesamtliteratur des In- und Auslandes," 1886-1930, 2,573 titles; "Meyer's Volksbücherei" 1886-1915, 1,698 titles; "Hesse's Volksbücherei" 1903-1920, 1,350 titles. The most significant series of similar type in Austria was "Die Deutsch-Österreichische Nationalbibliothek" which was founded by Hermann Weichelt in 1855 and had published 406 titles by 1916.[15]

Other, more specialized German series appeared in the late nineteenth and in the twentieth century, such as "Das Wissen der Gegenwart" (1882-1917), "Aus Natur und Geistswelt," "Wissenschaft und Bildung," "Verständliche Wissenschaft," as well as series of novels brought out by Fischer, Insel Verlag and many others.

It would be incorrect to assume that German inexpensive publishing proceeded only on a high plane of good literature. All through the seventeenth, eighteenth and nineteenth centuries Schundliteratur (gutter literature) was sold through various outlets outside the regular trade. There were overly-sweet romantic novels in the 1860's. In the 1890's Hintertreppenromane (backstairs novels), printed on coarse paper with a black and white title page, specialized in horror stories. Around the turn of the century, detective stories became popular, they had colored cover pictures and erotic themes as well as tales of adventure. Jeremias gives various figures for the sales of this type of material and states that in 1921 about 70 percent of all paper went into the manufacture of such books, which were sold through 30-40,000 outlets such as barbershops, stationers, and similar stores.[16]

Albatross Modern Continental Library

The "Tauchnitz Editions," which were unique in bringing English texts to German readers after 1841, could boast of an outstanding literary fare at a very low price. During the second and third decade of the twentieth century, they did not keep pace with progress made in typography and had little to recommend in this respect. In comparison to inexpensive German paperback publications, their appearance was dull and they began to lose a good deal of their sales appeal, particularly after World War I. Aware of these factors, the Albatross Modern Contenental Library was organized in Hamburg in 1932 as a competitor in this field. The new firm, under the management of J. Holroyd Reece, Kurt Enoch, and Max Christian Wegener, was owned by a holding corporation which was located in Luxemburg. The operations of Albatross were truly contenental in scope. Editorial offices were in Paris, first titles were printed in Milan, but manufacture was later switched to Leipzig. Sales and promotion departments were located in Hamburg.

Albatross followed the same basic pattern as "Tauchnitz Editions," but stressed contemporary writing and created a more attractive format for its series, which eventually included about four hundred titles. The conception of the series, and its restrained and dignified make-up, with good paper, typography and titles, was mainly Mr. Enoch's work. After Albatross had been in operation for two years, Tauchnitz felt the challenge so keenly that the old firm began negotiations with its competitors and by 1935 Albatross took over the management of Tauchnitz.[17] The success of the firm in that year coincided with the beginning of Penguin books in England and one wonders whether the name of the British firm was not suggested by the success of the continental publisher, as the Albatross format was adopted by Penguin. After the merger of Tauchnitz and Albatross the individual identity of each of the publications was maintained, but Tauchnitz was modernized by inclusion of more contemporary authors.

Mr. Enoch, who holds a doctor's degree in economics and comes from a family with a publishing background, left Germany in 1936 and directed the operations of both firms from the Paris office, but cut all connections with Tauchnitz at the outbreak of the war in 1939. The Nazi government forced Tauchnitz to publish German books and the firm was officially bought by Mr. Wegener. Albatross was produced for a short time by Collins in Glasgow and later during the war by Bonnier in Sweden. Schweizer Verlag in Switzerland attempted to fill the gap created by the demise of Tauchnitz and Albatross, but the demand declined and did not make such a venture worthwhile. The reading of English books by a soldier in Hitler's army during war time must have been, after all, a very isolated occurrence, and certainly was frowned upon by the Nazis. Mr. Enoch served in the French army, reached England after its collapse and, for awhile, distributed French books there and kept in close touch with Penguin. Later, he came to the United States where he made and is still making notable contributions to the American paperback field in his association with the American Penguin Branch and the New American Library of World Literature.

The recent American practice among hard cover publishers to print an inexpensive series in paperbacks was employed by German publishers in the 1920's and 1930's. Sometimes, these series were paperbacked, as "Die Gelben Ullstein Bücher," sometimes boarded, but small in format and limited in the number of pages, such as the "Insel Bücher," Another development in Germany was the "Volksausgaben" which represented cheaper editions, usually boarded, of works which had been successful over the years in regular clothbound trade editions, frequently published by the same firms. This parallels the movement started in the United States in 1954 by Knopf with "Vintage Books," which was followed by many similar series.

[1] John Carter, 'ABC for Book Collectors' (London: R. Hart-Davis, 1952), p. 51 and p. 71.

[2] "Annual World Production of Library Materials," 'Library of Congress Information Bulletin', Appendix (October 25, 1954), p. 1, pp. 3-5.

[3] Percy H. Muir, 'Book-Collecting as a Hobby' (New York: Alfred A Knopf, 1947), p. 93.

[4] Robert Brun. 'Le Livre Français' (Paris: Librairie Larousse, 1948), p. 113.

[5] Edith Diehl, 'Bookbinding, Its Background and Technique,' 2 vols. (New York: Rinehart & Co., 1946), v. I, p. 41.

[6] Brun, op. cit., p 119.

[7] H. Strehler, "Pocket-books on the Continent," 'The Penrose Annual, 1954,' v. XLVIII (London: Lund Humphries, 1954), pp. 33-34.

[8] Charles Ede, ed., 'The Art of the Book' (London & New York: The Studio Publications, 1951), p. 175.

[9] Strehler, op. cit., p. 34.

[10] Hans Widman, 'Geschichte des Buchhandels vom Altertum bis zur Gegenwart' (Wiesbaden: Otto Harrassowitz, 1952).

[11] Günther Jeremias, 'Das Billige Buch. Entwicklungs- und Erscheinungsformen.' Doctoral Dissertation, Friedrich-Wilhelm's Universität zu Berlin (Berlin: Triltsch & Huther, 1938).

[12] Johannes Tews, 'Geistespflege in der Volksgemeinschaft' (Berlin: Gesellschaft für Volksbildung, 1932), p. 150.

[13] Schmoller, op. cit., p. 38.

[14] 'Fünfzig Jahre der Verlagsbuchhandlung' (Leipzig: Bernhard Tauchnitz, 1887) and 'The Harvest, Being the Record of One Hundred Years of Publishing, 1837-1937' (Leipzig: Bernhard Tauchnitz, 1937).

[15] Annemarie Meiner, 'Reclam, eine Geschichte der Universal-Bibliothek zu ihrem 75 jährigen Bestehen' (Leipzig: Reclam Verlag, 1942).

[16] Jeremias, op. cit., p. 12.

[17] Kurt Enoch, "The Paper-bound Book: Twentieth Century Publishing Phenomenon," 'Library Quarterly,' XXIV: 3 (July, 1954), p. 211.

CHAPTER 3

AMERICAN INEXPENSIVE BOOKS -- 1639-1830's

Colonial Book Production

Less than fifty years after Columbus had landed in America the first book was printed in Mexico. It was another century before the first complete book was produced in the British colonies of North America in 1640. Unsettled political conditions, hostile surroundings, and lack of leisure time of an unsophisticated, parsimonious, and predominantly rural population resulted in a very limited demand for books which was readily satisfied by import. In 1638, the first printing press was brought to the colonies from England and the Cambridge Press was established by Stephen Daye in the comparatively more densely populated and urban New England. It is significant that the first products of this press were "The Freeman's Oath" and William Peirce's 'Almanack for the Year 1639'; the first book, 'The Whole Booke of Psalmes,' commonly known as "The Bay Psalm Book," did not appear until 1640. [1]

The colonial printer, who was also the bookseller and usually the binder, depended on various sources for his income. Most important for his trade was government patronage -- the printing of session laws, assembly proceedings, laws and other government documents. He also printed pamphlets, sermons, manuals, guides, almanacs, occasional advertisements, broadsides, and later on newspapers. He frequently held the position of postmaster. Only if his other printing was financially successful could he afford to devote time and materials to print and reprint and exhibit full length books for sale. In the early days they were mainly books of a religious nature; later on, he was able to add books of literary merit. In order to increase their selections, the booksellers still imported publications, particularly Bibles which could be printed only by a patent from the Crown or 'cum privilegio,' and traded their products with other printers. If Andrew Bradford, son of Philadelphia's first printer, William Bradford, can serve as an example, they also sold other completely unrelated items; he included in his merchandise, "whalebone, live goose feathers, pickled sturgeon, chocolate and Spanish snuff." [2] The rural population in the middle and southern colonies did not even have access to these shops -- their meager book needs were filled by the occasional traveling book agent.

The local printer-binder-bookseller carried on his shoulders the whole range of book production, including editorial work, and separation of these functions did not occur until after 1800. The first man known to be a bookbinder by profession who came to America was John Sanders, who arrived here from England about 1636, and purchased a shop in Boston in 1637. As the records are utterly incomplete it remains pure speculation whether he had any knowledge of or connection with the establishment of the first printing press two years after his arrival, whether or not he sold books in his shop and whether or not or for how long he engaged in his trade. G. P. Winship believes the evidence shows that he still followed the bookbinding trade in 1651. [3] American binding styles followed more or less the same pattern as those in Great Britain with a few characteristic exceptions. The "Bay Psalm Book", the earliest full-length book to be printed and bound in the Colonies, produced by the Cambridge Press in 1640, is preserved in only one complete and recorded copy. This volume is bound so exquisitely that most experts agree that the binding cannot be as old as the publication date of the book as they contend that no binder in the colonies before 1651 was such an excellent craftsman. It has therefore been ascribed to John Ratcliffe who arrived in Boston in 1661 and who did a number of beautiful bindings, most notably the "Indian Bible." He and the other outstanding binder of the period, Edmund Ranger, used a variety of leathers from undressed calf to imported morocco, including an inferior type of morocco which might have been domestic. The more expensive books were decorated with gold tooling and gilded edges. Towards the end of the century locally tanned leathers were used extensively as well as wooden boards which were more easily obtained and more sturdy than pasteboards. Decorations were simple and the leathers were plain, giving American colonial binding its characteristic qualities: solid, substantial and utilitarian. The

few more elaborate bindings were usually produced by crafts-
men who had learned their skill abroad and were located in
the large cities.[4]

The range of publications was considerably enlarged with
the appearance of the first magazines in 1740-41: Andrew
Bradford's 'American Magazine,' and Benjamin Franklin's
'General Magazine.' They became of primary importance for
the income of the printer, the spread of ideas and the distribution of literature. As they gained wider circulation, selling
by subscription came into its own, guaranteeing the printer a
predetermined number of sales and the possibility for advertisement, essential for this type of distribution.

From 1713 on book auctions gained popularity in the
larger cities such as Boston, Philadelphia, New York, and
Baltimore. Imported and second-hand books were offered at
these sales, as well as new books and publishers' remainders.

After 1750, the differentiation between small town and
city printer became more distinct. The small town printer
retained the publication of the local paper and sundry job
printing tasks, but the publishing of literature or "trade books"
developed more and more exclusively into the function of the
city printer-publisher who had begun to make use of mechanization and a better distribution system, thus being able to
make economies which were not available to the small town
shop.

Colonial Paperbound Publications

Various studies have attempted to assess book production
and reading habits in the American colonies. Due to the lack
of records none of these studies claims any degree of completeness, but they represent a picture which has to be accepted as it stands now since additional documentation seems un-
likely. Taken together, they permit a number of conclusions.
Charles Evans, who attempted in his 'American Bibliography'
to present a comprehensive listing, registers for the period
from 1639 to 1783, 18,300 separately printed books, broadsides and newspapers.

Wroth suggests that many of the early publications, particularly those of ephemeral nature like broadsides, ballads,
handbills, etc., completely disappeared and believes that the
ratio of known versus unknown printing may come to about 1

to 4.7 which brings the total production to an estimated 86,000 items. [5] Research by Arthur Benedict Berthold about the output of the American press from 1639 to 1763 indicates that 37 percent dealt with theology, 17 percent with social science, 19.5 percent with literature, and the rest with various subjects. [6] Religious publications were mainly sermons, pamphlets and some books, while the social science publications included laws, government proclamations, assembly proceedings and possibly some larger essays and treatises in book form. Other indications of the preponderance of religious and legal materials are found in estate inventories and bookdealer invoices of the seventeenth and eighteenth centuries. While the statistical approaches are incomplete, they seem to justify Wroth's generalization that the colonial printer produced for the most part "laws, pamphlets, and sermons which were issued in blue or marbled paper covers."[7] Mott says about the Cambridge Press that they were too "busy supplying needed almanacs, catechisms, and hymnals, and printing religious books in the Indian language to . . . get around to publishing more general books . . . until the 1660's."[8]

Therefore it can be assumed that colonial binding was not only plain and utilitarian, whenever bound books were produced at all, but that the bulk of colonial publications appeared in paperbound form, even though there exists an abundance of literature on colonial bindings and very little on the paper-wrapped items. Colonial publications fall into various types which will be discussed separately. They are: almanacs, government documents, tracts and sermons, catechisms, spellers and primers, chapbooks, and guides and handbooks. There was also a limited amount of belles lettres, which was more frequently bound in leather. Finally, there were broadsides, handbills, and other ephemera, as well as early newspapers and periodicals, which, due to their format and content, were never intended for binding. Government documents do not require consideration in the generic development of paperbacks, due to their content which sets them apart from today's paperbound books published by commercial publishers. In order to ascertain the correctness of the theory that paperback publishing has its roots in the earliest American publications rather than in the nineteenth century, as frequently maintained, a large number of actual colonial printings were examined, the most significant of which will be described in detail.

Sermons

Early sermons vary considerably in length, but were very popular reading material in colonial times and were generally published in the cheapest available form, in paper-wrappered pamphlets or books. An example of a sermon with an unintegrated wrapper is: 'A Plea for God and an Appeal to the Conscience of a People Declining in Religion.' A Sermon by William Williams. Boston. Printed by B. Green . . . for Daniel Henchman at his shop, 1719. This 42-page pamphlet has a marbled cover and a half-title page pasted to it; this is easily legible if held against the light and reads as follows: "Mr. William's Election Sermon on Wednesday, May 27, 1719."

An integrated wrapper appears on a sermon by Mather, published in 1724. Here the half-title page bears the following text: "The last Sermon heard by certain Pirates at a Conference with them." The title page is somewhat less sensational and reads: 'The Converted Sinner. The Nature of a Conversion on Real and Vital Piety.' Boston, N. Belknap, 1724.

One instance was found in which early sermons appeared as a series, called "Christian's Pocket Library" by John Stanford, M. A., assisted by other ministers of the Gospel. The series has several other characteristics of modern paperbacks. The individual titles are wrappered in light blue covers, showing an illustration. Examination of No. 5 of Volume I reveals the following statement on the verso of the back wrapper: "These publications serve the dissemination of the Gospel and the entertainment and instruction to the pious youth to be published in numbers, monthly, each containing 48 pages. As six numbers will form a neat pocket volume, with every sixth will be given a handsome title page and a copious index."

Another characteristic of present day paperbacks, the skyline, is also found in early sermons. This is a short sentence or phrase printed on the outside cover above the title, summarizing the book's content in a striking way and indicating why the book should be bought. As an example may serve: Adams, Abdiel, 'A Sermon Preached at a Lecture in Boston, New England . . . on August 27, 1772.' Boston, Isaiah Thomas, 1772. Above the title appears the following: "The happiness and pleasure of unity in Christian societies considered." The half-title page reads: 'Mr. Adams' Sermon on Christian Unity."

Government Documents

These publications are in content and manner of publication not related to today's paperbacks, but the binding style, in some instances, reminds one of today's practices. Many of the early laws were obviously published with the intention of being bound eventually and were, therefore, published without title page, covers, or even half-title page and have continuous pagination. Some were bound in rather heavy, unintegrated wrappers usually of blue or gray cartridge paper, apparently with the intention of leaving them in this condition more or less permanently.

One outstanding exception to the usual dull wrappers was found in the following twenty-five page pamphlet: 'The Articles of Confederation. The Declaration of Rights; the Constitution of this Commonwealth and the Articles of Definitive Treaty between Great Britain and the United States of America.' Published by order of the General Assembly, Richmond. Printed by Dixon & Holt, 1784. The wrapper of this document is dark blue paper with a very attractive abstract design in black and white. The wrapper is slightly smaller than the pamphlet, but since the publication shows no other signs of stitching or stabbing it can be assumed that it is the original cover. Harvard University Library has a copy of the 'Articles of Confederation' in a similar wrapper. According to Professor William A. Jackson of Harvard University, this wrapper has the same number as the one of the New York Public Library, and he believes that it is a binder's wrapper of commercial paper which could be bought in bales.[9] This unusual cover of an early American publication is remarkably similar to the abstract cover designs of many of today's higher priced paperbacks.

Almanacs

An almanac is defined in the 'Oxford English Dictionary' as "an annual table or book of tables containing a calendar of months and days with astronomical data and calculations, ecclesiastical and other anniversaries, and in former days astrological and astrometereological forecasts." This, however, does not quite characterize the American colonial type. William L. Andrews comes closer when he refers to it as

the curious hodge-podge of scraps of useful information, scintillations of native wit, and 'proverbial sentences which inculcate industry and frugality,' . . .
embodied in twenty to thirty small octavo or duodecimo
pages, which are all that most of these miniature
compendiums of knowledge contain. [10]

The earliest almanac located was dated 1685 and is listed in
Charles Evans' 'American Bibliography,' as item No. 27. The
most famous eighteenth century almanacs were the 'Poor
Richard,' begun by Benjamin Franklin in 1732 and continued
by him and D. Hall for over a quarter of a century. They seemed
to have been a lucrative venture as Franklin reports in his
memoirs that he sold about 10,000 copies annually. Other
famous almanacs were published by William Bradford in Philadelphia, Nathaniel Ames in Dedham, Isaiah Thomas in Wor-
cester, T. & J. Fleet in Boston, and Hugh Gaine in New York.
Some of them have survived to the present day and most of
them adhered to their original papercovered appearance. The
range of topics covered by them was very wide: cheap literature as well as selections from famous authors of the day,
revolutionary ideologies and instructions for projects such as
how to produce gunpowder at home.

As almanacs increased in size and content, they frequently
acquired protective covers, usually of blue or marbled paper.
After 1750, the covers became more elaborate in color and
design and a limited number used cover illustrations, to attract
prospective buyers. Two of the most remarkable almanacs
examined were printed in German for the years 1770 and 1779.
Both have illustrations on the integrated wrapper which cover
the entire page and the title appears on the recto of the second
leaf. These almanacs are: 'Der Hoch-Deutsche Amerikanische
Calendar. Auf das Jahr 1770,' Germantown, Christoph Saur,
and 'Der Gantz Verbesserte Nord-Amerikanische Calendar auf
das 1779ste Jahr Christi,' Lancaster, Francis Bailey. The
similarity of almanacs of two hundred years ago to current
paperbacks is striking because of make-up, the wide range of
topics covered, the large editions and the popularity which
brought them into most homes.

Chapbooks and Tracts

Chapbooks, popular in England in the seventeenth and
eighteenth centuries, were also widely sold in the colonies

during that time. They were carried by the traveling salesmen who had among their wares "pins, scissors, razors, lace,
perfume, cotton goods, pottery, spices, clocks, books and
many other small articles," [11] a traveling drug store. At first
the chapmen acted as independent hawkers who also carried
books. Later, their wares were specialized and many turned
into sales agents for printers and book dealers. In the early
days, most of the printed matter they handled was of religious
nature, but after 1750 books on spelling, geography, palmistry,
treatises on farming, almanacs, joke books, abbreviated legend-
ary romances and pamphlets on curiosa, etc., began to appear
and the number of religious books decreased consistently.
Already in 1713, Cotton Mather, the famous New England
divine, remarked in his diary: "I am informed that the Minds
and Manners of many people about the Country are much cor-
rupted by foolish Songs and Ballads which the Hawkers and
Peddlers carry into all parts of the Country." [12]

Chapbooks, as well as tracts, which treated subjects like
piety, goodness, sin and worship were issued sporadically
rather than continuously, and it is difficult to ascertain their
numbers or locate them exactly in time. Some chapbooks
were imported from England but they were also produced by
many colonial printers, from the best and most famous to
obscure small shops. Isaiah Thomas specialized particularly
in a type of chapbook for children, like 'Little Goody Two Shoes'
and 'The Juvenile Biographer.' Many of these were actually
reprints of originals published in London by John Newbery.
They were "clad in gay coats of gilt and brilliantly tinted
papers, with the intent to delight the eyes and conjure the pen-
nies from the pockets . . ." [13] Fowle & Draper, Andrew Bar-
clay and T. & J. Fleet were other famous chapbook printers.
Before and after the Revolution the political tracts were of
importance, and chapbooks continued to bring entertainment
and diversion as well as enlightenment to the lonely farms.
With the technical developments of the nineteenth century and
the profusion of magazines and newspapers distributed by
mail, chapbooks stopped being of any importance after 1830,
though occasional ones can be found as late as 1870.

Book Production During the Early Days of the Republic

After the Revolution, materials for book production were
more plentiful and techniques improved greatly. The leather

was tanned differently, producing a greater variety of binding materials, but the new staining processes contributed to their more rapid decay. Marbled paper was used for lining purposes and gilt-lettered red or black leather labels as well as more lavish decorations gave a richer look to the books produced in the first quarter of the nineteenth century, though the quality of the binding had actually deteriorated. It is noteworthy that cloth was used for some binding purposes earlier in the United States than in England, beginning in the 1790's. General widespread use of cloth was prevalent in the 1820's and found even faster acceptance here than in Great Britain. It apparently fulfilled the greater need for economy in the United States and allowed for faster handling and easier distribution in the larger, less densely populated country. By the 1830's, publishers' bindings were almost the rule, displacing expensive leather bindings rapidly. In the first third of the nineteenth century the trend toward specialization, which had started around the end of the seventeenth century, placed the publisher-entrepreneur clearly in the dominant position in book production. This trend is responsible for the emergence of the bookseller-publisher in the nineteenth century. Many of the firms started at that time are still in existence. Charles Wiley established a bookshop in 1807 which developed into a publishing firm. Harper, founded as a printing establishment in 1817, went into publishing. Appleton entered the field in 1831, J. B. Lippincott in 1836 and Little, Brown & Co., in 1837, to mention but a few. The essential characteristics and methods of the trade book publishers have not changed greatly since then.

At about the same time the movement for popular education made itself felt throughout Europe, the British Isles and America. Its aim was to include the large masses of the increasing urban population in this process. The drive for free and compulsory education, the wider dissemination of knowledge, and the spreading of literacy were the means towards accomplishment of economic and social betterment. As a result, the magazines and newspapers which catered to these newly felt needs gained great popularity.

The penny magazines went farthest in bringing regular reading matter to the masses. They started in the United States in the 1820s, came soon to England, and from here conquered the European continent.[14]

England transformed this medium somewhat and gave it a

higher cultural aim through the establishment of societies by idealistic educators who stressed the informational over the recreational aspects. A milestone in these educational trends was the founding of the Society for the Diffusion of Useful Knowledge in 1827 for which, among others, Henry, Baron Lord Brougham, was responsible. He established a model school for the poorer classes in London, became Lord Rector of Glasgow University and was also one of the founders of London University. Another early member of the Society was Charles Knight, the editor of 'Knight's Quarterly Magazine' who became superintendent of the Society's publications. In this capacity he published the very popular "Library of Entertaining Knowledge," the 'Penny Cyclopedia' which was later remodeled as the 'English Cyclopedia,' and the 'Penny Magazine.' The Society was influential in the establishment of similar enterprises on American soil.

In 1829, the Boston Society for the Diffusion of Knowledge was formed, which started in 1831 the "American Library of Useful Knowledge" whose objective it was to "issue in cheap form a series of works, partly original and partly selected, in all the most important branches of learning."[15] Freeman Lewis, in the sixteenth Bowker Memorial Lecture, entitled "Paper-Bound Books in America," stated that this series of books was probably the first low priced venture in America.[16] This lecture attracted a great deal of attention and Lewis is to be credited with having started the interest in the history of paperbacks. Most writers on the subject, in search of a date for the beginning of paperbacks, have erroneously used 1831 as their reference. Actually, a great deal of paperbound material had been published before, and while the "Library of Useful Knowledge" may have been the first low-priced series brought out in a large edition, neither its format, content or distribution justify this conclusion.

The purpose of the series, as described in the first volume, was to

> furnish a collection of such works on the most import-
> ant branches of knowledge as ought to be in the pos-
> session of every intelligent family . . . and is to em-
> brace in it only works of permanent value . . . Each
> work shall be written in a style which shall be intelligi-
> ble to the careful reader although he may have little
> other previous acquaintance with the particular subj-

ect . . . but the books will not be unworthy of attention
of the accomplished scholar and man of science . . .
It will be no part of their purpose to furnish works
of mere amusement. [17]

The subjects to be covered were given as Science, Natural
Science, Natural History, Moral Philosophy, Universal History, History of America, Geography and Statistics.

The four titles published by the Society between 1831 and
1832 were: Vol. I: 'Discourses Delivered before the Boston
Mechanics Institute'; Vol. II: 'Treatise in Mechanics'; Vol. III:
'Universal History', by John Von Müller, in four volumes;
Vol. IV: 'History of the United States', by Alexander H. Everett.
The format was "large duodecimo to be neatly bound in cloth." [18]
The original copies in possession of the Harvard University
Library are bound in fine grain purple cloth with printed labels
2 1/4 x 7/8" on the spines. [19] Each volume contained 320
pages and the announced price was five dollars per year or
$62\frac{1}{2}$ cents per volume, as the series was to consist of eight
volumes a year. Distribution was through regular trade
channels, with "liberal terms" granted to book-sellers, or
through subscription.

The above statement indicates clearly the Society's educational aim, but the readers who were to share in this cultural
bounty were unprepared to respond sufficiently to keep these
publications financially solvent. C. S. Rafinesque, the American
botanist, had similar plans in 1832 when he published his
'Atlantic Journal and Friend of Knowledge,' a serial which
failed in spite of its high aims to provide good literature at
a price nearly everyone could afford to pay.

The "American Library of Useful Knowledge" failed because it was nonfiction, distributed through regular channels
in a format which was similar to the regular products of the
trade; it was different merely by having been brought out in a
series and being offered through subscription, two features
which were not novel. Idealism could not supplant the keener
knowledge of trade publishers of what the public really wanted
to read and buy. Enlightenment had increased the demand for
reading matter and the industrial revolution, which at this
stage had not yet materially bettered the economic conditions
of a large segment of the population, had at least increased
their leisure time. Literacy was spreading rapidly and inexpensive publications, whether magazines or books, were

finding a widening market, particularly if they were geared to readers of moderate educational background. When publishers became aware of this situation, they lowered prices, bringing out reprints of British books. Such attempts were made by Harper around 1830 and were followed by Carey's "Library of Choice Literature."[20]

What occurred in the 1830's then is merely a broadening of the choice made available to a large segment of the population. The paperbound, inexpensive material of colonial days which consisted largely of almanacs, chapbooks, religious and political tracts, was channeled now more and more into the budding popular magazines, and regular full-length novels -- an expansion of the chapbooks -- were reduced in price. Even the physical differences between tracts and books now issued in series were not as great as would appear at first glance. Tracts, like those collected at the British Museum and referred to as Thomason Tracts in memory of their avid collector, came close to being issued in series -- not in fact, but certainly in appearance. In addition, they were sold and distributed like today's paperbacks. Even the revolutionary aspect of magazine distribution is not quite as new for the eighteenth and early nineteenth century when one considers that tracts and sermons actually stood midway between bound books and broadsides, the substitutes for the newspapers and magazines of our time. Techniques of production and methods of merchandizing have changed but there is more than a superficial similarity between the wares the chapman sold along with his books and those offered by today's drugstore, in which the rack with popular paperbacks is prominently displayed. Then, as now, the inexpensive, paperbound book was a medium reaching large groups and contributing towards democratization by providing reading material at a nominal cost.

[1] Lawrence C. Wroth, 'The Colonial Printer,' 2d ed. (Portland, Maine: The Southworth-Anthoensen Press, 1938), pp. 16-17.

[2] Ibid., p. 188.

[3] George P. Winship, 'The Cambridge Press, 1638-1692' (Philadelphia: University of Pennsylvania Press, 1945), p. 15.

[4] Hannah D. French, "Early American Bookbinding by Hand,"'Bookbinding in America,' edited by Hellmut Lehmann-Haupt (Portland, Maine: The Southworth-Anthoensen Press, 1941), p. 11, pp. 24-25.

[5]Hellmut Lehmann-Haupt, Lawrence C. Wroth, and Rollo G. Silver, 'The Book in America,' 2d ed. (New York: R. R. Bowker Co., 1951), p. 27.

[6]Ibid., p. 33.

[7]Ibid., p. 25.

[8]Frank L. Mott, 'Golden Multitudes'(New York: Macmillan Co.,1947), p. 11.

[9]Letter from Professor William A. Jackson, May 24, 1955.

[10]William L. Andrews, 'The Old Booksellers of New York and Other Papers' (New York: privately printed, 1895), p. 75.

[11]Weiss, op. cit., p. 123.

[12]Ibid., p. 125.

[13]William L. Andrews, 'Bibliopegy in the United States and Kindred Subjects' (New York: Dodd, Mead and Co., 1903), p. 51.

[14]Steinberg, op. cit., p. 227.

[15]Freeman Lewis, "Paper-bound Books in America," 'Bowker Lectures on Book Publishing' (New York: R. R. Bowker Co., 1957), p. 307.

[16]Ibid.

[17]"Discourses Delivered before the Boston Mechanics Institute," 'American Library of Useful Knowledge' (Boston: Simpson & Clapp, 1831), pp. 1-5.

[18]Ibid.

[19]Letter from William B. Todd, Harvard University Library, June 3, 1955.

[20]Raymond H. Shove, 'Cheap Book Production in the United States, 1870 to 1891'(Urbana: University of Illinois Library, 1937), p. vi.

CHAPTER 4

AMERICAN PAPERBOUNDS -- 1830-1930

The First Boom in Paperbounds:
Newspaper Extras, 1830-1845

In 1835, Carey & Lea brought out their 'Library of Choice Literature,' actually a magazine published weekly, which offered subscribers for five dollars a year or ten cents a copy a good collection of books in serial form, distributed through the mail.[1] A rise in postal rates in 1836 made the publication unprofitable and forced it to fold. In 1836, two journalists, Park Benjamin and Rufus W. Griswold, began a publication along similar lines which they called 'Brother Jonathan.' Though their intent was to publish serialized fiction, newspaper format was used and some news items were included in order to avoid magazine postal rates. In June, 1840, they were forced out of the editorship of 'Brother Jonathan' and started 'The New World.' Its aims and contents were identical with the first venture, but it appeared from the beginning in two sizes -- the regular edition in folio, the library edition in quarto. In answer to complaints by readers that the complete story could be read in book form long before it could be finished in the weekly, they began to bring out entire stories in folio-sized "supplements" in 1841. These supplements or "extras," as 'Brother Jonathan' called them, became a regular feature in 1842 and are often referred to as "the great revolution in American publishing."[2]

This first "revolution," preceding the second one by exactly 100 years, was made possible by the same ingredients which spelled undreamed-of financial success. Then, as now, they were technological advances in printing methods and a new system of distribution. Like modern paperbacks, the "extras" by-passed regular book distribution channels and were sold on newsstands as well as through the mails.

The first 'New World' supplement was Lever's 'Charles O'Malley' (Vol. 1), which was priced at fifty cents. 'Brother Jonathan' brought it out as an extra at twenty-five cents. Financial success attracted imitators and the 'Nation' in Boston, the 'Mirror' and 'Sun' in New York, and the Philadelphia 'Public Ledger' went into the field. Competition soon brought the price down to $12\frac{1}{2}$ cents.

The extras appeared in two editions -- in gay paper covers in New York for sale on the streets, and without covers for mail distribution to help maintain the newspaper pretext. The content of these paperbacks was primarily fiction, a good deal of it "borrowed" from French authors like Balzac and Hugo without the author's consent or the payment of royalties. American authors usually did receive payment. One of these was Edgar Allan Poe, who wrote the world's first detective story, 'The Murders in the Rue Morgue,' in 1841, followed by 'The Mystery of Marie Rogêt.' This story appeared first in Snowden's 'Ladies' Companion' as a three part serial in 1842-43, and in 1845 as part of 'Tales by Edgar Allan Poe,' in Wiley and Putnam's paperbound series "Library of American Books."[3]

Other publishing enterprises got into the low-priced, serially-printed book field and as a result the regular trade publishers were financially hard hit. Books that sold for one to two dollars could be obtained for twenty-five cents or less. Publishers who had built up large enterprises by pirating British material were now suffering from the same practice used by reprint publishers. Harper decided in 1843 to fight back by issuing a series of popular English novels in brown paper covers at twenty-five cents, and when this proved ineffective, they reduced the retail price to one-half, with one-third off to booksellers. Other publishers got into the price-cutting fight and by 1843 all the markets were overstocked and things came to a crisis. The Post Office Department changed its policy and charged book rates for supplements and extras. The increased cost and the oversupply of materials resulted in a rapid decline of sales.

'Brother Jonathan' sold out in 1844 to its competitor, the 'New World,' which was then owned by Jonas Winchester, who later sold the enterprise to his son and J. W. Judd. The size and format were changed several times, but by May, 1845, the 'New World' was forced to cease publication.

The Interlude in Paperbound Publishing -- 1845-57

The death blow to extras was struck by the Post Office Act of 1845 which lowered mailing charges for regular books. Publishers concentrated on cheaper books, selling for less than one dollar, and brought out many titles in cloth and paper covers simultaneously. The fifties saw the biggest boom American book publishing had ever known. American authors contributed 70 percent of the materials published, while thirty years earlier almost the same amount of publications came from British authors. Sales increased tremendously and book production, together with the general business expansion, took an unprecedented upswing. General prosperity and the bad experiences of the price war kept the inexpensive field quiet. "Trade courtesy," which was the practice of an unwritten gentlemen's agreement between publishers to leave the rights to further editions of foreign publications to the one who had brought it out first, also diminished competition. This went so far that even the additional works of a foreign author were considered the domain of the publisher who had introduced him, although these agreements were often broken in the case of exceptionally popular authors. The advantage of the "trade courtesy" system to the publishers was the maintenance of higher prices, and the public was assured a better manufactured book.

The Dime Novels

With the financial crash in 1857, the prosperity of trade publishers also suffered and there was again room for experimentation with cheap publications. Erastus Flavel Beadle, born in Pierstown, New York, in 1821, started with an idea along these lines which had a great effect on the entire future of the publishing industry. He had opened a print shop in Buffalo in 1852 where he also sold some sheet music published by his brother, Irwin P. Beadle. They brought out a 'Dime Song Book' which was an immediate success and followed this with several low-priced song books after their move to New York in 1858.

In 1860, Beadle & Co. issued its first dime novel in the famous orange paper covers. Whether this idea was inspired by a series published in 1857 by Ballou under the name "Novelette," or was Erastus Beadle's or his editor, Orville J. Victor's, is not known. At any rate, it was the first of a long series of short, 25,000 · to 35,000-word novels based on pioneer history and purely fictional legends. In 1862, Irwin P. Beadle withdrew from the firm. Robert Adams, Erastus Beadle's partner, died in 1866 and was succeeded by his brothers, William and David. The most successful years of the company were from 1870 to 1890. Erastus died in 1894 and the firm was bought in 1898 by J. M. Ivers, who continued the use of the Beadle name for several years. The firm published joke books, almanacs, biographies and some newspapers and periodicals, but was made famous through its dime novels.

The success of these stories is based on several factors, but originality was not one of them. They recognized an existing demand and satisfied it faithfully. The mixture of sensational-ism, nationalism and romanticism which glorified the pioneer and his heretofore unrecognized, unsung hardships and con-tributions to the nation's growth; the appeal of the gaudy cover with its frequently blood curdling and often artistically crude woodcut and the low price all combined to promote sales. John L. Cutler said about them: "[Their]. romantic sensationalism . . . flourished like a huge fungus for half a century and rotted speedily when its nutriment drained away. Out of its fragments was to spring another fungus . . . [flourishing] under the name of pulp paper fiction."[4] (Plates 4 & 5) This was the field in which Street & Smith domineered during the late nineteenth and early twentieth century. John McIntyre, discussing the merits of the dime novels, stated: "There are millions today who, in their youth, have seen the stirring of an undreamed-of-thing in these pages and have witnessed the gates of the imagination folding back showing a brave new world."[5] The truth as to their literary value lies probably somewhere be-tween these two extreme positions. The dime novels filled the popular demand for short, low-priced stories; serializa-tion added to this attraction by being less demanding on the reader's span of attention. That the basic pioneer theme of the Beadle formula still has selling power was recently demonstrated by Walt Disney's revival of Davy Crockett. king of the wild frontier, who delighted the boys of 1955.

Though Beadle & Co. had published over four million dime novels by 1865, the sales of individual titles ranged from 35,000 to 80,000 copies; thus few single dime novels ever had really large sales and only two can be placed on the overall best-seller list -- Mrs. Ann S. Stephens' 'Malaeska, the Indian Wife of the White Hunter,' which Frank O'Brien, a leading dime novel authority, estimates sold half a million copies, and Edward S. Ellis' 'Seth Jones,' which reached about the same number of sales and was reprinted occasionally as late as August, 1900. [6]

A branch of Beadle & Co. was established in London in 1861 and sixty items appeared in Great Britain, but after five years the branch closed and the rights to the British publications were sold. Until 1863, Beadle had the paperback market pretty much to himself, but from then until 1875 other firms entered the field and a wide expansion of paperback publishing occurred between 1875 and 1891.

Dime Novels During the Civil War

Like all other conflicts which try men's souls, the war between the States resulted in the publication of countless books and pamphlets on the political and philosophical issues of the day. The needs for the soldiers' recreational reading were at first supplied by many thousands of copies of dime novels presented to the Union army by Beadle & Co. Later, James Redpath, journalist, editor, lecturer, reformer, abolishionist became a publisher who released printed materials in various formats as a means to arouse interest in the causes he believed in. Beginning with the publication of Louisa M. Alcott's 'Hospital Sketches,' a series of letters which originally appeared in 'The Commonwealth' in 1863, he branched out into a hardcover series "Books for the Times" which sold very well. He expanded his operations with "Books for Camp and Home," and, after lowering their price, finally issued a ten cent series "Books for the Campfires," specifically designed for soldiers. They were bound in green paper covers and better printed than other dime novels. The first title was Louisa M. Alcott's 'On Picket Duty, and Other Tales,' followed by William Wells Brown, 'Clotelle, A Tale of the Southern States,' and reprints of foreign authors like Victor Hugo, 'Battle of Waterloo' and Honoré de Balzac, 'Vendetta.'

These and other titles which followed in 1864 were undoubtedly superior to other dime novels, providing the soldiers with good reading material, much like the "Armed Services Editions" during the Second World War. In 1864 James

Redpath closed his office in Boston and joined General Sherman's forces as war correspondent on his campaign in Georgia. He continued to fight for many causes and to pursue varied interests until his death in 1891, but never again returned to publishing. [7]

The Imitators: 1863 to 1870

The success of Beadle & Co. attracted imitators and by 1863 three firms were competing for second place in the production of cheap papercovered series. They were Irwin P. Beadle, a brother of Erastus who had decided to go into publishing for himself, Sinclair Tousey, and Elliott, Thomes & Talbot. James R. Elliott had been an editor of the Boston weekly magazine 'True Flag' which offered its readers adventure stories of the type characteristic for dime novels. Newton Talbot and William H. Thomes, after a roving youth, had settled down to publishing positions. Talbot became business manager for Frederick Gleason and later for Maturin M. Ballou. When Elliot, Thomes & Talbot was founded, their connection with Ballou was very close and they bought from him between 1861 and 1863 most of his literary periodicals. Among them was 'The Novelette' bringing out thirteen issues a year at a subscription price of $2.00, each of them containing one long and several short stories. [8] Elliot, Thomes & Talbot renamed Ballou's publication "Ten Cent Novelettes" and sold them singly or by subscription (twelve issues at $1.00). The first, Sylvanus Cobb Jr.'s 'Golden Eagle' appeared on November 10, 1863, one day in advance of "Irwin P. Beadle's Ten Cent Novels" and two days before the first of Tousey's "American Tales."

His brother's series was so similar in appearance and name that Erastus Beadle tried to stop them from appearing under this imprint, but did not succeed. (Pocket Books, Inc., in 1940, also tried unsuccessfully to stop their first competitors, Avon Books.) Sinclair Tousey's series was purchased by Erastus Beadle and it is believed that he may actually have started it and Tousey was only acting as his agent. [9]

In 1864, Irwin P. Beadle and his partner George Munro separated and "I. P. Beadle's Ten Cent Novels" became "Munro's Ten Cent Novels." R. T. Dawley & Co. came out with their "Fireside Library" and "Dawley's Ten Penny Novels."

In the same year, the American News Company was founded and began distribution of "Erastus Beadle's Dime Novels."

In the following years, Irwin P. Beadle issued several series, most of them short lived. George Munro started the "Backwoods Series" and Robert M. DeWitt & Co. "DeWitt's Ten Cent Romances." Hilton's "Dime Books" and Chapman's "Sunnyside Series" were also among the numerous competitors. Erastus Beadle opened two subsidiaries, Starr's American Novels and the Adams, Victor & Co. Numerous other series were started and dropped again. There were series planned specifically for boys, series in varying sizes, "Ten Cent Indian Novels," "Ten Cent Popular Novels," "Highway Novels," and many others.

The Second Boom in Paperbacks: Cheap Libraries -- 1870-1891

During the 1870's frequent changes in Beadle's dime novel series indicated that they were losing their grip on the market. The so-called illuminated covers, crudely colored from wood blocks or color stencils, were introduced by Beadle and imitated by others. They seemed to have some sales appeal, but as the frontier began to vanish the content of the series lost its attractiveness.

During the rise of the dime novels, the regular book trade had not been severely challenged. The stories were short and can be considered to stand between the magazine and the full-length novel. They appealed primarily to the less educated, unsophisticated readers, who were not regular trade book customers. However, in the 1870's the situation began to change. A great number of regular fiction titles were imported from Great Britain and sold at prices as low as twenty-five cents. These books were in every respect a threat to the American book trade. In 1873, a newspaper, the 'New York Tribune,' began to bring out "Extras," soon followed by full length "Tribune Novels," selling for ten and twenty cents.[10] These were both original works and reprints.

In 1875, the publication of the many series which were to call themselves "libraries" began with the "Lakeside Library" published by Donnelley, Lloyd & Co. in Chicago, which sold shorter novels at ten cents, longer ones at fifteen and twenty cents. At first they published one title a month, but soon stepped up production to one a week. The purpose of this series is well stated in their prospectus: "The great popular want today is for Cheap, Good Literature . . . Dime novels are issued by the million, and good books by the thousand, but to the mass of readers the one is as distasteful as the other is inaccessible."[11] The intent is clearly spelled out: good literature at a low price. This was accomplished by publishing reprints of foreign, particularly British authors, without payment of royalties. Beadle met the challenge in 1877 with the establishment of his "Fireside Library," containing reprints of British and some French authors, mostly cheap love stories, and with his "Half Dime Library," appealing to boys. During the same year, many other cheap libraries appeared, among them George Munro's "Seaside Library," Fergus' "Popular Library," the "Globe Library," etc. By October, 1877, there were at least fourteen such libraries in existence,[12] the most successful of which was the "Seaside Library," which was bringing out new publications daily.

Frank Leslie's "Home Library of Standard Works by the Most Celebrated Authors" was an outgrowth of his varied newspaper and magazine publishing activities. He had blanketed the newsstands with a flood of pulp and illustrated materials since 1854. Devoted to the glorification of railroad travel, he formed an alliance with the American News Company which was very profitable for both parties and provided the public with more reading material than ever before. These cheap reprints for railroad reading brought authors like Wilkie Collins, Annie Edwards, James Payn and Charles Read a wide audience. Another series, the "Chimney Corner," was planned and edited by his wife. Between 1876 and 1877 he released "Frank Leslie's Popular Library," bound in heavier covers and sold at twenty-five cents. For boys he added "Frank Leslie's Boys Library," but this overextension finally resulted in bankruptcy shortly before his death in 1880. [13]

There was growing concern among the trade publishers, as the libraries included "many of the best-selling and many of the best novels, largely from the list of Harper's "Select Library," but also from those of the Lippincott, Holt, and Appleton series . . . Of one line over a million copies have been sold, and 'Daniel Deronda' in the "Lakeside Library" is said to have reached a sale of about 60,000 copies."[14] It is estimated that the large sales of paperbound books lowered the sales of regular publishers.

As during the days of 'Brother Jonathan,' Harper & Bros. were in the forefront of the fight and began issuing their ten cent "Franklin Square Library" in 1878. Other publishers, like Isaac Kaufman Funk (founder of Funk & Wagnalls), Dodd Mead, Holt, and somewhat later, Houghton Mifflin, Appleton, Scribner, Cassell, and others followed suit. Soon the products of the cheap libraries and of regular trade publishers began to look more and more alike. Both used pirated fiction of foreign authors on which no royalties were paid, and as a result American authors were having a difficult time getting an audience. In 1880, the cheap libraries, which so far had been limited to fiction, began to conquer the heretofore exclusive domain of the trade publishers, non-fiction. The only field which had not yet been invaded by the publishers of cheap libraries was that of clothbound books, but in 1879, John B. Alden, a Chicago book dealer, moved to New York and brought out clothbound books at fifty cents and one dollar, called "Acme Editions" and "Aldus Editions." He went bankrupt in 1881, but Munro copied him and brought out a clothbound pocket edition in 1883.

During the 1880's the quarto paperbacks gave way to the duodecimos and a large number of libraries appeared in this format such as "Franklin Editions," "Standard Library," "Handy Series," "Household Library," "American Series" and "Echo Series." By 1887, a trend toward cheap clothbound books had definitely been established. No discussion of American inexpensive publishing in the last two decades of the nineteenth century would be complete without reference to John W. Lovell, capitalistic socialist, idealistic businessman, schemer, promoter, and always publisher. Starting out as a pirate publisher, he achieved success in 1882 with his "Lovell's Library," paperbound reprints at ten, twenty and thirty cents, offering readers better books with clearer type and more attractively designed than the cheaper series.

He offered fiction and non-fiction (mostly biographies, some books on history and travel) and had published close to 1500 titles after eight years. He used several devices in expanding his market. Many books came out in paper and clothbound editions. A second-class mailing privilege aided in distribution. He bought out some competing paperback series and introduced several new ones, among them the "Political and Scientific Series" which he used for the propagation of his radical and reform ideas, by publishing works by Albert K. Owen, Edward Kellogg, Friedrich Engels, Henry George and many others. [15]

Distribution of the cheap paperbound libraries in the 1870's was at first by mail at magazine rates. In response to trade pressure the Post Office denied them magazine rates and the libraries turned to the news companies for distribution. The cheap books were sold through newsdealers and smaller booksellers rather than through regular trade channels, as the profit of three cents a copy was not sufficient to induce booksellers to offer them in possible competition with the more profitable editions on their shelves. This situation was similar to one prevailing for current paperbacks, particularly until the higher-priced, more substantial series appeared from 1953 on. Other outlets for the cheap libraries were dry goods stores, the forerunners of the modern department stores. They obtained books from jobbers who also handled magazines and stationary supplies or bought them directly from the publishers at a 40 to 45 percent discount. The dry goods stores used books to attract customers, and many "holiday bookstores" were opened, catering to the Christmas trade only and drawing customers away from the regular book outlets. These stores, which had no all-embracing organization of the book trade to follow, undercut each other and the entire market picture became overcrowded and got completely out of hand. [16]

During the twenty years from 1870 to 1890, the American public was offered some very good books in addition to dime novels and cheap literature, but at the expense of the quality of the physical book, the art of typography, and the foreign authors who received no royalties, and the American authors who could not easily establish themselves. In 1891, the passage of copyright legislation helped to clean up the unwholesome situation; after a short period of expansion the cheap libraries were forced out of business. Piracy was coming to its end and the overexpanded book trade went through a period of readjustment.

Cheap Books -- 1891 to 1920

After 1891 the publishers of inexpensive books turned rather successfully to clothbound reprints, while paperbound editions fell more and more into disfavor with the public. John W. Lovell tried in vain to clear up the confusion caused by the Copyright Act and to save the cheap libraries by establishing the U.S. Book Company, which bought up plates of many of the libraries and thereby tried to eliminate competition, duplication and oversupply. However, the enterprise failed in 1893, and the clothbound pocket size reprint series of the type begun by John B. Alden in 1880 took over the market, though some paperbacks survived into the first decade of the twentieth century.

Among these were

. . . Hurst, Lovell, Coryell, Munro, Lupton and U. S. Book Company, [which] kept long series in print for such markets as were left, and Street and Smith took over others, but new readers were turning away from Mary J. Holmes and Mrs. Southworth to current best sellers . . . [17]

The most significant of these. links between nineteenth and twentieth century paperback publishers was the firm of Street & Smith, which is still in existence today as a magazine publisher. Established in 1855 as publisher of the 'New York Weekly Dispatch,' a serial dealing in light fiction, Street & Smith was immediately successful and began to publish all types of pulp magazines. Relying heavily on serialization, they engaged in as much pirating of British authors as their competitors, but paid their American authors better and, therefore, counted the most popular writers of the period among their contributors. After the Civil War, the firm began to publish the stories of Horatio Alger, Jr., which exerted a tremendous influence on the youth of the day. Edward Judson exploited the topic of the Wild West for the firm and wrote from 1869 on the "Buffalo Bill Stories" under the pseudonym of Ned Buntline. When he died, the stories were continued by Prentiss Ingraham.

In order to appeal to a male audience, detective stories were stressed. Many of the successful ones were contributed by Harlan P. Halsey, who had been lured away from George Munro's "Fireside Companion" and had acquired the penname of Judson R. Taylor in the change. From 1880 on John Russell Coryell, who had initiated the Nick Carter detective stories, contributed stories for a juvenile audience under various

pen names, among them Bertha M. Clay. The Nick Carter
stories were also written by Frederic Dey, Thomas C. Har-
bough, George C. Jenks, Frederick W. Davis and others.
Just as "Beadle's Dime Novels" were frequently reprints of
serialized fiction, Street & Smith often reprinted such novels in
their periodicals and, when popular demand was sufficient, came
out with a separate magazine which prominently featured
the name of the hero and often even used the name "library."
Thus, Street & Smith weeklies were distinguished from other
pulp fiction merely by their regular periodic appearance.
The first of the weekly libraries, the "Log Cabin Library" was
established in 1889, to be followed by others like the "Nugget
Library" (Plate 6). Weeklies carrying the hero's name were
"The Nick Carter Detective Library" (1891), "The Diamond Dick
Library" (1895), "The Klondike Kid Library" (1898). [18]

Irregularly published paperback series, continuing the
dime novel tradition, were started by Street & Smith in 1896,
and while the other pulp publishers of the nineteenth century
disappeared, Street & Smith continued, throughout the first
quarter of the twentieth century, to publish many such series
and distribute their popular ten and fifteen cent novelettes in
various outlets. The last series was "The Western Story
Library" created in 1927. While the firm eventually abandoned
paper pulp fiction in the 1930's, it continued to be active on the
American publishing scene and is today bringing out such
magazines as 'Mademoiselle,' 'Charm,' 'Living for Young
Homemakers' and 'Astounding Science Fiction.'

At the end of the nineteenth century, Grosset & Dunlap
tried to keep the low priced market alive by making best
sellers of the day available in inexpensive cloth bindings.
Many of these titles had been manufactured for the American
News Company as twenty-five cent paper editions. When these
paperbacks lost their sales appeal, Grosset & Dunlap tore
off the paper covers, bound them in cloth and wholesaled them
below forty cents. [19] This experiment was sufficiently successful to encourage the expansion of this operation. These books
sold well at various outlets and bookstores for 50 cents and
paperback publishing was additionally discouraged. There was
a concurrent change in the public's reading tastes and the
former paperback readers were now attracted by the new
illustrated magazines. Grosset & Dunlap was imitated by other
firms such as the A. L. Burt Company along with many of the

original trade publishers, though none of them quite matched Grosset & Dunlap's success.

The 1920's -- Experimentation in Paperbacks

In 1920, Emanuel Haldeman-Julius conceived the idea of publishing a "frankly paperbound booklet, not a 'little leather edition,' but just a cheap paper-bound book." [20] This was the beginning of the "Little Blue Books" which sold around 300 million copies. The first two titles were 'The Rubaiyat' and 'The Ballad of Reading Gaol' and their success started a publishing career which lasted until his death in 1951. He produced about 2000 titles on his specially designed presses and the prices of his booklets fluctuated from five to twenty-five cents. He occasionally changed titles of reprints for greater sales appeal (Maupassant's 'Tallow Ball,' for instance, became 'A French Prostitute's Sacrifice') but generally published for causes rather than financial returns and his favorite topics were socialism and sex education. At first, most of his books were reprints, but later many were originals, written to order (among these was Will Durant's 'Story of Philosophy'). His approach to paperback publishing was a one-man campaign and his success proved that the United States was sufficiently tolerant to permit him to express his ideas and while doing so even to make a good profit. It seems not unfair to compare his "Little Blue Books" with the chapbooks and tracts of preceding centuries in format as well as in much of their content. That he also made it possible for the public to buy for five cents works by Spencer, Huxley, Shelley, Balzac and Hugo along with Clarence Darrow, Havelock Ellis and Bertrand Russell, was one of his outstanding achievements, which earns him a place in American publishing. [21] The firm has been managed since 1951 by Henry J. Haldeman, the son of the founder; comparatively few bookstores or other outlets handle the booklets which were sold through coupon advertising. The price of all titles is ten cents. During August 1956 Henry J. Haldeman, whose primary interest does not lie in the management of the Little Blue Book Publishing Company, put the firm up for sale at $150,000, including the physical plant, bookstock and copyrights.

There were several other paperbound lines in the twenties which had avant-garde literary and politically leftist tendencies as their editorial policies -- "Pamphlet Poets" and "International Publishers" are examples. None of these enterprises were, however, successful. "Garden City Novelettes," published by a Doubleday subsidiary, also failed in competition with Street & Smith publications.

Public prejudice against paperbacks was considerable and advances in bookbinding techniques had made cloth bindings so inexpensive that any good line of paperbacks had to fight the competition from the scarcely more expensive clothbound reprints. Charles Boni tried in 1929 to bring out good books in paper covers, attractively designed by Rockwell Kent, selling for fifty cents a copy. "Boni Paper Books" were operated on a subscription basis of twelve books a year, but due to unsurmountable problems of distribution the series was discontinued in 1931. (Plate 7)

An entirely different type of publishing operation which aims at a specific audience rather than the general reader is exemplified by the releases of the John F. Rider Publishers, Inc., founded in 1929. The company specializes in manuals and texts in the radio, tape recording, television and electronics field for technicians, repairmen and students in schools and industrial training. These books, richly illustrated and brought out in paperback format since 1929, have been successful. They now sell in the $2.00 to $3.00 price range and are distributed to bookstores and to electronic parts distributors.

The 1930's -- Significant Failures and Accomplishments

Several new firms were established between 1930 and 1937 which, with the exception of Mercury Publications, did not succeed though their failures helped pave the way for the successful popular mass-distributed paperbacks of the forties. Other publications in paperbound format, more closely related to pamphlet than to book production, were also begun during the early and middle thirties.

In 1932, the National Home Library Foundation began to reprint literary classics. It was forced to change to cloth bindings in 1935 due to several reasons -- the independence of book dealers and librarians and difficulties in distribution.

Sherman Mitchell, president of the National Home Library, stated in 1938:

> After six years we have learned that a book that retails at 25 cents will sell about twelve times as fast and about twenty-five times as much as a book selling for $2.50 or more . . . People with fair incomes will buy inexpensive books and . . . folks with little or no income will buy them if they become interested in the subject. [22]

National Home Library was able to produce editions large enough to bring down production costs by running off twelve reprint titles in editions of 100,000 copies each as its first offering, costing 1½ cents per bound copy and selling at fifteen cents each. Yet the series did not succeed as a paperback.

In 1937, Richard S. Childs, an economist, started a paperback series under the name of "Modern Age Books." The titles dealt primarily with social and economic topics and current events, but also included travel and literature. The scheme was ambitious and it was planned to publish all titles "in strong paper bindings, good paper, and well designed at twenty-five, thirty-five and fifty cents . . . Their price plan required editions of fifty thousand, printed on magazine presses, to get the needed economies . . ." [23] The magazine presses were of the new rotary type installed by the Rumford Press to handle printing orders for the 'Reader's Digest;' cost production per copy was low, but great quantities had to be produced to make the enterprise profitable. The firm had a large sales staff, energetic promotion, and attempted distribution through book stores as well as newsstands and drug stores. The 33 to 45 percent discounts had to be split between the book dealer and the distributor making the discount too small to be attractive to regular book jobbers. The number of book stores was too small to support large editions. The formula was not right for newsstand sales, possibly because of a rather "highbrow" selection of titles, [24] and the prices of the books had to be raised to fifty, seventy-five and ninety cents, with editions cut to 15,000 copies. By December, 1939, Modern Age changed to clothbound books, with an occasional paperbound title.

Mercury Publications

In 1937, Mercury Publications started a series of

paperbacks, "American Mercury Books," which is the only pre-1939 line surviving to the present day and also the first series successfully employing magazine distribution.

The history of Mercury Publications goes back to the 1920's when 'The American Mercury,' edited by H. L. Mencken and George Jean Nathan and published by Alfred A. Knopf, was one of the most widely discussed magazines. The present publisher of Mercury Publications, Joseph W. Ferman, joined 'The American Mercury' with the first issue, in January, 1924. When the magazine was sold to Paul Palmer and later to Lawrence E. Spivak, Ferman continued with the magazine, first as business and then as general manager. In 1950, 'The American Mercury' was sold to Clendenin Ryan, while Mercury Publications retained the five other publications, among which were "American Mercury Books" and "Mercury Mysteries."

After thirteen years of magazine publishing, the firm brought out its first paperback in 1937, 'The Postman Always Rings Twice,' by James M. Cain. The introduction by Paul Palmer, the editor of the series, summarizes its aims and distribution system:

> There are millions of avid readers in this Republic and hundreds of good books are published every year; yet it is a rare volume that sells a hundred thousand copies, and a phenomenal one that sells a million. Most books find less than 3000 buyers. Why is this? We do not pretend to know the answer; but we do know that millions of Americans are assiduous readers of magazines. And we believe that among them are many who will buy books if the process of buying is made easier. It is chiefly for this magazine market that we now issue AMERICAN MERCURY BOOKS.
>
> These books will have a magazine price -- twenty-five cents; a magazine format -- the paper cover; a magazine distribution -- the newsstand; and a magazine endorsement -- THE AMERICAN MERCURY. Presenting both fiction and non-fiction, AMERICAN MERCURY BOOKS will be selected carefully from the hundreds of first-rate volumes published each year. They will be distinguished in style and engrossing in content. This first publication in the series . . . is an intro-

ductory example of what our standards of readability and literary quality will be . . .

The format of the books is the same as that of 'Reader's Digest,' and both publications are still produced by the Rumford Press. The idea of publishing the paperback series goes back primarily to Lawrence Spivak. "American Mercury Books" started as a bimonthly series and was changed into a monthly publication in 1938. Larger in format than other paperbacks, Mercury publications are not displayed on racks but are found alongside other magazines. They are available for one month only.

"American Mercury Books" contained in the beginning some nonfiction titles, but later changed completely to fiction and, from 1940 on, specialized in mystery novels; the name was changed to "Mercury Mysteries," but consecutive numbering continued and reached #204 in January, 1955. In March, 1940, another series was started by the firm under the name of "Bestseller Mysteries." These books, stressing the faster selling mysteries, appeared monthly, and 178 titles had been published by January, 1954. Both series are almost exclusively reprints and in many instances the limited exposure given to them enables the publisher to purchase reprint rights for thirty or sixty days only, after which all rights revert to the original publisher.

In 1942, a firm by the name of Jonathan Press was founded which is owned entirely by Mercury Publications. "Jonathan Press Mysteries" came out bimonthly until 1954, monthly since then, and stress somewhat tougher mystery novels. The publications are partly reprints and partly original collections. Some of the titles in this series are reissues of reprints -- titles previously published by Pocket Books or Dell.

Besides the paperback series, Mercury Publications also publish 'Ellery Queen's Mystery Magazine,' which is one of the most widely read and distributed magazines of this type and appears in Australian, French, British, German, Italian, Portuguese, Danish and three different Spanish editions. The firm also publishes 'The Magazine of Fantasy and Science Fiction.'

Early in 1943 the company released a special series of five books for the U.S. Armed Forces which was the forerunner of the "Armed Services Editions." The five books, reprinted under the heading, "The Mercury Library" were: 'A Yankee Doctor in Paradise,' by S.M. Lambert; 'Watch Below,' by William McFee; 'archy and mehitabel,' by Don Marquis; 'H.M. Corvette,' by Nicholas Monsarrat; 'Glencannon,' by Guy Gilpatric. These books were digest size and were supplied to the Special Services Division at cost.

Specialized Pamphlet Type Publications

How many publishers of this type of material exist is difficult to estimate, but several firms established in the 1930's and still operating successfully illustrate the variety of publishing activities related to but not actually a part of paperback publishing.

Pendle Hill, a non-profit educational institution maintained by the Society of Friends (Quakers) since 1930 started the "Pendle Hill Pamphlets" in 1934. Ninety-six have appeared in the last twenty-three years, selling for thirty-five cents each or, by subscription, at $2.00 for six per year. Although maintained by a religious sect, original writings from all sources on social and religious topics are represented. Average editions of 4000 copies have seen several reprintings particularly with Arnold Toynbee's 'Christianity and Civilization' and Simone Weil's 'The Iliad or the Poem of Force.'

Harian Publications released its pamphlets on travel starting in 1935 with the editorial policy of showing the reader that travel can be economical and comfortable. Selling mostly by mail but using Greenberg as trade distributor, Harian has been very successful with titles like 'Where to Retire on a Small Income' by Norman D. Ford, 'Florida' by the same author, and 'Travel Routes Around the World' by Frederic E. Tyarks. Most titles are priced at $1.00.

Bellman Publishing Company, established in 1934, produces career guidance material for use in trade and industrial training schools, high schools and colleges. Relying mostly on direct mail, Bellman grants dealers progressive discounts. The pamphlets, up to forty pages in length, are designed for occupational guidance counselors. There are currently ninety titles in print and twelve are being added annually, selling for $1.00 a copy.

Lane Publishing Company, publishers of 'Sunset Magazine,' released the 'All Western Foods Cook Book' in 1935 and has brought out sixty titles since, all staff written. Editions run from 15,000 to 50,000 copies. All titles deal with "how-to-do-it" information geared to Western living: travel and outdoor recreation, homebuilding and furnishing, cooking and gardening. Much of the material is reprinted from 'Sunset Magazine.'

[1] Shove, op. cit., p. vi.

[2] Lehmann-Haupt, Wroth and Silver, op. cit., p. 130.

[3] Irving Wallace, 'The Fabulous Originals' (New York: Alfred A. Knopf, 1955), pp. 173 and 182.

[4] John L. Cutler, 'Gilbert Patten and His Frank Merriwell Stories' University of Maine Studies, 2nd series, no. 13 (Orono, Maine: University of Maine, 1934), p. 11.

[5] Albert Johannsen, 'The House of Beadle and Adams and its Dime and Nickel Novels' (Norman: University of Oklahoma Press, 1950), vol. I, p. xxv.

[6] Mott, op. cit., pp. 149-150.

[7] Madeleine B. Stern, 'Imprints on History. Book Publishers and American Frontiers' (Bloomington: Indiana University Press, 1956), pp. 76-83.

[8] Ibid., p. 211.

[9] Johannsen, op. cit., p. 150.

[10] Mott, op. cit., p. 150.

[11] Ibid., p. 151.

[12] "The Cheap Libraries," 'Publishers' Weekly,' XII:13 (September 29, 1877), pp. 363-64.

[13] Stern, op. cit., pp. 221-32.

[14] "The Cheap Libraries," 'Publishers' Weekly,' XII:14 (October 6, 1887), p. 396.

[15] Stern, op. cit., pp. 259-89.

[16] Lehmann-Haupt, Wroth and Silver, op. cit., pp. 259-61.

[17] Frederic G. Melcher, "Paper Books at the Turn of the Century," 'Publisher's Weekly,' CLXVII:17 (April 23, 1955), p. 1948.

[18] Quentin Reynolds, 'The Fiction Factory' (New York: Random House, 1955), p. 272.

[19] Frederic G. Melcher, "The Publisher as a Factor in Popular Reading," 'The Practice of Book Selection,' L.R. Wilson, ed. (Chicago: University of Chicago Press, 1943), pp. 273-74.

[20] "Emanuel Haldeman-Julius," 'Publishers' Weekly,' CLX:6 (August 11, 1951), p. 564.

[21] Emanuel Haldeman-Julius, 'The First Hundred Million' (New York: Simon & Schuster, 1928).

[22] Leon Whipple, "Books on Main Street," 'Survey Graphic,' 27 (March, 1938), p. 174.

[23] Melcher, "The Publisher as a Factor in Popular Reading," op. cit., p. 276.

[24] "Books for the Masses," 'New Republic,' XCII (October 6, 1937), pp. 229-230.

Part 2

AMERICAN

PAPERBACKS:

THE CURRENT PHASE

1939-1957

CHAPTER 5

THE PUBLISHING SCENE

The Government and Paperback Publishing

Book publishing in America today is, with the exception of government publications and the releases of foundations, societies and associations, in the hands of private ownership. Since the government has never directly interfered with them, publishers have not been restrained in bringing out materials reflecting their own interests and preferences. As a result, the book industry in America has developed along lines of individual initiative, and there are no clear-cut distinctions between types of publishers and types of publications; publishers cross over freely from one field to another.

The government, on the federal, state, and local levels, has always brought out pamphlets and documents in paperbound form, but these publications do not fall within the scope of this study. The only exception is the cooperative effort between the government and private publishers which resulted in the "Armed Services Editions," "Overseas Editions" and the educational texts of the Armed Forces Institute during World War II. These activities formed a significant aspect of the paperback development and serve as an example of creative coexistence between private ownership and public interest at a time of national emergency which found the book industry prepared to fill unselfishly a sudden need. These paperback series carried American publications into the farthest corners of the globe. In spite of their expendable, transitory nature, they are a permanent monument to American culture.

The books of these series came into existence due to the efforts of the Council on Books in Wartime during World War II.[1] In a letter to its chairman, William Warder Norton, on December 1, 1942, President Roosevelt expressed his official recognition by saying that "all who write and publish and sell

and administer books . . . will rededicate themselves to the
single task of arming the mind and the spirit of the American
people with the strongest and most enduring weapons."[2]

Many Americans in the publishing industry, the library
profession, and governmental agencies, along with the general
public, felt that the Second World War was not merely a struggle for material goods or real estate but that it was also a war
of ideas, and that books were necessary for the sustenance
and entertainment of the men in the Armed Forces. The Army
had engaged in library service during World War I and the
machinery for book distribution existed in the Army Library
Service. Other agencies made reading material available. There
were Victory Book Campaigns, the Red Cross, private organizations and individual donors who contributed substantially.
John Jamieson estimates that some 25 million hardbound
and 200 million paperbound books were purchased or donated for
distribution to soldiers between the beginning of 1941 and the
fall of 1946.[3]

All those concerned with providing books for the Armed
Forces had come to the conclusion that paperbacks were the
most suitable format because they were light, small and inexpensive. Many paperbacks were distributed by the Red Cross
or mailed by civilians to friends in Army camps and overseas. The paperback firms in existence, Mercury Books,
Pocket Books, Penguin Books, Avon, Dell, Infantry Journal
Books and Superior Reprints, provided as many titles and
copies as possible for Armed Service consumption. Colonel
Ray L. Trautman, the Chief of the Army Library Section, used
all his personal vigor and devotion to procure a large amount
of books, but he was confronted with many difficulties brought
about by a shortage of paper and suitable titles. Only a small
number of books were being reprinted at the time, and most of
these were not current. Reprint rights for current titles were
not available. Several publishers considered bringing out
10,000 to 20,000 extra copies of their hardcover publications
in paper wrappers, but the reduction in cost was not sufficient
to make the project worthwhile.

The Army Library Section had used kits containing 500
books of commercially produced paperbacks for overseas distribution between 1941 and 1943. However, there were not
enough titles to choose from to make a wider selection possible.

Armed Services Editions

In 1942 a large quantity of a suitable English publication, 'Combined Operations: The Official Story of the Commandos,' was offered for sale to the Army Library Section. Colonel Trautman refused to buy more than a few copies unless this title could be made available in paperbound format. He consulted with H. Stahley Thompson, the graphic arts specialist of the Information Branch of the Special Services Division. In collaboration with Philip Van Doren Stern, who was appointed manager of the "Armed Services Editions" branch of the Council on Books in Wartime and had formerly been executive editor of Pocket Books, Inc., Trautman and Thompson worked out a solution which made the production of "Armed Services Editions" possible. They proposed in 1942, that books like 'Combined Operations' be printed on the rotary presses used by commercial printing firms for pulp and digest-size magazines and catalogs. These presses were not operating at full capacity because of wartime shortages. Furthermore none of the book industry's printing resources would be tied up, and costs would be less than ten cents per copy on runs of 50,000 and as little as five cents per copy on runs of 100,000.

Trautman and Thompson submitted their plan to the Council on Books in Wartime, and, after many concessions to various interests of the book industry, the project was established. No scientific books or texts were to be reprinted, and the Army was to take all possible precautions to avoid a postwar flooding of the market. A selection committee would choose about fifty books per month for reprinting from lists provided by various publishers, which would be predominantly current publications. Authors and publishers would get one-half cent royalty per copy, and the books would be sold to the Army and Navy at cost (approximately six cents plus 10 percent for overhead expenses). The point was made to the publishers that it would be of tremendous benefit to the book industry in the long run to provide books to millions of members of the Armed Forces, many of whom had never before done much reading.

The Army and Navy welcomed the project wholeheartedly. They were to procure 50,000 copies of each of the fifty titles published monthly. The final choice of titles, submitted by the original publishers and selected by a committee, was to be made by Colonel Trautman for the Army and Isabel Du Bois,

Librarian of the Navy, for her branch of the Service. Cuneo Press, Street & Smith, W. F. Hall Company, Rumford Press and Western Printing and Lithographing Company supplied the press work. As the equipment on hand had to be used, the books were printed two up, one above the other, resulting in two oblong formats, 5½ x 3 7/8" or 6½ x 4½", bound on the short side. (Plate 8)   This odd format had the additional advantage that the thinner books could be rolled up and fitted into any pocket or bag. Initial financial arrangements caused considerable complications, but two months after the contracts were signed, a million and a half copies of "Armed Service Editions" had reached the military establishments.

A total of 1,324 titles were published in "Armed Services Editions," of which only ninety-nine had previously been reprinted. They were a bargain for the government, which bought 123½ million copies at an average cost of 6.09 cents per volume before the project ended in the fall of 1946. The men in the services who got them free of charge welcomed them enthusiastically. Never before had so many books at such a low price found such a large number of avid readers.

Educational Texts for the Armed Forces

Shortly after Pearl Harbor the United States Office of Education and the National Committee on Education and Defense sponsored a conference of college and university executives which laid down plans for the operation and contribution of our educational institutions during the war emergency. By September, 1942 the Army had begun to put a program into operation which provided individual and group instruction through Army libraries. This and related activities drew the skill and resources of American textbook publishers into the war effort.

The Army Institute (later called the Army Forces Institute) provided correspondence courses and about seventy-five colleges came under contract to make instruction available through their extension divisions. The Army Institute set up an editorial staff under the auspices of the American Council on Education which created instructional materials to be used by students who had to work independently and rely on self teaching and checking. Publishers were asked to submit existing texts in elementary arithmetic, physics, electricity, radio and automotive mechanics which would lend themselves to publication in special editions. Added to these topics were English composition, algebra, plane geometry, trigonometry, blueprint reading, map reading and meterology.

William E. Spaulding, who is now president of Hougthon Mifflin Co., became director of the editorial staff of the Army Institute and developed an educational publishing program in which the selection of the format was guided "by the dimensions of the soldier's pocket . . . [so that he could] put all the material of one course into one book of pocket size."[5] If this proved to be impossible the text was compressed into two pocketsize books.

By July 1943 a large list of texts was in existence which was augmented by special book projects inaugurated by the Language Section, Educational Branch, Special Services Division. These and other educational text books in paperbound format accomplished three educational aims: they provided, in spite of the primary war effort, for the continuing education of the men and women of the armed forces; they helped to prepare service personnel for war-connected activities; they helped to maintain educational contacts of enlisted personnel and to ease the G.I.'s transition into college life or civilian occupations.

Overseas Editions, Inc.

Overseas Editions, Inc. was a joint project of the Office of War Information and the Council on Books in Wartime, which got under way in 1944. Chester Kerr, the chief of the book division of the Office of War Information, was the leader in many discussions and negotiations with various members of the Council, particularly with Stanley Rinehart. The project resulted in the distribution of 3,600,000 copies of thirty-five titles in three languages to the liberated civilians in Europe and Asia. The idea to supply American books in translation to civilians was of interest to the Office of War Information. The Psychological Warfare Division and the Office of Strategic Services were also drawn into the project. A list of 100 titles was first considered for translation. An independent corporation was formed and contracts between Overseas Editions, Inc., and the Council were signed. Difficulties arose over the financing, since the Office of War Information was not legally able to advance money on its contracts as the War Department could on "Armed Service Editions." This development stalled further progress until finally Robert de Graff of Pocket Books permitted the use of his firm's credit to finance the project. By November, 1944, production was under way, but foreign language composition created a new problem due to labor shortages. The books were 4 3/4" x 6 3/8" trim size, printed on rotary presses two-up and cut in two, wire stitched and with paper covers glued on. They varied in length from 96 to 544 pages.

The most amazing result of this project, which had such a slow start and faced at first many financial difficulties, was its economic success. Since the books were sold at prevailing retail prices in the various countries, this was a net profit operation for the U. S. government. Authors like Stephen Vincent Benét, Howard Fast, Ernest Hemingway, Walter Lippmann, David Lilienthal, Ernest Pyle and William Saroyan reached people in Austria, Belgium, Bulgaria, Czechoslovakia, Denmark, France, Germany, Greece, Holland, Italy, Norway, Poland, Rumania, Yugoslavia, North Africa, Syria, Turkey, China, Japan, the Philippines, and Thailand.

Postwar Cooperative Publishing Projects

Generally motivated by broader concepts than mere profit incentives, American publishers continued to bring books with and without government assistance through individual and cooperative efforts to underdeveloped areas in the post-World War II period. These projects were sparked by the realization that many foreign countries are not in a financial position to buy the books they want and need, that many of the people lack the ability to read English, and that millions in politically critical areas are receiving printed materials from the USSR. Paperbacks seemed the best means of supplying large numbers of books at low prices and shipping costs.

To make dollars available for book purchase, the U. S. government authorized the Information Media Guaranty Program under the Economic Cooperation Act of 1948 which permits American publishers to convert foreign currencies into

American dollars. Paperback overseas sales have been largest to countries covered by these contracts.

The Information Center Service of the U. S. Information Agency supplies missions in India and Southeast Asia with expendable libraries, self-contained units of one hundred paperbound books of which more than 3500 sets are in use.[7] Under the same project, translated American titles are produced abroad. The ICS also works with American publishers on low-cost export editions which are paperbound and sold abroad through regular trade channels. The Small Books Program makes inexpensive reprints available in the Near and Far East, South America, and other parts of the world at a price of ten or fifteen cents. These "Student Editions" are sold through local bookstores. Sixty-five titles were available in spring, 1957, and fifty more planned for the future. The "Ladder Editions" supply mainly non-fiction, some biographies and autobiographies depicting American life and culture in simplified English for those less proficient in our language. Distribution of "Student Editions" and "Ladder Editions" is made by regular paperback publishers through their normal commercial channels in foreign countries selected by U.S.I.A. CARE, a non-profit organization made up of twenty-six member agencies and supported by voluntary contributions, has developed the "American Bookshelf," a paperback presentation program.

Franklin Publications, Inc., a non-profit membership corporation, operating under a board of directors consisting of publishers and public interest representatives, arranges for the publication of American books in translation. Among its directors are Arthur S. Adams, president of the American Council on Education, Grayson L. Kirk, president of Columbia University, and Ralph R. Shaw, professor of Library Science at Rutgers University and former president of the American Library Association. Datus C. Smith, formerly director of Princeton University Press, has been president of Franklin Publications since 1952. Offices are in New York, Cairo, Teheran, Lahore (West Pakistan), Dacca (East Pakistan), and Djakarta (Indonesia). The first titles were released in 1953. American books by authors such as James B. Conant, Aaron Copland, Stephen Crane, John Dewey, William Faulkner, Nathaniel Hawthorne, Gilbert Highet, Henry James, Jack London, Edgar Allan Poe, William Saroyan, Benjamin Spock,

John Steinbeck and Thornton Wilder are being translated into Arabic, Urdu, Bengali and Bahasa Indonesia. Over two hundred titles have appeared and more than three hundred are in the process of publication.

Chekov Publishing House, established in 1951 by the Ford Foundation, produced and exported Russian-language books by contemporary Soviet emigré authors and the Asia Foundation, a private agency, supports the translation of American books into Asian languages and Asian books into English. The Chekov Publishing House ceased operation in April 1956 when its subsidy was discontinued.

Commercial Publishing

Paperback publications of agencies, organizations and commercial firms not engaged primarily in publishing activities will be omitted from further discussion. These pamphlets and brochures are usually done by job printers and form a large and amorphous group of ephemera, which has never been surveyed in detail.

The publishing scene under discussion consists of the following branches: Trade, university press, text, private press, vanity press, reprint, book club, reference and subscription, religious and Bible, art and architecture, music, law, scientific, medical and technical, and children's book publishing. Many firms in most of these branches engage in the release of paperbound titles or series. However, only books for adult readers are being considered. While a distinction between original and reprint publishing can be made easily, it blurs rather than delineates because most publishers tend to engage in both. Almost all firms branch out into different fields, at least occasionally, and are always willing to try a new line. These fluctuations are further stimulated by the ease with which publishers set up subsidiaries, establish new series and drop them again, merge or divide existing corporations, and change top personnel from one house to the other. This situation produces changes from day to day so that some of the information on various firms given in the following may soon be superseded by new developments. There is a great deal of mobility in publishing at mid-century for two reasons: -- the complete freedom from government control, and the intensely individualistic operations of publishers who follow their own inclinations and interests. Publishing as a profession has always attracted individualists and idealists who wanted to express their feelings and beliefs and, incidentally, also reap economic rewards if possible. This diversification of interests and freedom to compete poses a problem in the classification of the many firms which engage in paperback publishing, particularly if one realizes that the approximate number of paperbound books sold yearly rose from 6 million in 1940 to somewhere between 250 million and 400 million in 1956.[8]

In order to present a clearly discernible picture of the paperback production as it evolved in its current phase from 1939 to 1957, several approaches suggest themselves. These alternatives are: (1) a chronological account, (2) a treatment according to the type of publisher and publication. Since publications follow no historical sequence and do not stay within mutually exclusive categories, it was felt that, for the sake of completeness, both approaches were required. The historical year by year account synthesizes the developments as they occurred, (Chapter 6) while the treatment according to types of publications and publishers permits an analysis of the various firms (Chapters 8-14). Details as to various series, price structure, editorial problems and individual publications are incorporated into the accounts of the individual publishing houses. Problems of industry-wide significance, technical production, literary output, author-publisher relationship, distribution and censorship are treated separately (Chapter 7).

[1] Information on "Armed Services Editions" and "Overseas Editions" based on: Interviews with Colonel Ray L. Trautman; John A. Jamieson, 'Books for the Army' (New York: Columbia University Press, 1950); 'History of the Council on Books in War Time -- 1942-1946' (New York: Country Life Press, 1946).

[2] 'History of the Council on Books in War Time,' p. (vi).

[3] Jamieson, op. cit., p. 143.

[4] Henry C. Herge, et al., 'Wartime College Training Programs of the Armed Services' (Washington, D. C.: American Council on Education, 1948); "The Army Plans Big Educational Program," "Army Institute Starts Editorial Staff and Seeks Review Copies," 'Publishers' Weekly,' CXLII: 10 and 19 (Sep. 5 and Nov. 7, 1942), p. 835 and 1956.

[5] "Textbooks at War Discussed at Textbook Clinic Meeting," 'Publishers' Weekly,' CXLII:23 (Dec. 5, 1942), pp. 2309-10.

⁶ Dan Lacy, Charles G. Bolte and Peter S. Jennison, eds., "American Books Abroad," 'Library Trends,' V:1, (July, 1956), and Frank L. Schick, "American Publishers Share Our Problems," 'Publishers' Circiular and Booksellers Record,' CLXXI:4750, (July 13, 1957), pp. 831-33.

⁷Peter S. Jennison, "How American Books Reach Readers Abroad," 'Library Trends,' V:1, (July, 1956), p.11.

⁸"Good Year for Mass Market Paperbacks," 'Publishers' Weekly,' CLXXI:2, (January 14, 1957), p. 22.

PLATE 1 — *see p. 7*
Hans Schönsperger, 'Von Ordnung der Gesundheit,' 1482.
*Earliest known copy of an un-
integrated wrapper of the incunabula period, showing a
woodcut imitation of a blind-
tooled leather binding of the
time.*

PLATE 2 — *see p. 17*
S. H. Steinberg, 'Five Hun-
dred Years of Printing.'
Harmondsworth, Middlesex:
Penguin Books, Inc., 1955
(Pelican Books A343).

*Indicating the transition from
completely unadorned to illustrated Penguin covers, using
a design which is a modern
adaptation of the earliest
known printer's mark, the
double shield of Fust and
Schoeffer.*

PLATE 3 — *see p. 29*

A. Conan Doyle, 'The Memoirs of Sherlock Holmes.' Leipzig: Bernhard Tauchnitz, 1894 (Tauchnitz Edition, Vol. 2973).

The unadorned, typographically undistinguished volumes of the Tauchnitz Edition brought to non-English speaking countries some of the outstanding writings of English and American authors. A. Conan Doyle's 'Sherlock Holmes', strongly influenced by Edgar Allan Poe, found wide acclaim on the Continent and helped to introduce detective stories as a type of popular fiction the world over.

PLATE 4 — *see p. 51*

Ann S. Stephens, 'Esther, a Story of the Oregon Trail.' New York: Beadle & Co., 1862 (Beadle's Dime Novels, No. 45).

Ann S. Stephens, the author of the first dime novel of the Beadle series, uses in this and other books the pioneer theme, one of the basic ingredients also of many of today's Western novels.

PLATE 5 — *see p. 51*

'The Sheridan of Mexico or
the Fall of Maximilian.' New
York: American News Com-
pany, n.d. (Fireside Series,
No. 24).

*Dime novels, like today's
paperbacks, covered many
fields besides stories of the
Wild West; among them were
popularized historical novels.
The American News Com-
pany acted at times not only
as distributor but as publisher
of inexpensive paperbounds.*

PLATE 6 — *see p. 59*

Philip Reade, 'Tom Edison,
Jr.'s Prairie-Skimmer Team.'
New York: Street & Smith,
1892 (The Nugget Library,
No. 110).

*Science fiction, currently en-
joying a great deal of popularity in paperbacks, has
occupied imaginative writers
of the past as well, most notably Jules Verne, Edgar Allan Poe, and H. G. Wells. This
early example of a Street &
Smith "library" is distinguished from other pulp fiction
of the 1890's by appearing as
a periodical publication.*

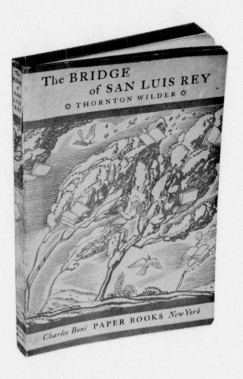

PLATE 7 — *see p. 61*

Thornton Wilder, 'The Bridge of San Luis Rey.' New York: Charles Boni, 1929 (Paper Books).

One of the bestsellers of 1927-28, this book has been frequently reprinted in various series. It appeared under the imprint of Charles Boni, who attempted to issue good books, attractively designed by Rockwell Kent, at the low price of fifty cents.

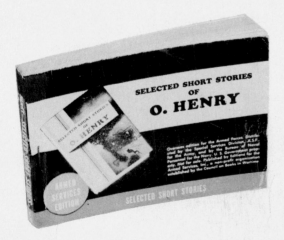

PLATE 8 — *see p. 72*

O. Henry, 'Selected Short Stories.' New York: Edition for the Armed Services, Inc., n.d. (Armed Service Editions, K-16).

One of over 1300 titles which were distributed in 123 million copies to soldiers of the Second World War free of charge. Produced at a cost of less than seven cents per book, they represent a singular achievement of voluntary co-operation between the publishing industry and various government agencies.

CHAPTER 6

CHRONOLOGY

The year 1939 is usually considered the beginning of the current phase of paperback publishing because "Mercury Books" was the only one of the paperback series started in the 1920's and 1930's which survived to the present time and does not compare in distribution and range of publication with the pattern now in existence. Reprints during the 20's and 30's were usually bound in hard covers, paper over board, or cheap cloth. A decided change occurred when Pocket Books entered the field in June of 1939 with its quality list of colorful paperbacks, distributed at newsstands with immediate and spectacular success. Robert F. de Graff, the founder of Pocket Books, had stated his reason for launching this venture in a letter to 'Publishers' Weekly' in April of 1939. He said:

> Has anyone ever considered publishing a special cheap edition . . . which people would buy instead of lend, that would not interfere with the sale of regular editions.
> It seems to me that might offer some solution, for then the author and the publisher through the sale of their cheap edition would get a revenue, however small, from each person who reads the book.[1]

Two months later, Pocket Books was in operation, and the future looked very promising. Penguin Books sensed the American sales potential and opened a New York office later in the summer, stocking 100 titles for a start. Before the year was over, Red Arrow Books had entered the field, and in 1940 Bacon & Wieck, a wholesaler specializing in pamphlets, became the agent for Penguin, Pelican, Pocket and Modern Age Books. Penguin expanded its sales and by fall began to produce books in the United States as shipments from Great Britain had become slow and unreliable. During this year, Pocket Books produced forty-nine, Penguin fifty-two, Red Arrow twelve, and

American Mercury ten titles. Department stores and other non-book outlets became steady customers.

By 1941, sales for all firms were satisfactory enough to consider exports to Canada, Central and South America. Newsdealers in urban and rural areas started to distribute paperbacks, and editions were selling well at the rate of 50,000 to 100,000 copies. By fall, Avon Books, with much the same appearance as Pocket Books, had entered the market and Pocket Books attempted to stem competition by taking Avon to court for imitating their format. However, Avon was upheld and other magazine and pulp publishers were encouraged to add paperback lines to their output. Pines Publication, Inc. started "Popular Library Books" and David McKay Company "The American Library" in 1942, but while "Popular Library Books" became one of the large paperback lines, "The American Library" failed in 1944. Dell Books, in cooperation with Western Printing and Lithographing Company, began their similar, and also highly successful, series in 1943, and other pulp and magazine publishers would have followed suit, but for the wartime paper shortages which made new ventures very difficult.

Due to purchases for the Armed Services and the limitations of consumer goods in general, the market for paperbacks was expanding and editions of 150,000 to 250,000 copies were selling well. In 1943, in spite of persistent demands, the acute paper shortage forced all companies to decrease the number of titles. In order to stretch available supplies, thinner paper stock and smaller type were used. Customers of old standing were supplied according to a quota system, and new ones were frequently turned away.

This was particularly exasperating as the paper shortage made hardback publishers more willing to offer attractive and newer titles to reprinters. Pocket Books solved its problems to some extent by establishing a Canadian firm which produced books from American plates. Demands for books for the Army were satisfied in part by diverting a large percentage of the production to them and by establishment of the "Armed Services Editions."

During the second half of 1945, paper and other shortages began to ease considerably. Another large paperback line, Bantam Books, was started by several of the top men of the American Penguin branch. They had resigned as a result of editorial difficulties and founded the new firm in cooperation with Curtis Publishing Company and Grosset & Dunlap. At the end of 1945 and in the spring of 1946, when the country returned to pre-war normalcy, a shift in sales techniques became necessary.

During the war the increased demand for books by soldiers as well as by civilians, due to enforced leisure time resulting from gas and travel restrictions, could hardly be met. Now all firms were publishing at full capacity, but drug stores and department stores suddenly had less space to devote to paperbacks because they began to stock items unobtainable during the war which they could sell at a higher profit. The millions of men returning from the Armed Forces were less interested in reading as recreational activities became possible. Pent-up demands for various gadgets and machinery helped the average American to use up some of his accumulated savings. As a result, paperback sales were unsatisfactory. The marginal firms were forced out and the large firms had to rid themselves of overstock, which in form of returns, may have been as high as one-third of the total production. While no accurate figures are available, many of the publishers recall that during the slump of 1946 the serious titles suffered less than the light reading fare. The number of copies produced during the year cannot be ascertained, but the number of paperback titles had grown from 112 in 1945 to 353 in 1946.

The industry tried to rise to the challenge and promotion was geared to a high pitch. The firms invested in racks which displayed more books in a smaller space, and new outlets were sought. As competition increased, covers became gaudier, colors brighter, and women's attire on the cover picture more scanty. The year 1947 proved to be better than 1946. The number of titles released went down to 297, and approximately 95 million copies were sold. Higher costs in labor and materials had forced some publishers to bring out their longer titles at thirty-five and fifty cents. Little sales resistance was found, if the book offered at a higher price was the one readers wanted. Some of the rising production costs were offset by technological advances in binding techniques, particularly the improvement of adhesives used for "perfect binding," which made this method standard with practically all publishers.

By 1948, the paperback industry had regained and expanded its market. Three hundred and twenty titles were produced and approximately 135 million copies sold. The physical appearance of the books was improved, but the quality of the contents of many of the reprints was interior and objections were heard from many quarters. The American Penguin branch cut its ties with the parent firm in Great Britain and continued as The New American Library of World Literature (referred to as NAL), taking over many of the Penguin policies and personnel, but shaping its publications to suit the American market.

The year 1949 saw several new firms enter the field: Graphic, Pyramid, Lion and Checker Books joined the paperback parade; Checker Books failed, the others stayed, offering much the same literary fare. Five hundred and thirty-eight titles were produced and sales approached 184 million. In search for wider sales, Pocket Books and Bantam established British firms as tney as well as NAL signed ECA (Economic Cooperation Administration) contracts to enlarge their exports. Pocket Books brought out a new $1.00 series called "Collectors Editions," with some of their outstanding titles produced on better paper and in hard covers. This series, however, did not sell well. NAL experimented with original hard cover editions. "Giant" editions of several firms were selling at thirty-five and fifty cents.

During 1949 and 1950 paperback publishers began to use more and more original publications. Authors felt that they were entitled to larger profits and that it would be to their advantage to write directly for paperback release. In May of 1950 Gold Medal Books, a subsidiary of Fawcett, was formed, which published exclusively original publications, specializing in light romantic novels, mysteries and western stories. This trend was also the result of increased competition for reprint rights, which had driven up prices, and a consequent dearth of books considered suitable for reprinting. Somewhat more attention was being paid to translations of foreign works, but there also the sensational, highly romantic book with sexual overtones received preference. Science fiction, a literary trend which goes back to Jules Verne, was beginning to gain increased recognition in the small book industry. Ian Ballantine is usually credited with having advanced this move. A corresponding drop of mysteries is noticeable.

In 1945, over half of all titles belonged in this category which had dropped to 26 percent by 1950 and to 13 percent in 1955.

Judging from the continuing ECA contracts to Pocket Books, NAL and Bantam, and the expanded arrangements of the larger firms for distribution abroad, particularly in Europe, paperback exports were becoming increasingly important and selling far more than American hardcover editions; they were actually the only books which Europeans could afford to buy in quantity. The heavy stress on exports suggests that the market was becoming somewhat crowded again, which is not surprising considering the number of new firms entering the field and the comparatively few which failed. In 1948 Doubleday had established a subsidiary, Permabooks, which published reprints in hard, glossy covers at first, but in 1950 abandoned the hard covers and switched to the same format as all other paperbacks. They offered fiction and non-fiction titles at twenty-five, thirty-five, and fifty cents. All in all, production during 1950 was estimated at 642 titles which sold about 214 million copies.

During 1949 and 1950 another trend in paperback publishing became more pronounced: the school and college market was found to have considerable sales possibilities for supplementary reading and use as text material. Barnes & Noble had published since 1939 a supplementary college series, "The College Outline Series," in paperbound format. In 1945, Barron's Educational Series entered the field, specializing more in examination and college preparatory materials. Supplementary reading for classics of American and English literature relied mostly on various clothbound series, most notably the "Modern Library." Since some of the suitable titles published by Penguin, Pocket Books and NAL had proved to be very successful for these purposes, Oskar Piest interested Walter Hafner in bringing out "The Hafner Library of Classics" in paper and cloth covers in 1947. In 1948, he opened his own firm, the Liberal Arts Press, specializing mainly in the history and literature of antiquity. Rinehart & Company came out with a paperbound series in English literature, "Rinehart Editions," in the same year, and Littlefield, Adams brought out their "New College Outline Series" in 1949. Modern Library joined the field in 1950 with the publication of the "Modern Library College Editions" -- a series of regular "Modern Library" titles in paperbound form, with introductions by subject specialists. The establishment of a second American Penguin branch in 1950 also added to the amount of serious material available in paperbound form, and "Lumen Books," published by the J. S. Paluch Company in Chicago, were the first religious paperbacks to appear. A new Pocket Book series, "Cardinal Books," was also bringing out high quality fiction and nonfiction titles in a somewhat more popular vein.

The serious paperbacks, published in smaller editions and distributed to a limited number of outlets, opened up a higher price range for this type of book, selling from fifty to ninety-five cents. In 1951, Dover Publications, a publisher of serious scientific and technical materials, began to issue highly technical, scientific and occasionally philosophical titles which sold at prices from one to two dollars, being the first books of this type obtainable at a comparatively low price. Otherwise, 1951 did not encourage any new firms to enter the crowded field of regular paperbacks, but production hit an all time high with 866 titles and over 231 million copies sold. Millions of copies, however, were returned to the publishers.

The year 1952 saw the first literary magazine in paperback format, NAL's 'New World Writing,' which was followed shortly by other similar enterprises. Ballantine Books appeared with the novel approach of simultaneous hard and soft cover releases of new titles. Trade publishers had done this previously on occasion. Simon and Schuster had started their series of "Readers Editions" in 1950, which appeared in regular book size in soft covers releasing some of the firm's successful titles. Ballantine was the first publisher to assure the author who wrote an original for paperback publication a simultaneous hard cover release, thus providing for reviews and added prestige. The only additional firm specializing in light fiction in paperbacks to begin operations in 1952 was Ace Books, Inc., offering two novels, bound together back to back for thirty-five cents. Several firms were bringing out collections of articles from various periodicals. One of the first was 'The Pocket Atlantic,' edited by Edward F. Weeks, which had been published by Pocket Books in 1946. Other firms continued this trend by releasing anthologies such as 'The Saturday Review Reader,' 'Harper's Magazine Reader,' 'Highlights of Modern Literature,' 'A Permanent Collection of Memorable Essays from the New York Times Book Review,' which not only sold well on their own merit but were used as inducements for subscriptions. They stayed in the thirty-five to fifty cent range until 'The Reporter' used the same technique for an attractive Doubleday publication, 'The Reporter Reader,' released in December, 1955, at one dollar.

The paperback industry received a great deal of publicity, favorable as well as unfavorable, during 1952. The Gathings Committee, a congressional committee on current pornographic materials, criticized the lurid cover art and the contents of some paperbacks, which show an overly strong representation of "the three S's" -- sex, sadism and the smoking gun. (Plates 9, 10, 11) Many of the books cited were works published by paperback firms which had always made an effort to bring out quality titles, like Pocket Books and NAL. Both Freeman Lewis of Pocket Books and Victor Weybright of NAL objected in their testimony to the efforts at censorship of materials which were freely sold in hardbound editions, often works of literary merit. An increasing number of periodicals devoted articles to the growing phenomenon of the paperback industry. The sixteenth Annual Bowker Lecture, delivered by Freeman Lewis, as well as many other speeches treated this subject. Bookstores began to realize the growing competition from small books and were seeking means to fight it. Eventually, most of them began to include selected titles in their stock and found in the next few years that they were rather an asset than a liability.

During 1952 and 1953, publishers seemed to realize that they were not only competing with each other but that their own titles were crowding each other on the valuable rack space. Reprint rights had gone so high through competitive bidding that it was hard to make a profit on any book which was not an excellent seller, and publishers were more inclined to call back slow-moving titles. "Lion Books" followed "Gold Medal" for a time in bringing out paperback originals, and Dell started its "Dell First Editions" which included a great deal of serious literature. This trend was continued by other publishers like the John F. Rider Publishing Company, which specializes in the technology of electronics, and began to bring out some of its books in paperback format. On the other hand, several firms started new twenty-five cent lines of popular light fiction, containing fewer pages, like Bantam's "Pennant" and Perma's "Star Books," neither one of which was successful. New outlets in chain supermarkets and department stores widened sales. About 252 million copies were sold in 1952, approximately the same as in the previous year, though the number of titles dropped from 897 to 882.

The year 1953 was one of expansion. One thousand sixty-one titles were produced and 259 million copies sold. Five paperback firms produced more than 100 titles: Bantam 129, Dell 120, NAL 110, Popular 107, and Pocket Books 104. Avon, Fawcett, Lion, Penguin and Ace Books issued between 50 and 100 titles. The outstanding publishing trends of the year were summarized in 'Publishers' Weekly' of January 23, 1954. There was a wave of censorship unparalleled in American history, proceeding on moral grounds undoubtedly stimulated by the Gathings Committee and on political grounds due to the efforts of Senator McCarthy and the investigation of the U. S. Information Libraries by the Senator's assistants, Roy Cohn and David Schine. Other developments of the year were a moderate increase in sales volume, an attempt to improve the techniques of book distribution, and the promotion of books and reading. Paperbacks were gaining a new foothold in the spreading number of supermarkets through rack jobbers who handle non-food items. The promotion of reading was served through Alfred Stefferud's widely read 'The Wonderful World of Books,' which appeared as a Houghton Mifflin hardbound edition and as an NAL paperback.

The effect of the Gathings Committee made itself felt during this and the following years in a certain amount of self control of the industry, demonstrated by a decrease in luridness of cover art and a somewhat closer relationship between the book's cover and its contents. Two more scholarly paperback lines appeared: "Academic Reprints" and "Schuman's College Paperbacks." The most important innovation of the year was the publication of a new Doubleday series, "Anchor Books" which, combining several elements previously used, established a pattern which changed the picture of the paperback industry considerably. "Anchor Books" are serious reprints in paperbound format, much along the line of Penguin, Dover and Liberal Arts Press. Providing them with modernistic and very attractive covers, relying on titles which would appeal to the mature and educated adult who could afford to pay from sixty-five cents to $1.45, and improving on the smaller firms' distribution and production methods, "Anchor Books" opened up a new price range and market. College campuses were considered their appropriate sales territory, but the textbook appeal was not stressed since the books were presented in their entirety without explanations or lengthy introductions. Since the titles were expected to appeal only to a limited audience, editions were kept around 30,000 copies; the price permitted the use of better paper and heavier covers than were found in the low price range; they were distributed through regular trade channels to book and department stores, as well as to selected non-book outlets. Between April, 1953, and January, 1955, "Anchor Books" sold over one million copies, with David Riesman's 'The Lonely Crowd' as the bestseller with over 60,000 copies. In January, 1955, Doubleday & Company received the thirteenth annual Carey-Thomas Award for creative publishing, one of the industry's most coveted recognitions, for the publication of "Anchor Books." Jason Epstein, the youthful editor of the series was honored for having conceived the idea and demonstrated the ability to carry it out.

The general trend towards higher priced, high quality paperbounds was followed with the distribution of Herman Wouk's 'The Caine Mutiny' by Doubleday & Company at ninety-five cents* and "Permabooks'" fifty-cent edition of Thomas B. Costain's 'The Silver Chalice.' On the other hand, the overproduction of cheap titles and the duplication of similar types of books offered by all publishers, produced a dangerous overstock during the year. By June, 175 million copies had piled up in the warehouses, and Freeman Lewis suggested that this overstock be gradually reduced through cooperation of all firms over a period of eighteen months.[2] Actually, this warning was not heeded and the oversupply resulted in a recession which made itself strongly felt in the spring of 1954.

The same five firms which had produced over 100 titles in 1953 were again leading the field in 1954; Bantam brought out 27 and Popular Library 14 more titles than the previous year, while Dell, NAL and Pocket Books produced approximately the same number. In the group producing between 50 and 100 titles, Fawcett and Penguin showed a considerable production increase. The general condition of the book trade in 1954 was aptly de-

---

*This edition was distributed by Permabooks but carried the Doubleday imprint and the unusual price tag because of the author's agent's insistance on a 10 percent retail royalty.

scribed by David Dempsey when he wrote: "It is the fate of the trade publisher in the United States to be chronically ailing without ever becoming critically ill."[3] This statement summarized his statistical conclusion that the average trade publisher turned an average loss of fifteen cents per copy on adult books into an actual profit of nine cents through the sale of subsidiary rights to reprinters, magazines, book clubs and the movie and TV industries. Other statistics indicate that the paperback industry represents about 9 percent of the total publishing turnover. Paperbacks were playing an increasingly important role and magazine wholesale distributors were deriving about 20 percent of their profits from this source. The most widely discussed development of the year was the growth of the higher priced lines following the beginnings of the previous year. In spite of this focal position of the industry, small book publishers were insecure because competition had created "a profusion of lines and titles and copies and a significant -- if not dangerous -- confusion at wholesale and retail levels of distribution, . . ."[4]

In their search for new sales possibilities, Pocket Books paid more attention to the science fiction field. The Atlantic Coast Independent Distributors' Association's 19th convention in the spring of 1954 reflected an alarming situation. Ballantine recalled fourteen of their titles and seeing some of the recalls and returns in editorial offices one could feel the gloom which came from these unopened boxes. Lion Books and several other firms declared publishing holidays and curtailed production, and key personnel was shifted or dismissed. Some publishers, like Bantam, changed some of their covers and paid increasing attention to the criticism voiced against their distribution methods. In order to relieve the difficult market conditions two solutions presented themselves: destruction of overstock and search for new outlets. The Bureau of Independent Publishers and Distributors, an organization of publishers, national distributors and wholesalers, set as its goal the opening of 2000 new magazine and book departments in supermarkets. Original paperback publishers showed great interest in the selling of subsidiary rights. Fawcett and Dell were successful in selling movie rights of their "Gold Medal Books" and "Dell First Editions." Five of the first sixteen titles of the latter series were sold to Hollywood. "Dell First Editions" also brought out several anthologies particularly suited for the college market, the most successful of which was 'Short Story Masterpieces' edited by Robert Penn Warren and Albert Erskine.

Total sales for 1954 were estimated to have reached close to 240 million copies, which was only slightly below the previous year, but production outran demand by a wide margin. Pocket Books, which is unusually frank about such matters in an industry which likes to keep its secrets, admitted that an abandoned canal near Buffalo was a burial ground for many volumes and Freeman Lewis believes that about 60 million copies found a similar fate in other parts of our landscape.[5]

As the year progressed, overcrowded conditions were cleared up and by fall the market was much healthier. Doubleday's "Permabooks" was taken over by Pocket Books, Inc., where it is now one of that company's paperback lines. Other stabilizing influences were: increased subsidiary rights, growing sales in drug stores, and reduction of production costs due to smaller reprint-right payments. The United States Information Agency received 3500 sets of miniature libraries consisting of ninety-nine paperbacks which were distributed to libraries, reading rooms, YMCA's and various educational institutions abroad. CARE was shipping paperback libraries overseas as American donations. With governmental assistance several publishers prepared special Book Export Editions, which consisted of regular trade books bound in paper covers to be sold abroad at one-third of the American price.

A large number of articles in various periodicals were being devoted to the topic of paperbacks and the first issue of the American Library Association's new publication 'Public Library Division Reporter' dealt exclusively with the use of paperbound books in public libraries. Radio Station KPFA-FM in San Francisco started a regular radio program under the name "Soft Cover World."

In spite of the temporary crisis, six new series entered the industry, more than in any previous year, except 1950. "The Catholic Home Library" of the Catechetical Guild and "Image Books" were the first religious paperback series, with the exception of the much smaller "Lumen Books" which had been started in 1950. "Image Books," a Doubleday line, followed in the footsteps of "Anchor Books" by appearing as higher priced and more durable paperbacks. Two other trade publishers, Knopf and Grove Press, came out with high quality paperback lines, "Vintage Books" and "Evergreen Books." Falcon Wing Press followed the Ballantine example of simultaneous publishing with the release of "Wing Books." Doubleday brought out its "Short Studies," a pamphlet series of supplementary text material, which was changed to regular paperback format when it was purchased by Random House in 1955. The absence of any new cheap lines of paperbacks and the surprising increase in scholarly and serious softcover publications significant for the year.

While during 1953 and 1954 five paperback publishers had brought out over 100 titles, in 1955 only three firms, Popular, NAL and Pocket Books, remained in this group. Bantam, Fawcett, Penguin, Avon and Ace published between fifty and 100 titles and were joined in this category by a newcomer Berkley Books, which brought out sixty titles in its first year. The very fact that Dell and Lion dropped below fifty titles is rather remarkable and the overall picture seems to conform to the statement in 'Publishers' Weekly' that "a great proportion of publishers' lists in 1955 were smaller than those in 1954, but so many publishers were active that the total of books published in the year was greater than in 1954."[6] The overall title production set a new record with 12,589, 1798 of which were soft cover publications, an increase of 388 over the previous year. Some three hundred titles were originals, created especially for paperbound publication. The most outstanding change occurred in the considerable rise of paperback, nonfiction publications which amounted to 28 percent of the total production as compared to 18 percent in 1954. This change was brought about by a shift in editorial policies of the already existing firms and by the fact that all new series entering the field, with the exception of "Berkley Books," belonged to the higher priced, better quality, primarily nonfiction type of publication, and were all paperback lines of established hardback trade publishers. They were Random House's "Modern Library Paperbacks," Noonday's "Meridian Books," "Viking Portable Library," "Beacon Press Paperbacks," Harcourt Brace's "Harvest Books," D. Van Nostrand's "Anvil Books," "New Directions Paperbacks," and "Gateway Books." Cornell University Press was the first publisher of its kind to enter the paperback field with its "Great Seal Books" in the fall of 1955.

In 1955, 'Publishers' Weekly' compiled for the first time the bestsellers of the year in paperback editions, an attention heretofore accorded only to hardcover books. Promotionwise, the year saw an increased use of movie tie-ins, which had risen from eight in 1954 to at least thirty. New outlets for paperback sales were found in book stores, which had originally been reluctant to take in paperback displays. Many stores were finding that particularly the higher quality lines brought potential customers for their hardcover books, especially younger people and professional groups with limited incomes. Kroch and Brentano in Chicago opened in its basement a Super Book Mart for paperbacks, where 7500 titles were on display and half a million copies kept in stock, waiting for readers to put them into their shopping baskets. Charles E. Lauriat's, one of Boston's well known book stores, opened display facilities for 1000 titles. Marboro in New York found that paperback racks displayed in the front of the store considerably increased the number of customers who came in to browse and eventually bought either soft or hard cover books. In Detroit, the J. L. Hudson Company's large suburban shopping center "Northland" welcomed to its many individual shops Marwil's Paperback Bookstore, which offers these books exclusively.

An exhibit was set up at Columbia University's School of Library Service with the cooperation of thirty-two publishers who chose the titles which they considered most representative for their firms. This exhibit, "The Evolution of American Publishing in Paperbacks" was taken over by Columbia University Library and afterwards by the New York State Library, which put the display on the road throughout the state. The U. S. Information Service displayed paperbound books in Ceylon in April, 1955.

The year saw probably more attempts at censorship than any previous one. Many state legislatures considered separate laws to cope with the problem, and the National Organization of Decent Literature put 342 titles on its proscribed fall list. The impact of these various restrictive actions resulted in a toning down of cover art which had previously leaned heavily on magazine type illustration, much of which was actually in bad taste. Since 1953, cover art has followed a new trend stressing abstract design and striking use of typography. (Plate 16) Advantages to the publisher included a reduction in cost over the original oil paintings depicting or elaborating upon a scene from the book. As the less expensive lines carried more serious titles than before, covers were adjusted accordingly, actually resulting in good poster or jacket art and including a much wider use of photographs than previously. The most noticeable change occurred probably in Dell and Bantam covers. (Plates 14 & 15)

The year 1955 may be regarded as the year of consolidation and maturing of the mass market. The 34th Annual Exhibit of the American Institute of Graphic Arts chose among the "Fifty Books of the Year 1955" Vernon L. Parrington's 'Main Currents in American Thought,' in Harcourt, Brace & Co.'s "Harvest Book" edition, John William De Forest's 'Miss Ravenel's Conversion' ("Rinehart Editions"), Langston Hughes' 'The Sweet Flypaper of Life,' published as a paperback by Simon and Schuster, Inc., and Alistair Cooke's 'The Vintage Mencken.'

There was no significant convention of booksellers or publishers where paperbacks were not discussed. Attempts were being made to keep production and consumption in some balance by setting up editions of 200,000 where there used to be 300,000, and by ordering reprint editions of 25,000 to 50,000 copies instead of much larger runs. More discretion in editorial policy was exercised, and some firms expanded their series to present a complete line of reprints. Fawcett, for example, added two new series, "Crest Books" and "Premier Books," both devoted to popular but more serious fiction. Simon and Schuster, which had abandoned its "Readers' Editions," started with "Scientific American Books" late in the year, and Knopf, which had entered paperback publishing with its "Vintage" books with the purpose of making some of its back titles available at greatly reduced prices, was considering occasional paperback originals.

1956 was an exceptionally good year for the publishing industry as a whole. While the total number of titles dropped for the first time in ten years, sales were excellent. 1572 paperback titles appeared, 198 more than the previous year, increasing their participation from 11 to 13 percent of the total output. Dollar sales also improved 12.4 percent for mass-marketed and 27.2 percent for trade-distributed paperbacks.[7] More old, well established trade publishers began to issue high quality lines. Viking added "Compass Books," a series of reprints from its backlist of outstanding authors to supplement its "Paperbound Portables"; Houghton Mifflin's "Riverside Editions," Grosset & Dunlap's "Universal Library" and Oxford's

"Galaxy Books" followed the "Anchor" pattern. The University of Chicago brought out "Phoenix Books," the leading scholarly series, and Indiana University, the University of California and the University of Michigan added similar lines. (Plate 13) Meridian's "Living Age Books" and Harper's "Torch Books," both predominantly Protestant, started their religious paperbacks patterned after Doubleday's Catholic "Image Books." A new firm, Hill and Wang, appeared with "Dramabooks" in a specialized field. All these books are higher priced (between $1.00 and $2.00), very well printed and attractively designed. Their serious, scholarly, sophisticated fare presents a challenge to the previous three S's -- sex, sadism and the smoking gun. Again two paperbacks issued by trade publishers were chosen among the "Fifty Books of the Year by the American Institute of Graphic Arts: 'Essays on Elizabethan Drama' by T. S. Eliot ("Harvest") and 'Poetics of Music' by Igor Stravinsky ("Vintage").

Pocket Books, Fawcett, Popular Library, Bantam, Dell and Avon Books produced over one hundred titles, NAL, Penguin, Ace Books, Ballantine and Pyramid Books over fifty titles. Promotionwise, increasing attention was given to movie tie-ins, following the trend of presenting successfully the same plot as a novel, a play, a movie, and a TV presentation. Many of these were on the publishers' bestsellers lists, such as 'The Man in the Gray Flannel Suit' by Sloan Wilson and 'Giant' by Edna Ferber (Pocket Books), 'Not as a Stranger' by Morton Thompson and 'Baby Doll' by Tennessee Williams (NAL), 'The Bad Seed' by William March (Dell), 'War and Peace' by Leo Tolstoy (Dell and Bantam), 'Picnic' by William Inge (Bantam). Erle Stanley Gardner remained Pocket Books' best-selling author and Dell felt that 'Bonjour Tristesse' by Françoise Sagan was one of the best-selling of all paperback titles. 'The Meaning of the Dead Sea Scrolls' by A. Powell Davies was the Signet Key sales leader. As a group, science fiction and mysteries seemed to lose somewhat in popularity while factual or fictional accounts of World War II gained.

The trend toward quality paperbacks published by trade publishers and university presses continued in 1957. E. P. Dutton's "Everyman Paperbacks" and the paperbound series of Sagamore Press, a new trade publisher, added to the titles available for college use and the serious reader. Abingdon Press and Association Press provided more material for

Protestant and interdenominational religious interest with their "Apex" and "Reflection" books.

The total number of titles decreased by over one hundred to 1469. Most of them were published by the established mass market series: Pocket Books 158, Fawcett 125, Bantam 110, Avon 107, Popular 101, and between fifty and one hundred by Dell, NAL, Pyramid, Ace, Ballantine and Berkeley. The decrease in title production and overall sales figures can be mainly attributed to the most important change in paperback distribution brought about by the complete withdrawal of the American News Company from magazine and paperback distribution. Dell Publishing Co. had shifted to independent wholesalers in the spring, followed by Popular Library and the Pines magazines. By late summer the shift was complete and independent wholesalers were expanding to take up the slack, but the sudden change in distribution suspended the production of approximately nine million copies.[8] Other factors contributing to the lower figures may have been the record-breaking sales of 1956 and the beginnings of the nation-wide recession. Prices were up, so much so that the original "quarter book" which had started the paperback boom in 1939 was virtually extinct except for a few mysteries, Westerns and very short romantic novels. A good number of short books were selling at thirty-five cents, but more and more mass market titles were priced at fifty and quite a few larger or very new bestselling items at seventy-five cents.

The new as well as the established firms seemed to stress more serious and religious books. While original paperback fiction was on the decline, the time lapse between the original hardcover and the paperback edition had narrowed to the point where publication announcement, sale of movie rights and adoption by a reprint house appeared almost simultaneously. Movie tie-ins remained the most widely used promotion device. 'Ten North Frederick' by John O'Hara (Bantam), 'Peyton Place,' Grace Metalious' sensational and controversial novel (Dell), 'Marjorie Morningstar' by Herman Wouk (NAL) and 'Auntie Mame' by Patrick Dennis (Popular) were the leading sellers of the year.

In the area of censorship, Michigan received national attention in three court decisions, paving the way for more enlightened censorship regulations in the state and country as a whole.

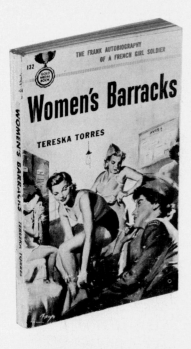

PLATE 9 — *see p. 85*

PLATE 10 — *see p. 85*

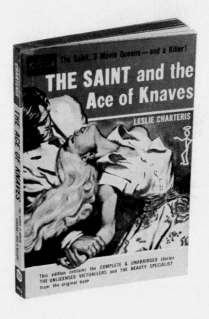

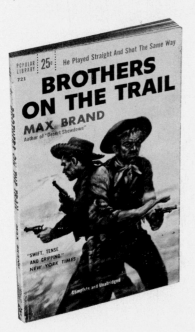

PLATE 11 — *see p. 85*

These titles illustrate the sex, sadism, and smoking-gun themes in cover art against which criticism of paperbacks has been primarily directed.

PLATE 12 — *see p. 146*

Stefan Zweig, 'Joseph Fouché.' Frankfurt/M: Fischer Bücherei, 1955 (Fischer Bücherei, No. 4).

A postwar German paperback breaking with the previous tradition of non-illustrated Tauchnitz, Reclam, and Albatross covers. The close similarity to the American format, particularly to NAL books, resulted in a court suit in Germany which, however, did not afford NAL any redress.

PLATE 13—*see pp. 93 and 230*

Edward Chiera, 'They Wrote on Clay.' Chicago: University of Chicago Press, 1956 (Phoenix Books, P2).

A university press paperback, representative of the creative art work done by this group of publishers which are using inexpensive editions to make the fruits of scholarship available at popular prices.

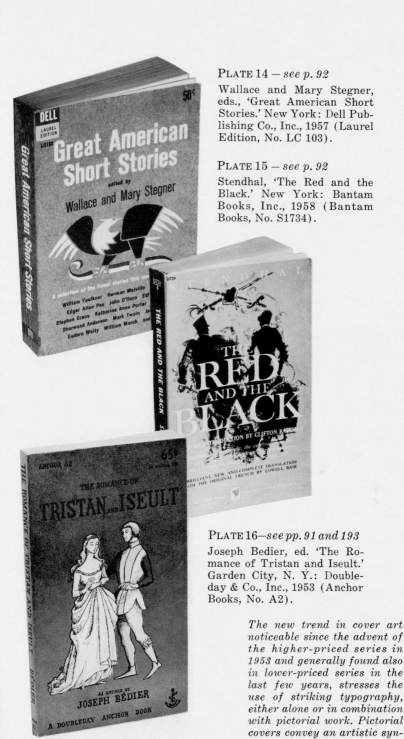

PLATE 14 — *see p. 92*

Wallace and Mary Stegner, eds., 'Great American Short Stories.' New York: Dell Publishing Co., Inc., 1957 (Laurel Edition, No. LC 103).

PLATE 15 — *see p. 92*

Stendhal, 'The Red and the Black.' New York: Bantam Books, Inc., 1958 (Bantam Books, No. S1734).

PLATE 16—*see pp. 91 and 193*

Joseph Bedier, ed. 'The Romance of Tristan and Iseult.' Garden City, N. Y.: Doubleday & Co., Inc., 1953 (Anchor Books, No. A2).

The new trend in cover art noticeable since the advent of the higher-priced series in 1953 and generally found also in lower-priced series in the last few years, stresses the use of striking typography, either alone or in combination with pictorial work. Pictorial covers convey an artistic synthesis of the book as a whole, avoiding clichés and stereotypes.

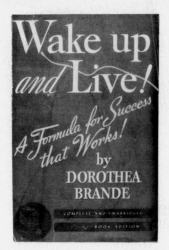

PLATE 17 — *see p. 128*

Dorothea Brande, 'Wake Up and Live!' New York: Pocket Books, Inc., 1939, 1953 (Pocket Book, No. 2).

PLATE 18 — *see p. 142*

Lillian Smith, 'Strange Fruit.' New York: New American Library of World Literature, 1948, 1953 (Signet Book, Nos. 665 and S1074).

Many publishers find in their lists titles which enjoy continuous sales over many years. These two from Pocket Books and NAL original lists have been reprinted and illustrate the changing trends in cover art.

Over the last eighteen years paperback publishing has grown from less than six to over six dozen firms representing virtually every type of publisher except private presses and reference and subscription book publishers and offering every subject in print. The growing significance of this type of publishing has been recognized by numerous articles and several dissertations and theses. Since 1955 a bibliography, 'Paperbound Books in Print' has been published, devoted exclusively to a listing of available titles which numbered some six thousand in the Fall-Winter 1957 issue. There is hardly a home or library in America today where some paperbacks cannot be found.

[1] Robert F. de Graff, "Cheap Editions to Widen the Ownership of Books," 'Publishers' Weekly,' CXXXV:16 (April 22, 1939), p. 1499

[2] "The Future of the Paperbound Book," 'Publishers' Weekly,' CLXIII:26 (June 27, 1953), p. 2664-68.

[3] David Dempsey, "The State of Business (1954) Along Publishers 'Row'," 'New York Times Book Review,' LX:1 (January 2, 1955), p. 23

[4] "A Real Survey of Small Books," 'Publishers' Weekly,' CLXV:8 (February 20, 1954), p. 1061.

[5] Freeman Lewis, "Books and the Mass Market," 'Publishers' Weekly,' CLXVI:16 (October 15, 1954), p. 1668.

[6] "Publishers' 1955 Title Output Analyzed," 'Publishers' Weekly,' CLXIX:3 (January 21, 1956), p. 197.

[7] '1956 Annual Survey of the General Book Publishing Industry,' (New York: American Book Publishers Council, Inc., 1957).

[8] "Paperbacks -- Publishing and Distribution," 'Publishers' Weekly,' CLXXIII:3 (January 20, 1958), p. 57.

CHAPTER 7

PRODUCTS, PRODUCTION AND DISTRIBUTION

Technical Production

The technological advances which were responsible for the change of binding styles from the incunabula period to the twentieth century, and the emergence of the paperbound book have been covered in Part I.

"Penguin Books" and American paperbacks during the 1920's, 30's and early 40's were almost exclusively sewn. This technique is still used in series of smaller editions of scholarly content. The advantage for the publisher lies in the fact that a specified number of copies may be bound in cloth while the others receive paper covers. Occasionally, one finds paperbacks which have been wire stapled, a process still frequently used for inexpensive publications in Europe and exclusively for the "Armed Services Editions."

The basic ingredients which go into the making of books were greatly affected by advances made in the field of plastics, which contributed nylon thread and plastic-coated cloth and papers during the last decade. Until the late 40's, most American paperback covers were laminated with transparent plastic sheets, giving them a highly glossy appearance. In 1947 Pocket Books discontinued the use of lamination, which was rather expensive and had the disadvantage of peeling off easily. In its place, Pocket Books adopted a technique of applying lacquer under heat, which resulted in a more durable and better looking cover. Other firms followed and covers remained unchanged until the early 1950's when Dover and Anchor began to use unvarnished, heavy paper stock, a trend followed in most higher-priced series. These "cardboard cover" books, which use smooth, dull stock, seem preferable to coated papers which are more subject to abrasion.

Today, most paperbacks, inexpensive as well as higher-priced, are bound by a process known as "perfect binding" which, until recently, was neither perfect nor notably similar to binding as previously practiced. Single leaves, not signatures are bound together, not with thread but with adhesive applied to the inside edge of the pages. As long as animal glues were used in this process, the results were by and large unsatisfactory because cracking of the glue resulted in loose pages and broken spines. Paperback publishing is frequently referred to as a revolution, yet the only sudden and startling physical change which occurred over the last decade is rarely mentioned. The physical quality of the paperback and the efficiency with which it can be produced has been changed tremendously with the replacement of animal glues by synthetic adhesives. Their quick-drying quality permits assembly-line procedures and eliminates temporary storage problems; they are resistant to moisture and temperature changes; they retain adequate flexibility, eliminating the breaking of backs and loosening of pages, and are almost impervious to mildew, fungi and insects, thus guaranteeing the adhesive a longer life than the paper they bind. Their disadvantage lies in their fast setting, which necessitates the use of new and expensive machinery.[1] Hot-melt adhesives based on poly-vinyl acetate were developed during 1944 and the following years when W.F. Hall, one of the largest paperback manufacturers, approached the DuPont Company for the perfection of an adhesive material which would speed up and improve existing production methods. Because of difficulties involved in the handling of hot-melt adhesives, cold adhesives have been developed to a point where their practical and advantageous use was reported in October, 1955.[2] Regardless of the type of glue used, the technique of "perfect binding" consists of properly assembling the pages, slicing off the fold, dipping the whole spine by machine into the adhesive, and slapping on the paper covers. How many readings these bindings permit is still open to question, but they seem to vary from six to twenty-eight.[3] Approximately, 18,000 single books can be bound in this fashion per hour.

The printing of paperbacks is also undergoing rapid and far reaching changes. Typesetting is still done mainly on slug-casting machines, but photographic composition and the use of photopolymer printing plates adapted to offset rotary presses are under trial and should further speed up production. At the present time rubber plates are used, made of synthetic Buna-N, and the speed of the presses is such that 16,000 to 18,000 impressions of a 128-page book can be made in one hour.[4]

Literary Production

Two of the most interesting aspects of current paperbound book publishing -- the exact statistics of production and the actual literary merit of the titles published -- cannot here be treated exhaustively. Production and even sales statistics are well guarded secrets and existing data do not permit exact measurements and comparison. The ephemeral quality of many titles and their fast turnover at the newsstands makes it impossible to compile a strictly exact list of all titles in print at any one time. The demands of publishers and librarians for some bibliographic tool, however, resulted in the publication of 'Paperbound Books in Print' by the R. R. Bowker Co. in May, 1955. This index by author, title and selected subjects lists titles submitted by the publishers because they are considered of sufficient popularity or value to be kept in print. The Fall-Winter 1957 issue lists 6000 titles of almost 100 publishers. A picture of the currently available titles can be obtained from this source. The literary history of the preceding years has been told by Frank Luther Mott in his 'Golden Multitudes, the Story of Best Sellers in the United States' (New York: Macmillan Company, 1947), and James D. Hart in 'The Popular Book, A History of America's Literary Taste' (New York: Oxford University Press, 1950).

Titles of literary merit in the opinion of a panel of librarians and college professors may be found in a section of 'Good Reading,' prepared by the Committee on College Reading under the chairmanship of Atwood H. Townsend (New York: New American Library, 1956); that book's "Checklist of Paperbound Editions" lists more than 1300 selected titles which were in print in August, 1956.

Some indication of the type of materials published and the increasing trend toward works of greater literary value can be obtained by the random comparison of 'Publishers' Weekly's' forecasts for January, 1954, January, 1956, and January, 1958. These listings are selective, but they were compiled under similar conditions and for the same month. In 1954, twelve (or 30 percent) of the forty titles were nonfiction; in 1956, thirty-six (or 73.5 percent) of forty-nine titles and in 1958 twenty-eight (or 55 percent) of fifty-one titles belonged in this category.

Fewer Westerns, mysteries and science fiction are listed for 1956 and 1958; this does not necessarily indicate that fewer books of this type are being published but rather that more outstanding works deserving to be mentioned have appeared, which did not leave space for a listing of lighter fiction. In January, 1954, Rachel L. Carson's 'The Sea Around Us,' Emil Ludwig's 'Napoleon' and Tallulah Bankhead's 'Tallulah' were the most outstanding nonfiction titles; fiction included works by Thomas B. Costain, Edna Ferber, Erskine Caldwell, George Orwell and Colette. Most of these were brought out by mass-market paperback publishers at popular prices. In January, 1956, we find several good nonfiction titles at popular prices, the first three of a new series of "Bantam Biographies," Milton Cross' 'Stories of the Great Operas,' Robert Lindner's 'The Fifty Minute Hour,' and 'The Way of a Woman,' edited by J. E. Fairchild. Nineteen of the nonfiction titles are of the higher-priced series and include authors like Denis Diderot, Jacob Burckhardt and Richard B. Morris. Fiction titles are primarily by popular writers, but include Fyodor Dostoyevsky's 'Crime and Punishment,' Morton Thompson's 'Not as a Stranger' and John Steinbeck's 'Sweet Thursday.' The 1958 selection shows a slightly stronger emphasis on science and psychology as represented by Fritz Wittels' 'Freud and His Time' and Alexander Koyre's 'From the Closed World to the Infinite Universe' in the higher-priced lines, and Bishop Fulton J. Sheen's 'Life is Worth Living' and Elbert Tokay's 'The Human Body and How It Works' in the lower-priced books. Religion is strongly represented by books of wide interdenominational appeal. Reprints dominate the field of fiction with literary classics and serious collections appealing to the college market, such as Thomas Hardy's 'Jude the Obscure' and 'The Viking Portable Poets of the English Language,' edited by W. H. Auden and Norman Holmes Pearson. Mass-market paperbacks include Meyer Levin's 'Compulsion' (Pocket Books), originally released by Simon and Schuster in September, 1956.

At this writing there were signs of a trend towards more prompt reprinting of fiction and nonfiction bestsellers. Grace Metalious' 'Peyton Place' appeared as a Dell publication in September, 1957; original publication date by Messner was

September 24, 1956. (Reprint rights had been assigned before it was realized that the hard cover edition was to enjoy a long and sensational vogue.) William H. Whyte, Jr.'s 'The Organization Man' appeared as a Doubleday "Anchor Book" in September, 1957, less than a year after its release by Simon and Schuster.

The Relationship Between Authors and Publishers

According to the 1950 census there are about 15,000 professional authors in the United States, but hardly more than 200 of them earn the major portion of their incomes, year after year, by writing hardcover books.[6] The earnings of authors depend on royalties, a fixed percentage being geared to the number of copies of their books sold. "Before the First World War, twenty percent of the retail price was a common royalty for popular hard cover novels ... After 1925, fifteen percent became the maximum and it was reached at the end of a sliding scale."[7] Contracts are usually drawn up to start with a 10 percent royalty for the first 1000 to 2500 copies sold, and reach the 15 percent maximum at 5000 copies. This arrangement is necessitated by the economic facts of publishing which are pushing the break-even point for hard cover books steadily upward. Various hard cover book publishers estimated in discussions in 1954 and 1955 that this point is reached between 5000 and 8000 copies sold. In 1951, the average total sale per title of a trade book came to 6500 copies.[8] Actually, many hard cover titles do not result in profits for the publishers, who -- to cite a representative survey group -- were able to turn in 1951 an overall deficit of 0.6 percent for the average adult trade book into a 5.4 percent profit before taxes only by relying on subsidiary sales rights.[9] By 1956 the net profit from all operations for a comparable survey group had climbed to 6.6 percent, but again the sales from various rights remained a substantial source of revenue.[10]

Some books which were adopted for reprinting have earned authors rather spectacular subsidiary royalties -- for example, $40,000 for Norman Mailer's 'The Naked and the Dead' and $100,000 for James Jones' 'From Here to Eternity.' Mickey Spillane's 'The Big Kill,' reprinted by NAL, brought royalties of $45,000 with its first printing of three million copies. However, in most instances the author receives 50 percent of these subsidiary earnings, while the other 50 percent go to the original publisher.

Reprinters generally offer writers similar types of contracts, namely, one cent per copy royalty for the first 150,000 copies of a twenty-five cent book sold, one and one-half cents per copy thereafter, and correspondingly higher figures for thirty-five, fifty and seventy-five cent books. Smaller firms pay somewhat less, but no publisher admitted to payments of less than $1000 per title to his authors. Pocket Books estimates that at 250,000 copies per printing, its authors get $3000 for twenty-five cent books, $4200 for thirty-five cent books, and $6000 for fifty cent books, with the average per title amounting to $4500 to $5000. Other firms confirmed these figures and all agreed that authors' incomes for Western novels are lowest, averaging about $1500 to $2000 per reprint.

Authors had not been satisfied with the reprint royalties given them and were looking forward to greater financial rewards when Gold Medal was launched as a line confined to originals, and Dell and Avon also began to publish original paperbacks. Actually, these firms pay minimum advances of $3000 on first printings of 250,000 copies. Ballantine Books, with those of its books that are simultaneously released in cloth and paperbound editions, offers its authors a combined royalty of 10 percent on cloth and 8 percent on paperback editions. If a Ballantine book sells 250,000 paperback copies at thirty-five cents and 3000 clothbound copies, it brings the author $7450.

The vast array of titles which are in the public domain after the expiration of copyrights give a small income to introductions and comments. It is customary to pay a flat fee for these services, as well as for translations, regardless of the number of copies produced or sold; this ranges from $150 to $300 for editorial work and approximately double these figures for new translations.

Malcolm Cowley, in speaking about the American literary situation, states that "in the early 1950s there were more apprentice novelists than ever before, and fewer of them were breaking into print; only about half as many new novels were being published each year as in the early 1900s." [11] There are many reasons why this may be so, but the generally low financial return for true intellectual efforts such as the publication and writing of books is undoubtedly one of them.

Distribution in the United States

The basic characteristic of American book publishing is its diversity which "lies partly in the limitless variety of subject matter it must deal with . . . [and partly] in an economic structure generally conceded to be chaotic since the market potential is inadequately known and even less adequately realized."[12]

During 1956 over 539 million copies of books were sold for at least 743 million dollars. Of these, paperbacks accounted for more than 253 million copies sold for over fifty million dollars. In 1957, more than one thousand publishers produced 13,142 titles; of these 1469 were paperbacks[13] which sold close to 240 million copies for more than fifty-two million dollars. The largest increase among paperbacks in terms of production and sales was reported for the higher-priced series.

In line with the general pattern of diversity, books reach their ultimate consumers by various routes. They may be obtained directly from publishers, book clubs, mail order houses, wholesalers, bookstores and a variety of non-book outlets. When they are out of print and no longer available from publishers, they can be purchased from second-hand, antiquarian, remainder and rare book dealers and at book auctions.

There are about 9000 outlets of all kinds and sizes for hard cover books in the United States, of which about half make an effort to handle new, nonspecialized books but only 500 can be considered to be effective stores, adequately stocked; an additional 1000 stores attempt to offer a fairly good general book service; and 3000 stores provide at least the most popular modern books.[14] This appallingly small number of stores for an adult population of 98,000,000 is justified because only 1-2 percent of the population use them. Barely one-fifth of one cent of each consumer dollar after taxes in 1956 was spent by individual readers on books. (This does not include, however, institutional purchases by schools, libraries and so on.) Only 17 percent of the Americans questioned admitted in 1955 to Dr. Gallup that they were currently reading a book. Rough as some of these data are, they add up to the unmistakable conclusion that Americans on the average are not heavy readers -- at least, not heavy readers of adult hard cover "trade" books. Correspondingly the book industry is a small segment of our national economy, of which it represents a paltry one-five hundredth of nearly 400 billion.

In spite of the limitations of its operations, publishing is exceedingly competitive. Not only do publishers vie with each other for a comparatively small number of individual and institutional buyers, but competition extends all the way down to the organizations which distribute and sell books. Libraries and book stores purchase their hard cover titles either directly from the publishers or obtain them through wholesalers who specialize in adult books. Prebinders provide juvenile books with more durable covers than the publishers and wholesale them to libraries. Paperback titles of predominantly hard cover publishers are distributed with the other materials of these firms.

The distribution facilities of mass-market paperbacks are much more adequate because they include nearly 110,000 retail outlets ranging from newsstands on street corners, in subway and railroad stations, bus and air terminals, drug and department stores and supermarkets, to exclusive paperback stores and general and college book stores. The books reach these sales outlets through national distributors who carry the merchandise from printing plants or publishers' warehouses to about 850 independent local news wholesalers who cover the cities and metropolitan areas of the country which can be profitably serviced by truck deliveries. Some 10,000 retailers which cannot be reached in this manner are covered by galley wholesalers, a group of regional jobbers who make distribution through the mails. Sometimes local accounts are directly covered by the publishers themselves.

Until May, 1957 this "independent" system of distribution existed side by side with the completely integrated operations of the American News Company (ANC) which handled distribution operations of magazines and paperbacks from printing plants to retail outlet deliveries by means of their network of nearly 400 local branches. When ANC discontinued this part of their business in 1957 it abandoned a field which it had virtually controlled from 1846 to 1904. This firm had been instrumental in the distribution of the many paperback series, "dime novels" and "cheap libraries" so prevalent during the 1870-1890 period and had helped to distribute the publications of Street & Smith, who moved, after the turn of the century, to independent distributors.

The breakup of this near-monopoly came about gradually and without legal intervention from the government. Smaller independent news wholesalers were able to establish themselves in less densely populated areas and developed a reputation for efficiency which attracted first some of the smaller and later even the larger magazine publishers. In 1919 the McCall Corporation and Popular Science Publishing Company joined in the formation of the S-M News, Inc., which 'Reader's Digest' made its distributor in 1929. Curtis and Hearst began to use the independent distributors and Curtis organized its own circulation subsidiary in 1932.

When Pocket Books began its operations in 1939 it asked ANC to handle its book distribution, but shortly thereafter the new firm began to manage its own national distribution and turned to independent newsdealers for local distribution. In less than three years, contracts with 600 of these provided some of the most efficient sales organizations for inexpensive books ever devised in this country. Other paperback firms followed the Pocket Book example or joined the ANC or established their own circulation divisions or created more independent distribution subsidiaries like Curtis and later Fawcett. S-M News changed eventually its name to Select Magazines, Inc. and is now owned by six publishers. Another large circulation organization is International Circulation Co., a Hearst subsidiary; smaller ones include Publishers Distributing Corp., Capital Distributing Co. and Kable News Co.

Many of the large publishers of popular magazines, pulp magazines, one-shot releases, and paperbacks -- among them Dell and Pines Publications with "Popular Library" -- remained with ANC.

During 1955, 'Time,' 'Life,' 'Fortune,' and 'Sports Illustrated' moved from ANC to Select Magazines, Inc., 'Look' signed up with Curtis, followed by the publications of Condé Nast -- 'Vogue,' 'Glamour,' 'Home & Garden' and 'Vogue Pattern Book.' The next calamity for ANC came when Crowell-Collier discontinued its magazines, 'Woman's Home Companion' and 'Collier's.' During the spring of 1957, 'Newsweek' and the 'New Yorker' moved to Curtis and Dell Publishing Company cancelled its contract.

ANC's decision to leave the magazine distribution field did not curtail its other profitable and unrelated activities. Among these are the operations of the Union News Co., one of the largest magazine and newspaper retailers, which owns also a string of restaurants, barber shops, lending libraries and book stores; the American Match Co. which distributes various drug store supplies, and the book department of the ANC which wholesales primarily hard cover trade books. At the end of the year ANC declared dividends of 40 cents a share because of "the size of . . . earned surplus, the continuing profitability of the remaining divisions and . . . the liquidation of the unprofitable wholesale periodical division."[15] The demise of ANC's magazine wholesaling strengthened independent newsdealers and created new opportunities for library jobbers. Paper Editions Corporation, emerging out of the ill-fated Paper Editions Book Club, established itself as a national wholesaler of inexpensive and higher-priced paperbacks and even hard cover books.

Many paperback firms solicit in their advertising direct mail orders from individual customers, though they all agree that mail requests for single titles do not pay because of the time involved. For public relations reasons and for testing the market they still feel that it is worthwhile to accommodate the individual buyer in this way.

In addition, many of the larger paperback publishers are "willing to supply . . . libraries at discounts ranging from 10 to 40 percent, regardless of number of titles ordered. Several preferred that libraries order no less than five titles at one time. The discount most frequently offered was 20 to 25 percent . . . Several indicated a sliding scale -- the more titles ordered, the greater the discount."[16]

Local news wholesalers receive substantial discounts; they pay sixteen cents for a twenty-five cent book. For the retailer, only a small profit is left, which is sufficient in the case of drug stores and supermarkets where no service is connected with the sales; book stores, which depend exclusively on the sale of books and have a larger overhead, find that the handling of paperbacks is profitable only if they can rid themselves of the middleman's services. Partly for this reason, and partly to obtain selective stock, book stores attempt to establish direct connections with the publisher. Some paperback firms permit such direct contact, granting the book dealer a larger discount; others feel that such practices are unfair to their national distributors and local wholesalers.

Book dealers have welcomed the higher-priced lines of

paperbacks of regular trade publishers because their distribution takes place through regular trade channels. They consider them substantial traffic builders which bring new customers to their stores and have relented in their objection to the cheaper mass-market series which help them to round out their offerings of inexpensive publications of high literary quality.

The significance of an efficient distribution system is stressed by every publisher, and even in the absence of statistics, there remains no doubt that the personnel engaged in advertising and sales far outnumbers those concerned with editorial and art work. Hard cover publishers use their own sales force which travels in certain territories and maintains contacts with book stores, libraries and faculties in all types of schools from the elementary to the college level. They not only sell but act as the eyes and ears of the organizations they represent. They channel manuscripts to their head offices and learn about shifting trends among general book buyers and teachers.

Publishers devoted decisively to paperbacks employ sales staffs to supervise, supplement and assist the sales agents of the independent local newsdealers. They supply them with promotional materials and see to it that good and bad sales are quickly reported to the head office, that the supply of required materials continues in an even flow, and that sufficient and desirable rack space is allotted to the releases of their firms. The salesmen of the newsdealers are engaged in retail merchandising and the products they happen to handle are three-quarter magazines and one-quarter books.

These men who drive the trucks and stack the racks in the thousands of outlets across the land do not promote knowledge or literature but they do try to do an efficient job in season and out. They read books and magazines but don't let their personal tastes interfere with their assigned tasks, and they are just as resentful of the banning of books as of receiving tickets for traffic violations. Both of these are considered occupational hazards which reduce their hard-earned incomes.

The organizations which employ these men are not to be blamed for the worthless, useless and sometimes damaging material which often overshadows the better books. The critics of the industry fail to recognize paperback publishing as one aspect of mass production and mass marketing, in which output is geared directly to public demand. Changes in taste, of course, occur. They tend to be national in scope and slow in developing, but in mass-market publishing as in other mass-production fields, the producers are quick to respond, once a shift in demand is indicated. Mass production, which has given Americans better, cheaper and more homes, cars and other material goods than people enjoy elsewhere, has made countless books of high value available to more readers at lower prices than at any previous time during our 300 years of publishing history. For this achievement the publishers and merchandisers of paperbacks deserve the country's appreciation.

Distribution Abroad

From the seventeenth to the twentieth century the United States imported far more books than it was able to sell to foreign countries. Between the two World Wars a trade balance was reached and imports and exports each amounted to about five million dollars per year. Since 1945 U.S. exports have increased considerably and reached forty million dollars in 1956.[17] In the mid 50's, the average export of U.S. books came to about 7 percent of the total production and some individual text, technical, scientific, and medical book publishers and university presses ship out as much as 30 percent of their output. Many of the exported books are sent as outright gifts or through special arrangements which are usually subsidized by the government or foundations (See chapter 5).

Some American publishers, including the larger paperback firms, own European subsidiaries which act as independent agencies and serve as the distributor of the products of the parent firm. This practice is found most frequently in the British Isles. Other publishers rely on the services of a foreign agent whom they share with a number of other firms. W. S. Hall & Co. and Henry M. Snyder & Co., Inc. represent a large segment of the paperback field. Small publishers maintain direct contacts with book importers and larger book stores which distribute and promote their products. Visits by American publishers and their staffs help to follow up on sales methods and changing demands for American titles.

The shift of emphasis to more serious and nonfiction paperback titles since 1953-54 widened the foreign market for these books. Titles usually listed as being in greatest demand in foreign countries fall into the following categories: physical sciences and applied fields such as engineering, electronics, chemistry, medicine; the theoretical sciences like mathematics and physics; technical fields including international banking and agriculture; the social sciences with particular stress on international affairs, economics, transportation, psychology, sociology and anthropology.[18] Apparently the need for books in the humanities and the arts is less acute and considered more of a luxury with the possible exception of Western Europe. The cooperative publishing projects have done a superb job in giving readers in underdeveloped areas a balanced view of the United States through its literary productions.

Paperback publishers will find encouragement in the Report of the Princeton Conference of the National Book Committee which stated in September 1955 that "in many important areas, especially in Asia and Latin America, even a quite reasonably priced hard cover book is beyond the means of any but libraries and similar institutions, and a very few individual purchasers . . . A retail price of 25 cents to 50 cents probably represents the maximum limit for popular sale."[19]

While serious paperbacks sell well abroad because they are really needed, the market for very light fiction is also considerable, as its sale at a much lower price brings a small profit to the publisher for his remainder stock which is completely valueless in the U.S. market. Unfortunately, the cultural interest of the United States and the economic interest of the paperback publishers do not always coincide insofar as the latter promote the widest sales of our least enduring literary efforts. Paperbacks as a format have found widespread imitation outside the Anglo-Saxon book world and our technological advances in inexpensive book production have stimulated similar efforts in many other countries.

Censorship

Freedom of communication, the right to free speech and a free press, are based on the First and Fourteenth Amendments to the Constitution which enjoin Congress from enacting such restrictions and prohibit the states from enacting legislation depriving any person of life, liberty, or property without due process of law. Restrictions of freedom of speech or of the press have been exercised on grounds of protection of individuals against falsehoods, common standards of the community, security against internal violence and disorder and external aggression. Literary expressions were primarily affected when they offended the common standards of the community through obscenity, blasphemy, sedition, libel, and other variations from communal standards. [20] With the exception of the Alien and Sedition Acts of 1798, which were exceedingly unpopular, no restraints on reading were imposed by Congress until the Tariff Act of 1842, which prohibited the importation of obscene literature. Thirty years later, the Comstock Act "barred obscene literature from the mails." [21] These two laws granted the right of censorship to the Customs Service and the Post Office. The Tariff Act of 1930 subsequently expanded the laws dealing with the importation of books.

The present condition of censorship has been summarized by Paul Blanshard:

> We may not publish or distribute reading matter which is seditious or treasonable, or which interferes with the draft, or which advocates the overthrow of the government by force, or which threatens to kill the President, or which incites to insurrection, or which is obscene.
>
> We may not send any reading matter through the United States mails which advocates treason, sedition, insurrection, forcible resistance to American law or the overthrow of the government by force. Nor may we send through the mails anything which is obscene, lewd or lascivious, or anything . . . which tends to incite arson, murder or assassination, or anything which solicits money by fraud and misrepresentation.
>
> We may not import from abroad any reading matter which is obscene, or which advocates treason, insurrection or resistance to federal law, or which contains any threat to inflict bodily harm upon anyone in the United States. [22]

Legal censorship then occurs on the federal, state or local level when a book enters the United States, when it goes through the mails, or when legal proceedings are instituted through complaint of an individual or a group. Private citizens rarely take the initiative unless they act as spokesmen for a group of

volunteer censors. They take their complaint to the police, the
local prosecutor, or a federal district attorney. Usually,
matters are settled at the level of complaint; a warning of
possible confiscation or court action usually results in a voluntary withdrawal of objectionable titles and few in the community
will ever know that complaints were lodged and that the publications in question are locally unavailable. Exceptions occur
only when the law enforcement officers consider it necessary to
set the legal machine into motion and when individuals or
groups inform the press, and public opinion is aroused in the
ensuing controversy.

On the local level of censorship, city ordinances usually
require the inspection of newsstand materials, magazines,
comics and paperbacks, but are not concerned with hardbound
books and regular book store merchandise. As a result, an
anomalous situation exists today in which, in a local area, the
original clothbound edition of a book may be freely obtained in a
book store and possibly in most public libraries, but not in the
paperbound format at newsstands, in drug stores or railroad
stations. This type of suppression of reading matter puts the
hardbound editions beyond the attention of the local censor
while inexpensive paperbacks of identical content are made
subject to different treatment. The inherent rationalization is
that the inexpensive editions find a wider market and are more
easily accessible to children and adolescents. These arguments
undoubtedly have some merit and explain the particular interest
of individual vigilante groups and the Gathings Committee in
these publications. It is significant that this does not result in
a clear-cut pattern of enforcement. It seems deplorable that
the existing system of censorship substantially works in the
secrecy of police offices, where spokesmen of various groups
represent their members, but the public at large remains
excluded from the discussion. The main reason why this
atmosphere of silence is possible is the system of distribution
used for paperbacks.

If a local group has objected to a book or it has been found
undesirable by a police official, the police or the prosecutor's
office will contact the retailer or wholesaler and suggest that
he cease and desist from selling a particular title. The distributor usually drops the title quietly and eventually returns the
undistributed copies to the publisher. He usually has more titles
to distribute than he needs, paperbacks are only part of his

business, and he does not want to jeopardize the good will of the community by having his name dragged through the newspapers. The retailer, owner of a drug store or newsstand, may or may not read the books he sells, but he, like the wholesaler, is primarily a businessman and not a literary authority. He is even more susceptible to local intimidation and will not risk antagonizing any of his customers for his other wares by selling a book that has been found objectionable; he cannot be expected to let the concepts of constitutional liberty or freedom of the press interfere with his business. Usually the only person or firm with a tangible economic interest in such a problem, and the only one with professional pride in books as well as the resources to take a case of unjustified censorship to court is the publisher. Hard cover publishers do this occasionally, paperback publishers rarely. In studying some of these court cases one finds that the most reputable firms with the smallest percentage of objectionable titles are the ones which have most frequently been involved in litigation of this type, because these firms have the necessary means and convictions to see a case through court. In these instances, extra-legal pressures against books have been sternly rebuked, as occurred in 'New American Library of World Literature v. Allen,' 114 F. Supp. 823 (N.D. Ohio, 1953), 'Bantam Books v. Melko,' 25 N.J. Super. 292, 96 A 2d 47 (1954)[23] and 'Butler v. Michigan,' 352 U.S. 380 (1957). In spite of this, court cases are usually avoided because the publishers, even after having won a victory in one community or state may still have to face repeat performances in other legal jurisdictions. The costs are high and the publicity value is usually not worth the effort because their product is so inexpensive. Publishers of original hard cover books may find it more profitable to fight it out and they will enlist an occasional bookseller to cooperate with them.

When a case reaches the courts and is tried on grounds of obscenity, criminal law is applied, being still the sole legal means for checking obscenity in books, magazines and newspapers everywhere except in the State of Massachusetts.[24] This is the only state which, since 1945, allows an equity suit.

The system of controlling books by warnings from persons without legal authority aroused so much indignant criticism that Boston booksellers drafted legislation

and succeeded after eighteen years in getting it enacted in much improved form . . .[25]
This law provides for action against the book after adjudication by the Supreme Court and replaces criminal action against the bookseller or purchaser of the book by civil procedure and transfers responsibility from the police to the attorney general. Besides the booksellers, library associations and other organizations were instrumental in the adoption of this law. It has many advantages as it removes the function of censorship from police officials, who are usually neither by training nor avocation literary experts. Since only the book and not a person is on trial, the case goes before a single judge unless a jury trial is requested by one of the interested parties, the author or publishers for example. The declaratory judgement of the court may be appealed to the Supreme Judicial Court. The same book will be assured of uniform treatment throughout the state.

It is undeniably true that a considerable amount of pornographic material is being published in the United States and that some of it -- depending on one's definitions -- appears in paperbound books. The latter, among other material, were scrutinized in detail by the Gathings Committee on Current Pornographic Materials in pursuance of House Resolution 596, Eighty-second Congress, Second Session, May 12, 1952.

> [The committee was] authorized and directed to conduct a full and complete investigation and study (1) to determine the extent to which current literature -- books, magazines, and comic books -- containing immoral, obscene, or otherwise offensive matter, or placing improper emphasis on crime, violence, and corruption, are being made available to the people of the United States through the United States mails and otherwise; and (2) to determine the adequacy of existing law to prevent the publication and distribution of books containing immoral, offensive, and other undesirable matter.[26]

The majority report of the committee, signed by six members, made three recommendations: (1) That Congress enact legislation to prohibit interstate and international transport of obscene, lewd, and similar materials, not only by public but also by private carrier. (2) That the Postmaster General receive even broader powers than he holds now to restrict or withhold mailing privileges for certain specified items or under certain conditions.[27] (3) That the industry engage in self-censorship. These seem to be rather meager results for a congressional expenditure of $25,000.

The minority report agreed with the majority report's "condemnation of the printing and dissemination of obscene and pornographic materials whose only purpose it is to cater solely to the lust and wantonness of its readers."[28] However, it stated that the committee had

> sat as a high Congressional tribunal which has arbitrarily labeled as 'obscene' a vast array of books, magazines, and other publications . . . [and not only blundered] into the area of literary criticism but also into an area which the Supreme Court of the United States has declared to have a preferred position in our entire scheme of constitutional government.[29]

In referring to 'Hannegan v. Esquire, Inc.,' the minority report stated that a requirement that literature or art conform to some norm prescribed by an official smacks of an ideology foreign to our system. The minority singled out Erskine Caldwell's 'God's Little Acre,' James T. Farrell's 'Studs Lonigan,' and John Steinbeck's 'Wayward Bus' as titles which received an undue amount of criticism. The minority report agreed with that of the majority "that the covers of many of these volumes are extreme and in bad taste," and went on record "that in many instances the covers do not reflect the content of the book and are designed to promote sales by catering to the sensational."[30]

Other objections to the majority report have come from many quarters, but were most ably summarized by Victor Weybright in his 'Complete and Unabridged Statement to the Gathings Committee by the New American Library of World Literature, Inc.' [New York: New American Library of World Literature, Inc., 1953 (?)] which was only partly quoted by the committee report. In connection with pressure groups, Mr. Weybright referred to 'Burstyn v. Wilson' 343 U.S. 495, better known as the "Miracle Case," where the movie by this name was regarded as sacrilegious and blasphemous by the League of Decency, but the court decision pointed out that what is acceptable to one group may not be acceptable to another. Victor Weybright stated that at the point where one group seeks to impose its own private standards upon members of the general public, the activity of such a group becomes vicious.[31] In connection with the influence of paperbacks upon children, he pointed out that reprints are not essentially designed for children or aimed at the juvenile, but rather the popular adult market. Father John Courtney Murray went a step further by stating that if "adult standards of literature would be dangerous for children, a child's standard of literature is rather appalling to an adult. If therefore any censorship is to be administered in the interest of society, the professional competence of the literary critic must play a role in the process."[32] The main problem of the Gathings Committee's literary censorship lies in the fact that it ignored the decision in the famous "Ulysses Case" in 1933 which rejected the concept of using isolated passages as proof of obscenity.

Reviewing the censorship situation in general, Douglas M. Black, president of Doubleday & Company and chairman of the American Book Publishers' Council Anti-Censorship Committee, referred at the Council's Annual Meeting in May, 1955, to the situation in Michigan as the

> most acute and serious, particularly as the pattern established there has a tendency to spread . . . One feature of the Michigan law is that it is a 'containing' statute, i.e., passages in the book are sufficient for censoring action; another feature is that if a book could be considered as tending to corrupt the morals of minors, it cannot be sold to adults.[33]

In this way, the Hicklin test, established in the 1868 case of 'Regina v. Hicklin' in Victorian England and refuted by the Ulysses case, still lives on in contemporary America. According to the Hicklin rule, the test of obscenity is "whether the tendency of the matter charged as obscenity is to deprave and corrupt those whose minds are open to such immoral influence, and into whose hands a publication of this sort may fall."[34] The best example for the perpetuation of the Hicklin rule is the Detroit License and Censor Bureau, established in 1937. The municipal code of the City of Detroit contains several statutes which deal with obscene and libelous publications, but the books are judged strictly according to the Michigan State Statute, Section 343, which prohibits publications or anything else containing obscene, immoral, lewd, or lascivious language, or obscene, immoral, lewd, or lascivious prints, pictures, figures or descriptions manifestly tending to the corruption of the morals of youth.[35] As a result of the Detroit Police Department listing, fifty-seven books and forty-six magazines were banned during 1955. After inspection of some samples of these magazines no fair-minded person could possibly object to their withdrawal. Many of the fifty-seven books indicate by their title obscenity and lewdness, and many of their authors have never shown any literary merit; their publishers are not listed in any serious publication dealing with book production in the United States. However, some of the other authors have gained national and international reputation and fame, their works are of great literary merit, and they could be considered obscene only by lifting isolated passages out of context. Among the books, banned in Detroit were:

> Niven Busch, 'The Hate Merchant'
> *Erskine Caldwell, 'God's Little Acre'
> *Erskine Caldwell, 'Tobacco Road'
> James T. Farrell, 'An American Dream Girl'
> James T. Farrell, 'Gas-House McGinty'
> *James T. Farrell, 'Studs Lonigan'
> *Gustave Flaubert, 'Madame Bovary'
> *Ernest Hemingway, 'Across the River and Into the Trees'
> Ernest Hemingway, 'The Sun Also Rises'
> Evan Hunter, 'The Blackboard Jungle'
> *Aldous Huxley, 'Antic Hay'
> Christopher Isherwood, 'The World in the Evening'
> *James Jones, 'From Here to Eternity'
> *D. H. Lawrence, 'Lady Chatterley's Lover'
> Norman Mailer, 'Barbary Shore'
> *Norman Mailer, 'The Naked and the Dead'
> *John Dos Passos, '1919'
> Jules Romains, 'Lord God of the Flesh'
> *Jean Paul Sartre, 'Intimacy'
> *Lillian Smith, 'Strange Fruit'
> John Steinbeck, 'The Wayward Bus'
> Leon Uris, 'Battle Cry'
> Frederick Wakeman, 'Naked to My Past'
> Kathleen Winsor, 'Forever Amber'
> *Émile Zola, 'Nana'

Undoubtedly, some of these are of greater literary value than others. The ones marked with an asterisk were listed in the

1954 edition of 'Good Reading,' edited by the Committee on College Reading.

In going through the Detroit lists, one notices that no distinction is made between authors of literary repute and those who cannot make such claims. Also, Western and detective fiction and blood-curdling mysteries seem to get scant attention even though many of these works are without value and show strong tendencies of sadism, violence and bad taste. This is the more surprising because this area, "the pornography of violence," would appear most deserving of restraining action, for here, "sex is associated with, and becomes symbolic of, the hatreds and hostilities, the angers and cruelties, that lie deep in men and women; the profanation of the most sacred thing in sex -- its relation to love and the hope of human life -- is almost complete." [36]

Several court decisions helped to clarify the confused censorship situation in Michigan which had assumed the position previously held by Massachusetts. In 'Butler v. Michigan,' the case involving the banning in Detroit of John H. Griffin's 'The Devil Rides Outside,' the United States Supreme Court in 1957 unanimously ruled that the state's obscenity law, which attempts to restrict adult reading to the level suitable for juveniles, was unconstitutional. The Wayne County Circuit Court in Detroit in the same year issued an injunction against the police ban of John O'Hara's 'Ten North Frederick' without court decision. A change in the censorship laws of the state is unavoidable in consequence of the Supreme Court decision.

Attempts at censorship through private group pressure come from many quarters. One of the best organized of these is the National Organization for Decent Literature (NODL) which was formed in 1937 by a group of Catholic bishops. It publishes monthly lists of "Publications Disapproved," which are widely distributed. Many of the titles listed have certainly little to recommend for either young people or adults, but the lists include books by Ernest Hemingway, William Faulkner, John Dos Passos, George Orwell, John O'Hara and Emile Zola. The enforcement of their withdrawal from sale is frequently brought about through extra-legal channels by pressure upon distributors. Lately, NODL, along with other, similar groups, has realized the greater promise of a positive attitude and, since 1957, is issuing a "List of Acceptable Pocket-Size Books for Youth" which states in its foreword: "Never before has it been so easy to accumulate a library of lasting interest at very small cost. Never before, therefore, has it been so easy to develop the reading habits which enable one to live a fuller life."

The question of who shall censor what in a free and democratic society is a perplexing one and seems to have been solved in the most satisfactory fashion in Massachusetts. Judges and juries, in conjunction with prosecutors operating under an adequate law, are best suited to settle problems of censorship.

Institutional Sales

Paperbacks were originally conceived as books to be bought on the spur of the moment by individual customers. After the war, the growing student population and the teaching trend of stressing survey courses made increasing use of serious titles brought out by firms such as Penguin, Pocket Books and NAL, which found a significant source of revenue in quality titles that sell over a long period of time. In the 1950's other mass-market publishers including Dell and Bantam followed their lead and as an ever greater number of excellent reprints, often unobtainable in any other format, as well as some worthwhile originals appeared, the problem of purchasing, processing and conserving paperbacks for library use became more and more prominent. Various articles on this topic appeared with increasing frequency after 1952-53. Library reactions were first summarized by the 'PLD Reporter' (Public Library Division of the American Library Association) of September 1954.

The interest of libraries and schools created problems for them as well as the publishers. The larger houses recognized these special needs by creating educational departments which circularize lists emphasizing titles of particular significance and also handle direct sales. Selection, which was very difficult until a few years ago, has recently become comparatively simple with the help of 'Paperbound Books in Print,' Orton's 'Reprints in Series,' 'Publishers' Weekly's' monthly Forecast of Paperbacks and the reviews of selected titles appearing regularly in the 'Saturday Review,' the 'New York Times Book Review,' the 'Nation,' and other publications. In spring, 1958, the R.R. Bowker Co. released 'Paperbound Books, College

Edition,' which is the subject index section of 'Paperbound Books in Print' and lists 1900 titles suitable for use in colleges. It was distributed free of charge to thousands of college teachers.

Acquisition has also been facilitated recently. Most publishers now deal directly with libraries. Local newsdealers will also supply titles of series handled by them. Hard cover book publishers make their paperback lines available in the same way as their other titles, either through direct sales or library jobbers. Paper Editions Corporation is effective as a national jobber of mass-market as well as higher-priced paperbacks to book store and library purchasers and issues stock lists of a large number of series. 'Paperbound Books in Print' provides a directory of sources which supply paperbacks on request, arranged by geographical regions.

The technical processing of paperbacks requires special simplified techniques. Most libraries using inexpensive titles of wide popular appeal consider them as "expendables" and shelve them separately; they are often circulated on an "honor" system and in some institutions borrowers may take out one book and return a different one from their own collection. Higher-priced titles are usually handled in the same manner as hard cover titles. Several studies of this topic have been made and experimentation on a larger scale would be in order.[37]

Permanent preservation requires a technique of rebinding. Paperbacks issued in small editions of about 5,000 copies are still sewn and occasionally stapled. They lend themselves to rebinding like any other book, except that the margins are frequently so narrow that they complicate the process; this can, however, be overcome by skillful library binding. The rebinding of "perfect bound" books presents greater difficulties because signature folds have been sliced off and oversewing is therefore impossible. Bindings are at best patch-up jobs, but as most paperback series use cheap pulp paper such bindings by the various means of reinforcement are likely to last about as long as the paper of the book. Experimentation along these lines by individual binders and librarians led to the creation of the Paperback Subcommittee of the Bookbinding Committee of the American Library Association which, in cooperation with the Library Binding Institute, the American Book Publishers Council and the Book Manufacturers' Institute, is working on specifications for the most economic and durable process.

The preservation of original paperbacks and titles which are unobtainable in any other format poses a more difficult problem. A certain number of uncut signatures, printed from the same plates but on better paper could be made available for edition or library binding. Explorations into this field are made by the above-mentioned group. The growing interest of various types of libraries in many aspects of paperback preservation and use was convincingly demonstrated by a cooperative survey conducted by several paperback publishers with the approval of the Public Library Division and the assistance of the Reprint Expediting Service of the American Library Association. [38]

Projection into the Future

Looking into the future would lead one to believe that the shape of books to come will approximate the paperbound rather than the leather or clothbound volume. It seems probable that an increasing number of manuscripts will be excluded from the likelihood of being preserved between two stiff covers. Light fiction, Western stories, light romances, mysteries, detective stories and science fiction are written to be hastily and superficially indulged in and seldom to be remembered or reread. They neither require nor deserve more permanence than the same type of material which flashes rapidly across the movie or TV screen or attracts temporarily the listener's attention when carried over the radio. As mass media seem to supplement rather than supplant each other, the demand for impermanent reading matter seems to grow and may reach the point where most, if not all, fiction will appear in this temporary format. Only, perhaps, when such writing is recognized to be of enduring value will it be granted the coat of distinction, in a reversal of the current practice, and appear as a reprint in cloth binding.

Another possibility may be brought about by technological developments. A simplified process through the use of plastic materials may eliminate binding entirely and reduce the price of the hardbound book to a point where a flexible, yet solid, fused-on cover will wipe out the difference between the two types of publications. Such advances, however, are too far off to be coped with at mid-century.

It seems likely that photomechanical reproduction processes, involving a combination of microfilm and Xerography, will solve the problem of publishing a limited number of copies at low cost in paper covers. "Perfect bound" books, held together with synthetic adhesives and produced with type set by photographic composition systems using plastic plates on high-speed rotary presses, will probably become the accepted format for large editions, upwards of 150,000 copies.

It is hoped that this history of inexpensive publishing indicates that the shape and price of books have had significant influence on their use. Paperbacks have democratized the approach to learning, self-improvement and entertainment. They fit well into the smaller American homes of today. Clifton Fadiman stated two years ago that Americans had consumed approximately two billion copies of about 12,000 paperback titles in sixteen years and were slowly becoming a nation of readers.[39] Two years later another five or six hundred million copies of about 3,000 additional titles had been bought and probably read. In the spring of 1958 more than 6,000 titles were being kept in print and approximately 120 titles released every month by about 100 firms and the number of serious titles had grown considerably. Paperbacks hardly ever outlast the life of their purchasers, but the ideas they convey often do. If they are worth the reader's attention this alone justifies their existence and expansion.

[1] "Hot Melts Bind a Market," 'Chemical Week,' LXXIII (July 18, 1953), p. 68 and "Resinous Adhesives for Book Binders," 'Chemical Age,' LXIX (September 12, 1953), pp. 547-48.

[2] "Reading Plan and Cahen's Report on Cold Adhesive Are BMI Highlights," 'Publishers' Weekly,' CLXVIII:19 (November 5, 1955), pp. 2004-08.

[3] Donald E. Strout, "Paperback Books -- Boon or Bane?," 'The Nature and Development of the Library Collection' Urbana, Ill.: The University of Illinois Library School, 1957, p. 50.

[4] "Problems of Paperbacks Cited at Trade Book Clinic," 'Publishers' Weekly,' CLXXI:9 (March 4, 1957), pp. 126-30.

[5] Barbara Bannon, "Popular Market Forecast for January," 'Publishers' Weekly," CLXIV:21 (November 21, 1953), pp. 2122-28, CLXVIII:21 (November 19, 1955), pp. 2151-54, and "PW Forecast of Paperbacks," CLXII:21 (November 18, 1957), pp. 53-57.

[6] Malcolm Cowley, 'The Literary Situation' (New York: The Viking Press, 1954), p. 170.

[7] Ibid., p. 173.

[8] Harold K. Guinzburg, Robert W. Frase, and Theodore Waller, 'Books and the Mass Market' (Urbana: University of Illinois Press, 1953), p. 26.

[9] Ibid., p. 27.

[10] '1956 Annual Survey of the General Book Publishing Industry.' American Book Publishers Council, Inc., May, 1957, Table 2, p. 5.

[11] Cowley, op. cit., p. 161.

[12] Chandler B. Grannis, "Structure of a Diverse Industry," 'What Happens in Book Publishing' New York: Columbia University Press, 1957, p. 5.

[13] 'Publishers' Weekly,' CLXXII: (October 14, 1957), p. 18, CLXXIII: January 20, 1958), p. 54.

[14] Grannis, op. cit., p. 9.

[15] 'Publishers' Weekly,' CLXXII:22 (November 25, 1957), p. 13.

[16] Strout, op. cit., p. 51.

[17] '1956 Annual Survey of the General Book Publishing Industry,' Table 1, p. 3.

[18] 'A Manual on Foreign Trade for University Presses (n.p.: The Association of American University Presses, 1956), p. 11.

[19] 'American Books Abroad, A Report of a Conference Called by the National Book Committee, Princeton, N. J., September 29-30, 1955' (New York: R. R. Bowker Co., 1955), p. 17.

[20] Zechariah Chafee, Jr., Government and Mass Communications, Vol. I (Chicago: University of Chicago Press, 1947), p. 196.

[21] Paul Blanshard, 'The Right to Read' (Boston: Beacon Press, 1955), p. 36.

[22] Ibid., pp. 36-37.

[23] R. McKeon, R. K. Merton, and W. Gellhorn,'The Freedom to Read' (New York: R. R. Bowker Co., 1957), p. 11.

[24] Chafee, op. cit., p. 219.

[25] Ibid., pp. 228-29.

[26] 'Report of the Select Committee on Current Pornographic Materials' (Washington, D.C.: United States Government Printing Office, 1952), p. 1.

[27] Frank Walker refused in 1946 the second class mailing privilege to 'Esquire Magazine' until the Supreme Court ruled in 'Hannegan v. Esquire, Inc.' against this decision. In 1954 the Post Office attempted to exercise the same censorship against a translation of Aristophanes' 'Lysistrata' but eventually backed down. To strengthen the powers of the Post Office in this direction does not seem to be in accord with previous Supreme Court decisions or the basic functions of Post Office service.

[28] 'Report of the Select Committee on Current Pornographic Materials,' p. 121.

[29] Ibid.

[30] Ibid., pp. 124-25.

[31] 'Complete and Unabridged Statement to the Gathings Committee by the New American Library of World Literature, Inc.,' p. 15.

[32] John Courtney Murray, S.J., "Literature and Censorship," 'Books on Trial,' June-July, 1956, p. 5.

[33] "Reading Promotion Is Stressed at Publishers 'Annual Meeting'," 'Publishers' Weekly,' CLXVII:24 (June 11, 1955), p. 2653.

[34] Blanshard, op. cit., pp. 148-149.

[35] 'Report of the Select Committee on Current Pornographic Materials,'

p. 54.

[36] Murray, op. cit., p. 5.

[37] ·Strout, op. cit. and Elinor C. Kuhns, "Paperback Expendables," 'Library Journal,' LXXIX:19 (November 1, 1954), pp. 2059-62.

[38] Aaron L. Fessler, "Paperbacks in Libraries -- '58," and Harold H. Laskey, "A Survey of the Survey," 'Library Journal,' LXXXIII:8, pp. 1137-42 and pp. 1143-45.

[39] Clifton Fadiman, "Party of One," 'Holiday,' XIX:3 (March, 1956), pp. 6-14.

Part 3   PUBLISHERS

OF

PAPERBACKS

CHAPTER 8

POCKET BOOKS, INCORPORATED

The Beginnings

The British development of large scale, mass-produced paperback publishing can be traced to Sir Allen Lane, whose vision and broad conception started an old branch of publishing on a new road by building on a foundation laid by others. In the United States, the publication of "Pocket Books" in 1939 marked the beginning of the "paperback revolution." Four men were responsible for the success of this venture -- Robert F. de Graff, M. Lincoln Schuster, Leon Shimkin and Richard L. Simon. The exact role played by each is impossible to establish as they worked so closely together. De Graff, as president, was the active managing head and contributed particularly to the procurement and packaging of the product. Shimkin, as treasurer, was largely responsible for the financial and business arrangements of the firm. By 1957 of the original four only one remained active, Leon Shimkin, who had become president and chief owner.

During the mid-thirties, Richard Simon observed on one of his trips to Europe the wide display given to "Penguin Books" in bookstores and in Woolworth 3d and 6d stores and discussed their success with Sir Allen Lane.[1] The attempts at paperback publishing during the 1930's by Modern Age Books, National Home Library, Boni Paper Books and others have been previously discussed. Robert de Graff states that he

> personally had nothing to do with the Boni Paper Books but knew the two brothers and watched their experiment with interest . . . In my opinion, their book was definitely a quality product physically but did not have the editorial selection adequate to insure its success.[2]

Other publishers showed interest in the paperback field but

nothing came of their plans. The depression undoubtedly made them less inclined towards taking chances, yet their attention was attracted to the sales possibilities of low-priced books. Simon and Schuster pursued this line of reasoning by bringing out a series of one dollar volumes in paper covers in 1930. Since success did not seem assured this series was soon discontinued. Simon, however, remained interested in the subject and discussed the possibilities of such a venture with various parties, among whom were Nelson Doubleday, who had been successful with reprint publishing, and Robert F. de Graff, who had acquired his publishing experiences at Doubleday, Page & Co. where he had started to work in 1922.

About 1923 the Garden City Publishing Company, a wholly-owned subsidiary, was formed because it did not seem desirable to use the Doubleday, Page imprint on a series of paperbound novelettes which were 128 page reprints of articles appearing in short story magazines. They were made originally for Sears, Roebuck sales and then later offered to the general public by direct mail by the Garden City Publishing Company -- 12 for $1.98. So many dealers wrote in saying that they could sell the books through their stores that they were offered in that way at 15c each. These proved inadequate in competition with the then popular Street and Smith novels at the same price. [3]

Street & Smith, which had been founded in 1855, had long experience in dime novels and cheap libraries and had survived their competitors, most of whom had been wiped out by the adoption of international copyright by the United States. They had just begun to sell their books through independent distributors when Garden City started a similar line to be sold through the American News Company. Various series were tried unsuccessfully and the sales of Street & Smith continued to decline

. . . as the taste for this type of book was changing. The market was dwindling. Further attempts by Garden City were made by reprinting older novels to retail for 25c but these were duodecimo in size . . . and bulky. The covers were not durable, they damaged easily in the stores and they did not compare in value . . . with the cloth bound remainders that were offered for about the same price. [4]

Since cheap fiction was difficult to sell, de Graff originated the Garden City experiment with cloth bound non-fiction reprints in the 1920's which became the "Star Dollar Books." This series went through "a difficult first year, because the jackets of semi-uniform design were not sufficiently attractive; . . . when the books were rejacketed with attractive individual picture jackets the sales increased . . . tremendously."5 When de Graff left Garden City in 1936 he and Richard Simon engaged in discussions about publishing a paperback series, but Simon and Schuster were too involved in trying to keep the trade business above water to spend much time in launching a different kind of publishing program. Robert de Graff became president of Blue Ribbon Books, Inc., a hardcover reprint firm which had been founded in 1930 by Harcourt Brace, Harper, Dodd Mead and Little, Brown. Alfred Harcourt was the moving spirit behind the joint enterprise. Eugene Reynal left Harper to manage Blue Ribbon Books and bought out the original publishers in 1933. De Graff resigned from his position in 1938 in order to study the public's reading tastes and to find the answer to the question, "Why won't the American public buy paperbound books?" He states in his letter:

It had almost become an axiom in publishing that they wouldn't because there had been so many failures in the last thirty or forty years. Possibly it was my persistent nature that urged me to prove once and for all that it really wouldn't work that tempted me to try it. I really did feel on analyzing various efforts that had been made that they had obviously been 'cheap' books -- cheap editorially and cheap physically. Another procedure in past experiments that I thought was wrong was that it had been based on giving the wholesaler and retailer such a large margin that it left little for the physical book and adequate royalty. I felt that if a first-class book, editorially and physically, could be made, the turnover would be sufficiently rapid that the wholesaler and retailer would not require the usual large margin . . . Everyone knew that paperbound books had been successful on the continent and recently through Penguin's efforts in England. It seemed logical that if properly handled it could be successful here. Rather than attempt organizing a business of my own,

preferring to have the backing of an established publisher, particularly one that I considered as astute as
any, I approached Simon and Schuster. They had been
considering a similar product, only their plan was to
sell books at twenty rather than twenty-five cents.[6]
They had tentatively chosen a series title: "20th Century Books
(or Library) -- at 20 cents." A company was formed into which
de Graff and Simon and Schuster each put $15,000. The common
stock was held 51 percent by de Graff and 49 percent by
Simon and Schuster. De Graff suggested the name "Pocket
Books," which prevailed. He says:

> I picked this name because I felt it should be made
> clear that this was a book that could be carried in the
> pocket and, at the start, we did a good deal of promo-
> tion in selling the public on the convenience of a book
> that could be carried in a man's pocket or a lady's
> purse. We stressed the desirability of a portable book
> and went against tradition by using the lightest possible
> paper rather than a bulky paper which heretofore had
> been common practice.[7]

The Success Story

Towards the end of 1938, serious consideration was given
to the selection of titles, and de Graff gathered information
regarding costs of supplies, printing, binding and art work.
'The Good Earth,' by Pearl S. Buck was offered as a sample
volume in mail order tests. Preparation had been so careful
that the makeup of "Pocket Books" has remained nearly the
same. During the preparation of the first ten titles in the spring
of 1939 one of the cover artists made the sketch for "Gertrude,"
the bespectacled kangaroo with a book in her paws and another
in her pouch, which became the Pocket Book trade mark. It
was later redrawn by Walt Disney.

The first list of ten titles was published in June, 1939, in
editions of approximately 10,000 copies each. These titles remained excellent sellers over the years. The figures in paren-
theses indicate the number of copies sold by June 1957:

James Hilton, 'Lost Horizon' (1,759,000)
Dorothea Brande, 'Wake Up and Live!' (420,000) (Plate 17)
William Shakespeare, 'Five Great Tragedies'
(2,101,000)
Thorne Smith, 'Topper' (1,546,000)

Agatha Christie, 'The Murder of Roger Ackroyd'
(653,000)
Dorothy Parker, 'Enough Rope' (210,000)
Emily Bronte, 'Wuthering Heights' (1,176,000)
Samuel Butler, 'The Way of All Flesh' (210,000)
Thornton Wilder, 'The Bridge of San Luis Rey' (431,000)
Felix Salten, 'Bambi' (289,000)

'The Good Earth' became title number eleven. In order to test sales in non-book outlets, "Pocket Books" were distributed to drug stores, newsstands, five-and-ten-cent and department stores. Actually, the books were produced at a higher cost than they could be sold for to demonstrate the new markets. A small cigar store near the Pocket Books office sold 110 copies of 'The Good Earth' in one day, Macy's 695. Out-of-town orders came in rapidly and by July, 1939, Pocket Books was nationally established. By the end of the year, Robert F. de Graff had "published thirty-four titles and sold 1,508,000 copies. In 1940, he published fifty-three titles and sold 4,554,000 copies."[8]

At first, there were certain difficulties in distribution. Wallis E. Howe, Jr., was brought in as sales manager for the company. De Graff recalls that his firm was not getting sufficient cooperation from the American News Company, which was their newsstand distributor at the time. As he had been successful with some of the independent distributors at Garden City with the fifteen-cent novelettes, he decided to try them and was able at first to persuade four wholesale magazine distributors to handle the new pocket-sized books. By 1941, 600 independent distributors had signed up to carry "Pocket Books" together with the rest of their quick-turnover merchandise, thus realizing the vision of "Pocket Books" on sale in subways, trading posts, backwoods stores and other outlets all over the country. It was this approach to distribution, with the country divided into territories and an individual sales force supervising distribution, display and sales all the way down to retail level, rather than the publication of inexpensive paperbound books, which has to be considered the radical departure from past practices brought about by Pocket Books. Titles which did not sell were dropped quickly and popular titles were reported back to headquarters for reprinting. Fiction led in sales, but a Bible edition sold 75,000 copies in one month. The firm has followed this basic distribution plan to this day, using about 850 independent wholesalers in 1957.

In spite of competition, the firm continued to prosper. Avon Books, which had been started in November, 1941, was taken to court by Pocket Books for using a similar format. The first decision was in favor of Avon; it was later reversed by the Appellate Court of New York; finally, after a year, the battle ended in the Court of Appeals where Avon Books was again upheld.[9] The war and the ensuing paper shortage curtailed the production of paperbacks. Pocket Books continued publication all through the war, bringing out anthologies and dictionaries and selling many titles to the Armed Forces.

In 1944, Marshall Field purchased Pocket Books, Inc. and acquired an interest in Simon and Schuster. The editorial policy and control of both firms remained unchanged. The end of the war and of government restrictions on paper allowed for expansion of the publishing program. With the favorable court decision for Avon on record, many new twenty-five cent book ventures deluged the market; "Pocket Book" sales had skyrocketed from 4½ million in 1940 to 35 million in 1944, apparently limited at that time only by paper restrictions. Fast action was needed to meet the rising competition. In the spring of 1946, Freeman Lewis, formerly director of "Blue Ribbon Books" and later of "Triangle Books", a thirty-nine cent hard cover reprint series run as a separate division of Doubleday, became executive vice-president of Pocket Books. He is commonly referred to by his colleagues in the trade as "Doc" and holds a position of high esteem which seems to penetrate all the way down the line to the sales force in the field. In 1950, Robert de Graff became chairman of the board of the firm and Leon Shimkin, president. In 1954, de Graff retired and in August of the same year Pocket Books acquired "Permabooks," Doubleday's low-priced paperbound series.

In 1955, a wholly-owned subsidiary, Affiliated Publishers, Inc., was formed to handle sales and distribution activities not only for its own publications but also for other books and allied items, of which the "Little Golden Books," published by Simon and Schuster, were the largest series. By 1957, Affiliated Publishers was handling sales and distribution of more than fifty million units per year in addition to the publications of Pocket Books, Inc.

The death of Marshall Field in November, 1956 resulted in a change of ownership. Leon Shimkin and James M. Jacobson purchased the company from Field Enterprises, Inc. No major changes in policy or personnel occurred. In September, 1957, Affiliated Publishers concluded an arrangement with Select Magazines for distribution of its products through independent magazine wholesalers.

The firm covers a wide range of subjects. The percentage of Western stories and mysteries is comparatively small, and basic information books like dictionaries (Merriam-Webster), atlases (Rand McNally), thesauri (Roget), foreign language dictionaries, anthologies and handbooks are very important and have sold well throughout the years. Pocket Books stresses serious literature of all times and languages and paved the way for the acceptance of paperbacks as collateral reading material in schools and colleges, a trend which was later followed by others.

Production, Management and Distribution

Freeman Lewis feels that paperback publishing is not greatly different from hardcover publishing, insofar as each firm's individual traits are expressed in its editorial policy. When he took over the vice-presidency of Pocket Books, Inc., he sensed the approaching glut of the newsstand market due to over-production of books and magazines at the end of the war. He recalled 275 titles from newsstands and wholesalers' warehouses. With the distribution line cleared and a carefully selected list of titles, Pocket Books, Inc., broke all sales records in 1947.

Pocket Books has kept about 50 per cent of its titles in print and six of the original ten titles can still be obtained. Sometimes, if necessary, reprints are made on runs as low as 10,000 copies. The company publishes general and selected lists of available titles at frequent intervals and will sell individual titles from their backlist to people who write in or come to their office. The Mail Service Department is operated on a cash-with-order basis and a handling charge of five cents per book above retail price is made. A limited amount of business also is done with individual accounts without intermediary distributor, but in comparison with total sales this is a small operation.

By the summer of 1957, Pocket Books (including "Permabooks") had published over 1850 titles with approximately

85 percent reprints and 15 percent originals. In the earlier years, most of the originals were anthologies or reference works. Recently, the firm has been publishing an increasing amount of original fiction, particularly Westerns and mysteries.

"Pocket Book" sales have been continuously high over the years, beginning in 1939 with one and one-half million copies, reaching about thirty million in 1945 and selling about fifty million annually throughout the 1950's. The firm's best-selling author is Erle Stanley Gardner whose thirty-eight titles have sold more than one million copies each, seven of them reaching over two million. The best selling book is Benjamin Spock's 'The Pocket Book of Baby and Child Care' which was approaching the ten million mark in early 1958. It has been selling at the rate of nearly a million copies a year. 'The Merriam-Webster Pocket Dictionary' has sold close to seven million copies and 'The Pocket Cook Book' nearly four million. Among the firm's twenty-five best-sellers are only ten novels (Émile Zola's 'Nana' tops this group with 2,637,000 copies) and two anthologies. Authors who sold most copies have not necessarily been authors of best-sellers or even of good literature, but rather reached their high figures through a prolific output of titles.

Few of the outspoken critics of paperbacks are aware of the fact that the firm made readability tests and experiments with various kinds and sizes of type to lessen eye strain and to get as much on a page as possible. The Times Roman 9/10 point has seemed to give the best results. It is important to get as much on a page as possible because the paper -- and not very good paper at that -- amounts to about 50 percent of the production cost.

The manufacture of "Pocket Books" has undergone some significant changes over the years. In 1939, the volumes were sewn, with end sheets pasted to laminated covers. Later, "perfect binding" replaced sewing and instead of lamination application of lacquer under heat was used for covers beginning in 1947. Originally, the printing was done by Colonial Press but is now handled by the J. W. Clement Co. in Buffalo and the Hall Printing Co. in Chicago. Both of these firms use rubber-plate rotary presses. The presses used in 1940 ran at a rate of 1,100 sheets per hour, while the new equipment handles 15,000 sheets in the same time.

At first, American manufactured "Pocket Books" were exported to Canada, but transportation and taxes made it necessary to charge thirty-nine cents for a book which sold for twenty-five cents in the United States. In order to reduce costs, Pocket Books of Canada, Ltd. was established in 1943 and prices were reduced to match those in the States. Canadian production began in 1944 and distribution followed the same pattern as the parent firm, using fifty-five independent magazine wholesalers. Canadian sales amount to approximately 10 percent of American sales. During the Second World War Pocket Books began to export to Latin American countries, selling books through local wholesalers. After the war, similar arrangements were made throughout the free world with usually one wholesaler handling the distribution for each country. In 1949 a British Company, Pocket Books, Ltd., was formed and books were produced and distributed in Great Britain. This arrangement was discontinued in 1951 and "Pocket Books" are now exclusively produced in the United States and Canada.

Additional Pocket Books Series

After the war, it became apparent that some titles could not be profitably published to sell at a retail price of twenty-five cents, and Pocket Books issued half a dozen such "Specials," before finally starting a new series in 1950: "Cardinal Editions." These books sell at thirty-five cents, and have a distinctive format. They have the bird "Cardinal" as a trade mark. Exceptionally long books come out as "Cardinal Giants," priced at fifty and seventy-five cents.

In September, 1953, another new series, "Pocket Library of Great Art," was started. These are published in collaboration with Harry N. Abrams, Inc., who brings out the same works in hardbound two dollar editions. Pocket Books had done art books before, but did not publish them as a series. The paperbound editions cost fifty cents and go under such titles as 'French Impressionists,' 'Rembrandt,' 'Matisse,' and 'Gauguin,' and include a great variety of classical and modern painters.

In May, 1954,: "The Pocket Library" appeared. These are new printings, with attractive covers, of the great books of all times, from Plato to twentieth century fiction. The books sell for thirty-five and fifty cents and are printed on heavier stock than usually found at this price. The covers are not glossy and their distinctive designs give the impression of leather or cloth bindings; striking labels are used for the titles. The first titles were transferred from the regular "Pocket Book" and "Cardinal" lists and include: Robert Louis Stevenson, 'Great Short Stories'; Jane Austen, 'Pride and Prejudice'; Emily Brontë, 'Wuthering Heights'; Lin Yutang, 'Chinese Short Stories'; Thomas à Kempis, 'The Imitation of Christ'; and 'The Golden Ass of Apuleius,' translated by Robert Graves.

During the post-war years, several other series were begun, but failed for one reason or another. The Teen Age Book Show Program, exhibiting good books from all publishers for teen-agers in 1945, and directed by Martha Huddleston, resulted in the formation of a Teen-Age Book Club in 1946 which offered five different "Pocket Book" titles selected by a committee of distinguished educators and librarians every month. In 1949 the Club was extended to include other paperback publications, from the lists of Bantam, New American Library, etc. In December, 1951 Pocket Books turned the active management of the Teen Age Book Club over to Scholastic Magazines. The club has flourished and become one of the major distribution agencies for paperbound books. In line with the interest in reading for young people, "Comet Books" were started in November, 1948. They were reprints of good titles published by original juvenile publishers, designed for ten- to sixteen-year-olds. Somewhat larger in format than "Pocket Books," these releases required separate racks and proved to be expensive to handle. In January, 1950, the series was changed to "Pocket Book Jrs.," with the same format as regular "Pocket Books." However, they did not prove to be profitable and were discontinued in 1951.

In September, 1950, Pocket Books brought out a higher priced series called "Collectors Editions." Successful books of literary value, which had previously been published for twenty-five cents, were reprinted from the same plates but on better paper with wider margins and bound in boards covered with reproductions of eighteenth and nineteenth century handmade paper patterns. The series was designed for book store sales and forty titles priced at one dollar were brought out. As rising manufacturing costs made it impossible to maintain this price and the books did not sell at $1.25 in sufficient quantities, the series was discontinued in October, 1951.

In the summer of 1954, "Permabooks", the inexpensive Doubleday reprint line, which had released nearly 300 titles between 1948 and 1954, was merged with Pocket Books. [10] Pocket Books undertook a dual job in this merger:

1) to operate as agent in the collection of outstanding accounts receivable, and the disposition so far as possible of inventory in existence at that time, and

2) to continue publication of the line, to use up as many as possible of the titles under contract between Permabooks and various publishers and authors. [11]

Under Pocket Books "Permabooks" maintained a publishing program of between four and six titles a month which had resulted in a total sale of about thirty million copies by the end of 1957.

Pocket Books had been repeatedly successful in the publication of literary anthologies. The idea of an anthology brought out periodically was realized with the first issue of 'Discovery' in May, 1952. This publication was conceived as a paperback literary magazine. The editors stated in the introduction:

It is our intention that it shall at last fulfill the terms of the American writer's perennial vision of a magazine: large audience, fair pay, and the freedom to write as he pleases . . .

We reject the kind of practicality which dictates that the contents of a large circulation magazine must be inoffensively general, meeting the romantic needs of the pablum set at both ends of the human life span and leaving nothing of merit for the adults in the middle . . .

Just before 'Discovery' was launched, The New American Library distributed its first issue of 'New World Writing' in April, 1952. Meanwhile, Penguin had been publishing a similar publication, 'New Writing,' in Great Britain for several years. This development in the paperback field is of interest as it actually represents a merger of the two different branches of publishing -- yet it is not as startling as it appears. Historically, paperbacks developed out of periodical publications during the 1840's, and both Pocket Books and The New American Library had published single anthologies for a long time. The

new feature, from the magazine point of view, is the format.
From the point of view of paperback book publishing, it is the
avant-garde content actually, a "little magazine," published in a
different format, mass-produced and mass-distributed. Six
issues of 'Discovery' were published, the last in July, 1955.

A different type of magazine was published by Pocket
Books in the fall of 1954 as a counterpart to 'Discovery': 'PB,
The Pocket Book Magazine,' containing nonfiction articles,
stressing "ideas, inspiration, information, issues." Franklin
Watts, the editor, said in the introduction to the first issue that
the idea of starting this publication originated at Pocket Books
because there was

> no magazine composed of articles of permanent value
> on important ideas and issues readily available to the
> public in small book format . . .
> [The] editorial approach should be that of a book
> publisher rather than that of a magazine or newspaper
> editor or of a radio or television commentator.

With this in mind, original contributions rather than reprints were offered. 'PB,' like 'Discovery,' was a critical but
not a sales success. After three issues it was discontinued.

Pocket Books has been in the forefront of resistance against
censorship attempts of local police officials. The firm decided
to run a test case in Detroit where censorship of newsstand
materials was considered particularly stringent and arbitrary. Seizure of the book, 'The Devil Rides Outside' by John
H. Griffin, was arranged and the case went to court in Detroit
in summer, 1954. (See Chapter 7, page 116)

[1] Bennet Cerf, "Trade Winds," 'Saturday Review,' XXXVI:51 (December 19. 1954), pp. 5-6.
[2] Letter from Robert F. de Graff, December 16, 1954.
[3] Ibid.
[4] Ibid.
[5] Ibid.
[6] Ibid.
[7] Ibid.
[8] Freeman Lewis, "Paper-bound Books in America," 'Bowker Lectures on Book Publishing' New York: Bowker, 1957, p. 311.
[9] "First Class Mail," 'Publishers' Weekly,' CXLII:1 (July 4, 1942), pp. 19-20; "Pocket Books Wins Unfair Competition Appeal," 'Publishers' Weekly,' CXLII:19 (November 7, 1942), p. 1951; "Court of Appeals Upholds Avon Books," 'Publishers' Weekly,' CXLV:5 (January 29, 1944), p. 495.
[10] For the history of "Permabooks," see Doubleday & Co., infra. p. 180.
[11] Letter from Freeman Lewis, February 2, 1955.

CHAPTER 9

OTHER EXCLUSIVE PAPERBACK PUBLISHERS

The inner core of paperback publishing is represented by the small group of firms which devote their efforts exclusively to this field. The basic foundations were laid by Pocket Books and Penguin. The New American Library of World Literature (NAL) was the direct successor of the first American Penguin branch; Bantam Books and Ballantine Books were established by former Penguin executives; the top men of all five firms are pioneers and recognized representatives of their profession. Of the 1469 paperback titles issued in 1957, these firms contributed 470, or 32 percent (Pocket Books 158, Bantam 110, NAL 80, Penguin 69, Ballantine 53). [1] They have had a significant share in every phase of production, distribution, design and choice of titles and deserve credit for having brought high quality books to the mass market. They also share, at least in part, in the blame for the selection of poor titles and gaudy covers which has occasioned much criticism of the lower-priced paperbacks.

The First American Penguin Branch

Penguin Books Ltd. had been so successful in Great Britain during the first few years of its existence that Sir Allen Lane decided to open an American branch in 1939. The firm was incorporated with 51 percent of the stock owned by the British parent organization and 49 percent owned by Ian Ballantine, the first American manager. Offices were located in New York City and the trade was informed of the event in 'Publishers' Weekly' of August 12, 1939. 3 Books were to be imported from Great Britain and distributed through regular book channels. Sir Allen hoped for an annual sales volume of two million copies at twenty-five cents per copy. The established policy was to sell books which were not copyrighted or had a courtesy copyright, having been published after the ad interim period by American publishers, and courtesy royalties were to be paid to these publishers. The firm began with a stock of one hundred titles and planned to add ten every month.

Sales of the American Penguin branch during 1939 and 1940 were very satisfactory, but the war and increasing transportation difficulties, as well as the need for some more specifically American titles, suggested the desirability of printing at least some of the books in the United States. The firm distributed "Penguins," "Pelicans" and "Penguin Specials" during 1940 and added "Puffin Picture Books" and "King Penguins," as well as the "Penguin Hansard Series" in 1941. More printing was done in the United States and in Canada and, after Pearl Harbor, the demand for war titles published in Great Britain since 1939 increased, not only from the general public, but also from the Armed Forces, the Red Cross and the United Service Organizations. Penguin Books, Inc. entered into arrangements with the Military Service Publishing Company and the 'Infantry Journal,' issuing titles under a joint imprint. Usually Penguin contributed the text, 'Infantry Journal' the paper, and the Armed Forces used the books for orientation courses and recreational reading of its personnel.

By 1942, American production had reached such proportions that some of the titles were exported to England.[4] In 1943 and 1944 paper and manpower shortages affected all publishers severely. The public had become used to illustrated and more striking covers than the regular Penguin format and, to attract readers, some of the new books were published with cover illustrations and drawings.

In 1945, shortages began to ease and the demand for paperbacks increased greatly. Editorial differences between the mother firm in England and the American personnel developed, and Ian Ballantine, Walter Pitkin, Jr., and Sidney Kramer left Penguin to establish a new, American owned paperback firm, Bantam Books, Inc. With these men also went the cooperative agreement with the Military Service Publishing Company which was taken over by Bantam.

Kurt Enoch, formerly editor of the German Albatross Books, replaced Ian Ballantine as the head of the American Penguin branch. The output of titles was stepped up from four to six per month, and Fawcett Distributing Company began to handle Penguin's distribution, an arrangement which remained in force until the fall of 1955. Kurt Enoch created an editorial advisory board and brought new leadership to the firm. By 1947, titles were again imported from England and some of the more serious ones were distributed only to bookstores. Sales for "Penguin Classics," a new series, "King Penguins" and "Puffin Story Books" were excellent.

In 1948 connections between the American Penguin branch and the British parent firm were severed and all British-owned shares were bought by Americans. The assets of the firm were taken over by newly-founded New American Library of World Literature, Inc. British "Penguins" were exclusively imported from England until the establishment of the second American Penguin branch in 1950. Penguin, however, had made a lasting contribution to the American paperback field by leaving behind a group of trained experts.

The Second American Penguin Branch

In January, 1950, a new firm was incorporated under the name Allen Lane, Inc. which was shortly thereafter changed to Penguin Books, Inc. Offices were set up in Baltimore, Maryland, with Harry Paroissien as manager.

The bulk of "Penguin Books" are imported directly from Great Britain, but approximately 20 percent of the books are sold and produced in the United States. Printings range from 40,000 to 85,000 copies and prices from fifty cents to over one dollar. "The Pelican Shakespeare," a series of plays edited with introductions by American scholars, is entirely an American Penguin venture. Translations of the classics sold particularly well during 1957, especially Robert Graves' translation of 'Suetonius: The Twelve Caesars.' Other notable titles are 'The Penguin Book of French Verse,' edited by Anthony Hartley, and Éric de Maré's 'Photography,' a "Penguin Handbook."

The firm handles distribution directly to book stores, college book stores, selected drug stores, and other individual outlets across the United States. Their success on college campuses paved the way for the sale of other quality paperbacks in college book stores.

The New American Library of World Literature [5]

NAL demonstrates most clearly in its origin   and

management the influence of continental and British paperback publishing in the United States. The result is a combination of European and American features. The management and ownership of the new firm, established as the successor of the first American Penguin branch in 1948, was taken over by Kurt Enoch as president, treasurer and general manager and Victor Weybright as editor-in-chief and chairman of the board. [6] Mr. Weybright was engaged in writing and editorial work before World War II, being connected with 'Survey Graphic' among other publications. During the war he served on the staff of John G. Winant, American Ambassador to the Court of St. James's. While in England, he met Sir Allen Lane, had frequent contacts with him and towards the end of the war told him that he would like to enter the paperback publishing field. Sir Allen suggested a meeting with Kurt Enoch. Subsequently Weybright joined Kurt Enoch in the ownership and management of the firm.

The complete separation from the British Penguin and the establishment of the new firm, was necessitated by complications brought about by British import and export regulations, by the competition on the world market between British and American Penguins, and by differing opinions on editorial policy. The arrangement was worked out amicably and in an atmosphere of mutual respect. At first American Penguins came out as "Penguin-Signet" for fiction and "Pelican-Mentor" for non-fiction titles; however, the words "Penguin" and "Pelican" soon were dropped. The first list of titles of the new firm had been decided on before the American Penguin branch changed hands, and the editorial advisory board was retained.

Enoch and Weybright cooperate smoothly and closely in the management of the company and are united in the strong feeling of confidence that in the long run the good book outsells the bad, and the so-called mass audience reader is not basically different from the one who has access to a limited number of book stores or the means to purchase higher priced hardcover books. Any reversal of this principle tends to upset them, even if it means a financial gain. They are both very vocal as spokesmen for the educational possibilities of the mass distributed book and have made many speeches on the topic. Their interest in the author is greater than in the cover of the book. This attitude is expressed in the wall decorations of their New York offices, which consist largely of photographs and letters from their many outstanding authors.

The first "Penguin-Signet" titles were characteristic of the type of fiction published in the Signet series. Among them were: Carlo Levi, 'Christ Stopped at Eboli'; William Faulkner, 'Sanctuary and Wild Palms and the Old Man'; Erskine Caldwell, 'Tragic Ground'; Lillian Smith, 'Strange Fruit'; (Plate 18) James Joyce, A Portrait of the Artist as a Young Man.' The firm's bestseller, taken over as a Penguin imprint, was Erskine Caldwell's 'God's Little Acre,' which sold three and one-half million copies between March, 1946, and January, 1948. Originally published as a Viking imprint in 1933, it had sold 8,300 copies by 1939, and 66,650 as a "Modern Library Edition." The Grosset & Dunlap reprint in 1940 sold 150,000 copies. The paperback title sold over six million copies between 1946 and 1957. Other Penguin best-sellers taken over by NAL included Erskine Caldwell's 'Tobacco Road,' 'Journeyman,' and 'Trouble in July,' each of which had sold several million copies, and D. H. Lawrence's 'Lady Chatterley's Lover' and James T. Farrell's 'Young Lonigan,' which also exceeded the one million mark. By December, 1957, 821 "Signet" titles had been released.

All "Signet Books" at first were priced at twenty-five cents, but in 1950, following the rise in production costs and in order to issue important but very long books NAL initiated "Signet Giants" at thirty-five cents and "Signet Double Volumes" at fifty cents and in 1953 "Triple Volumes" at seventy-five cents. The Signet list contains so many outstanding titles by famous authors that it is hard to single out a few without doing injustice to many others of similar excellence. To mention some: Erich Maria Remarque's 'Arch of Triumph,' Arthur Koestler's 'Darkness at Noon,' James Jones' 'From Here to Eternity,' Thomas Mann's 'Confessions of Felix Krull, Confidence Man,' John Steinbeck's 'Tortilla Flat,' MacKinlay Kantor's 'Andersonville,' Norman Mailer's 'Naked and the Dead' and Thomas Merton's 'Seven Storey Mountain.'

The most outstanding sales of any NAL author were achieved by the detective stories of "Mickey" (Frank Morrison) Spillane. While his 'I, the Jury,' 'Kiss Me, Deadly' and other Mike Hammer mysteries are devoid of any literary merit, they have become America's most famous and best-selling detective stories except those by Erle Stanley Gardner.

The firm's "Mentor Books," of which 168 had appeared by the end of 1957 are a continuation of the "Penguin Classics" and "Pelican" series. The first "Pelican-Mentor" titles included Marquis Childs's 'Sweden, The Middle Way' and Susanne K. Langer's 'Philosophy in a New Key,' as well as two original anthologies. The series is subdivided into various categories: Classics and the Arts, with titles such as Dante's 'Inferno,' Whitman's 'Leaves of Grass,' Homer's 'Iliad' and 'Odyssey,' Cervantes' 'Don Quixote,' 'Great Dialogues of Plato.' Anthropology and Psychology include Sigmund Freud's 'Psychopathology of Everyday Life,' 'Psychology of Sex' by Havelock Ellis, and 'Patterns of Culture' by Ruth Benedict; Economics, with Thorstein Veblen's 'The Theory of the Leisure Class'; and Philosophy and Education with Albert Schweitzer's 'Out of My Life and Thought' and John Dewey's 'Reconstruction in Philosophy.' A series on all major religion offers among others 'The Holy Bible in Brief,' edited and arranged by James Reeves, 'The Living Talmud' translated by Judah Goldin and 'The Meaning of the Glorious Koran,' translated by Marmaduke Pickthall. Due to the extensive interest in the latter title, the firm decided to release it in cloth binding at $2.75 in 1955.

In 1955 a new series was added to the Mentor imprint, the "Mentor Philosophers." These are six volumes published over a two year period, priced at fifty cents, and covering the basic writings of the leading philosophers of each age from the Middle Ages to modern times, with introductions and commentaries by noted present-day authorities, such as Henry D. Aiken and George de Santillana. In 1956 a series of books on archaeology was begun.

In April, 1952, NAL published the first issue of 'New World Writing,' a periodical publication which had its eleventh issue in May, 1957. It is a "little magazine" in paperback form, containing essays, poems, literary criticism, art, cartoons and drawings.

In 1954, a new series, "Signet Key Books," was started. To quote the company's announcement these are, "a series of authoritative lucid nonfiction, especially designed to meet the reading requirements of the vast audience for inexpensive, mass-distributed books at 25 cents." (later also 35c & 50c) By 1957, 55 titles had appeared. They are nonfiction, somewhat less scholarly than "Mentor Books" and written in a way to be understandable to the layman and include: Joseph Gaer, 'How the Great Religions Began'; Louis Fischer, 'Gandhi: His Life and Message for the World'; David C. Coyle, 'The United States Political System and How It Works'; Horace Coon, 'Speak Better -- Write Better English'; Samuel Rapport and Helen Wright, editors, 'The Crust of the Earth'; A. Powell Davies, 'The Meaning of the Dead Sea Scrolls'; John Langdon-Davies, 'Seeds of Life.' NAL also issues a series of "how-to-know" nature books, with color illustrations, 'How to Know Minerals and Rocks,' by Richard M. Pearl, 'How to Know the Birds' by Roger Tory Peterson.

Distribution of NAL books was handled by independent wholesalers in the United States through Fawcett Publications, Inc., as the national distributor. Special book store sales and export was managed by NAL directly. The firm's export activities have been rather extensive and Enoch has made frequent trips abroad in efforts to organize new markets and to increase foreign sales. Most notable was an extensive survey of the Middle East and Southeast Asia, where a chain of distributing agencies for inexpensive paperback books was set up, which increased NAL's sales in those territories.

NAL books have always sold well on college campuses, and the company is exceedingly interested in this particular market. In 1952, 171 of the 453 titles on the firm's list were used as required or supplementary reading in schools and colleges throughout the country.[7] A special educational department, with Harold Laskey as director, keeps in close contact with schools, colleges and universities and organizes exhibitions at professional and educational conventions. The department also issues lists of 'Books for Schools and Colleges,' and 'Titles for Use in Adult Education Classes.' In 1955, New American Library Bookshelves were introduced. These were 100 selected titles, delivered to libraries in a sturdy corrugated cardboard unit which can easily be displayed and used as a library shelf for paperbacks. The titles for Fiction for Public Libraries (twenty-five dollars) and Non-fiction for Public Libraries (thirty dollars) were selected by Francis St. John, librarian of the Brooklyn Public Library; the Fiction for High School Libraries shelf is selected by Eleanor R. McKinney, then librarian of the Montclair, New Jersey, High School Library.

Promotional efforts included a number of successful movie tie-ins which in 1956 and 1957 covered titles such as

Tennessee Williams, 'Baby Doll,' Robert Anderson, 'Tea and Sympathy,' Richard Bissell, 'Pajama (7½ Cents),' Marcelle Maurette, 'Anastasia,' Claude Anet, 'Love in the Afternoon.'

In 1957 the NAL released two spoken records, Judah Goldin's translation of 'The Living Talmud' and Walter Starkie's translation of 'Don Quixote' under the "Mentor" imprint. NAL expects that the editorial material contained in this series could be usefully adapted for spoken records and widen the value of NAL's activity in the educational field.

New American Library has been involved in several censorship cases and some of its titles were cited by the Gathings Committee on Current Pornographic Materials in 1952. Weybright defended his company's position in a detailed statement in which he also summarized the type of books published by the firm, the attitudes and problems of the paperback industry in general, and the literary merit of the individual titles cited, which included James T. Farrell's 'Young Lonigan' and Erskine Caldwell's 'God's Little Acre.'

In 1950, the Federal Trade Commission issued a complaint against NAL and its chief officers charging that abridgement notices on "Signet" and "Mentor Books" were "false, misleading and deceptive."[8] The complaint asserted that the firm's books were "usually" abridged from about 90,000 to 180,000 words in the original to about 60,000 to 120,000 words. Weybright explained in his reply that of more than 300 titles in print in October, 1950, only thirty-five had been abridged, that there had been a special reason for abridgement in each case, and that the book had been so labeled. He conceded only one case in which an abridged book through the error of the printer was mistakenly labeled as complete and unabridged. In April, 1951, the larger part of the original charge was dismissed in a court decision, but the ruling was handed down that the word "abridged" had to appear on the front cover and title page of the book and that, if a new title was used, the original one had to be shown in close proximity and in equally conspicuous type. NAL appealed, and the final decision was reached in May, 1954, which appears to avoid arbitrary direction to a publisher about where he must place his notice, so long as the notice is given and is clear to the reader.

In 1952, NAL brought suit against the Fischer Verlag in

Germany because it had introduced a paperback line which bore a striking resemblance to "Signet Books" and "Mentor Books" in make-up and covers. (Plate 12) It is interesting to note in this connection that Christian Wegener, who had once been associated with Kurt Enoch in the publication of "Albatross Books," is one of the publishers of this series. The suit did not come to trial since the court in Frankfurt refused a motion for a preliminary injunction against the Fischer Verlag. The series in question seems to bear a strong resemblance not only to NAL but also to other American paperbacks. It is one of the many successful items with which West Germany is attempting to reconquer the world market.

Bantam Books, Inc.[9]

Bantam Books, Inc., was founded in the summer of 1945, but the events which led to its formation preceded this date by several months. In 1944, the reprint firm of Grosset & Dunlap was purchased jointly by Harper & Brothers, Little, Brown & Company, Random House, Charles Scribner's Sons, and the Book-of-the-Month Club. In the spring of 1945, Sir Allen Lane came to the United States to discuss the editorial policy of the American Penguin branch. Differences of opinion finally resulted in the resignation of Ian Ballantine, Walter Pitkin, Jr., and Sidney B. Kramer, who were director, editor and counsel and business adviser, of the Penguin branch. Ian Ballantine, looking for a new position in the mass market field, and Grosset & Dunlap, in search of a man to direct its operation, came together upon the recommendation of Bennett Cerf and founded Bantam Books, Inc., with the assistance of the Curtis Publishing Company. The Curtis Publishing Company was to assume responsibility for distribution and sales, Grosset & Dunlap for editorial policy and selection of titles. Reprints were to be acquired from all publishers, not just from those of the Grosset & Dunlap group. Ballantine brought with him to Bantam "Infantry Journal Books" and "Superior Reprints," published by the Military Service Company. Their distribution was to be handled as before by independent magazine wholesalers but supervised by Curtis.

The stock of the new corporation was divided into three parts: 42½ percent went to Curtis, 42½ percent to Grosset & Dunlap, and the remaining 15 percent was divided between Ian

Ballantine, president of Bantam Books, Inc.; Walter Pitkin, Jr., vice president; and Sidney B. Kramer, treasurer and comptroller. The Board of Directors consisted of a number of outstanding personalities in the publishing field, representing a great deal of experience as well as competing interests. The original Bantam Board of Directors was made up of the following:

Ian Ballantine, president of Bantam Books; Cass Canfield, chairman of the board, (later chairman of executive committee), Harper & Brothers; Bennett Cerf, president, Random House; John O'Connor, president, Grosset & Dunlap; Meredith Wood, president, Book-of-the-Month Club; Charles Scribner, president, Charles Scribner's Sons; Arthur H. Thornhill, president, Little, Brown & Company; Lewis W. Trayser, director of manufacture, Curtis Publishing Company; Benjamin Allen, vice president, Curtis Publishing Company; Robert E. Mac-Neal, secretary, (later president), Curtis Publishing Company; R. C. McLarty, assistant circulation manager, and two other members from the Curtis Publishing Company.[10]

Ballantine directed the firm until September, 1952, when he left to form Ballantine Books, Inc., and Pitkin continued as executive vice president until June, 1954, when he resigned. In a reorganization Sidney B. Kramer became executive vice president. Walter Pitkin was succeeded by Oscar Dystel who came to paperback publishing from the magazine field, where he had held various positions with 'Esquire,' 'Cornet,' and 'Collier's'; he was also founding editor of 'U.S.A.,' the OWI magazine during World War II.

Originally "Bantam Books" were planned as twenty-five cent reprints with laminated glossy covers. The first twenty titles were distributed to outlets in December, 1945, and were sold from coast to coast in January, 1946. Publishing schedules called for four new titles every month thereafter. Bantam started with an unusual sales campaign. The December 1, 1945, issue of 'Publishers' Weekly' carried advertisements for the twenty titles, including an offer of two free copies of any of the books to book sellers and buyers who would participate in voting on the most popular titles of the first release. Among the twenty titles, were the following: Mark Twain, 'Life on the Mississippi'; Rafael Sabatini, 'Scaramouche'; John Steinbeck, 'The Grapes of Wrath'; F. Scott Fitzgerald, 'The Great Gatsby'; Elliot Paul, 'The Last Time I Saw Paris'; Antoine de St.

Exupéry, 'Wind, Sand and Stars'; Booth Tarkington, 'Seventeen'; Budd Schulberg, 'What Makes Sammy Run?' Alice Tisdale Hobart, 'Oil for the Lamps of China.' Half of these twenty titles were originally published by members of the Grosset & Dunlap Group. The other ten were reprints from Houghton Mifflin, Farrar & Rinehart, Morrow, Knopf, Bobbs Merrill, Reynal & Hitchcock, and Viking. Apparently, they were chosen on the basis of availability and suitability for the reprint market. Half of the books appeared for the last time in hard covers during the 1930's, and half between 1940 and 1944.

Bantam's outstanding sales promotion of 1946 occurred in connection with MGM's production of 'Captains Courageous' by Rudyard Kipling which appeared in November of that year, a few months after the release of the paperback. The movie and book posters were planned jointly by both firms and the promotion was very successful. Ian Ballantine as well as other publishers brought out the fact that this type of joint publicity can be very helpful to both the movie and the book.

Tie-in promotions were used to a considerable degree by Bantam during the first few years of the firm's existence. In 1947, when Hollywood produced the movie 'Joan of Arc,' based on Maxwell Anderson's play, Bantam reprinted Frances Winwar's 'The Saint and The Devil' under the title of 'Joan of Arc,' featuring illustrations from the movie. During 1951 Bantam's reprint of Edmond Rostand's 'Cyrano de Bergerac' was featured jointly with the José Ferrer movie and the publicity was very successful for both media. Richard Gerstell's 'How to Survive an Atomic Bomb' brought another tie-in promotion with the author's radio talks on the topic sponsored by Civil Defense on many stations throughout the country.

Another example of joint promotion by Bantam was George Axelrod's 'The Seven Year Itch,' which had been a successful Broadway hit for several seasons and was released as a movie in June, 1955. At the same time, the reprint appeared with Marilyn Monroe's picture on the cover. This play, incidentally, is of interest to paperback publishing. Its hero is the editor of a paperback series who, besides his extracurricular activities, changes the title of a book he accepts for publication and plans to bring it out with a sensational and partly misleading cover portrait of which the author disapproves. During 1956 and 1957 thirty-three titles were published for which movie tie-in promotion was used. The costs of the "read the book -- see the movie" posters are shared by both media.

Other novel promotion ideas included radio dramatizations of Bantam titles. These fifteen-minute programs were heard over 200 ABC stations in 1947 and were an outgrowth of the original Curtis program "The Listening Post." For a short time, good reproductions of original cover paintings which had been commissioned by the firm were sold to readers for two dollars. Another first was scored by Bantam when they sold advertising space in Betty Smith's 'A Tree Grows in Brooklyn' to the Book-of-the-Month Club in 1947. In November, 1947, Bantam and 'Scholastic Magazine' joined in a project aimed at secondary school teachers and teachers in training. Twenty-six Bantam titles, already published, but withdrawn from general circulation, were reserved for sales to schools through 'Scholastic Magazine.' Some of the unusual advertising ideas were the work of Arthur Hale, who was formerly promotion manager of Bantam and later editorial consultant of the "Mass Market" section of 'Publishers' Weekly.'

Bantam was the first company to raise the price of the quarter book to thirty-five cents in 1950 and to fifty cents in 1951; the trade looked upon this experiment rather skeptically, but eventually the other publishers also increased the prices of many of their books to this amount as increased production costs made this almost mandatory. In June, 1950, a new series, "Bantam Giants," was started, which were priced at thirty-five or fifty cents. Many excellent titles have been published in this series, among them: Thomas B. Costain, 'High Towers'; Archibald J. Cronin, 'The Keys of the Kingdom'; John P. Marquand, 'Point of No Return'; James Michener, 'Return to Paradise'; Samuel Shellabarger, 'The King's Cavalier.'

One of the most interesting "Bantam Giants" was Robert E. Sherwood's 'Roosevelt and Hopkins, An Intimate History.' It was published originally by Harper in 1948 as a clothbound, 979 page volume, and appeared in a slightly enlarged and revised edition of 1002 pages in 1950. Bantam issued this publication as a two-volume paperback at thirty-five cents a volume, in a first edition of 500,000 copies. Forty-five percent of this edition was sold within ten days after its release.

"Bantam Books" as well as "Bantam Giants" cover a wide range of popular and historical fiction, science fiction, Westerns, and some mysteries, as well as very good nonfiction and anthologies. Some of the titles, especially the anthologies, are originals. Approximately 10 percent of the titles are of British origin. In the past two years, Bantam has had a program of bringing back into print many best-sellers of previous years and literary classics which are in demand for school use such as Leo Tolstoy's 'War and Peace,' Victor Hugo's 'The Hunchback of Notre Dame,' Aldous Huxley's 'Antic Hay.' In 1956 two special series were established: "Bantam Biographies," including titles like Emil Ludwig's 'Cleopatra,' and "Bantam Frontier Classics," a line of Western nonfiction. "Pennant Books," primarily a series of Western fiction reprints selling at twenty-five cents, which was started in 1953, has been discontinued; some of the more attractive titles reemerged as regular "Bantam Books." Recent bestsellers include 'The Fifty Minute Hour' by Robert Lindner, 'Sweet Thursday' by John Steinbeck, 'Picnic' by William Inge, 'Island in the Sun' by Alec Waugh.

Art director Leonard Leone is responsible for a new trend in cover art. He believes that a cover has first of all to be honest and should represent the book as a whole, not just one isolated incident. Secondly, in order to accomplish the purpose of the paperback cover to sell its contents, it should be arresting, persuasive, and, if possible, entertaining.[11] He has discarded the misleading design, the obvious cliché, the sensational and the literal approach. As a result, covers convey the feeling of the book through an over-all poster effect; by abstractions, if this is feasible; and by making people "real" and not just "stereotypes." He tries to encourage the creativity of his staff artists and they have succeeded in achieving unusually effective and artistic results. (Plate 15)

From the very beginning, Bantam has been extremely conscious of the importance of exports. Overseas distribution in Belgium, Holland, Scandinavia, and Portugal started in 1946; in 1947, the Middle East was added. In 1949, arrangements with Bantam Books, Ltd., of London, an independent British firm, provided for publication of American Bantam titles and export of American manufactured copies to Europe and the British Empire. By 1952, Bantam had organized a British subsidiary, Trans-World Publishing Company, which handles exports and publishes the paperback series "Corgi" books.

One of the court cases in which paperback publishers were involved, concerns Bantam's release of Vivian Connell's

'The Chinese Room.' In 1950, a Committee on Objectionable Literature was formed in Middlesex County, New Jersey, which, with the assistance of the prosecuting attorney of the county, passed on a proscribed list of twenty paperback titles to two local newsdealers who considered it best to stop distributing them to their local accounts, even though there were no direct threats of legal action. Five books were Bantam publications; after some correspondence, four of these were removed from the list, leaving only 'The Chinese Room.' Originally been published by Dial Press in 1942, it was reprinted by Bantam in 1949, and had sold over two and one-half million copies without interference prior to the Middlesex County incident. Bantam went to court and an injunction was issued against the prosecuting attorney prohibiting him to engage in censorship "without the due process of arrest and trial or other legal means." [12] An appeal by the prosecutor to the New Jersey Supreme Court sustained this decision but deleted from the lower court's opinion all rulings regarding the prosecutor's right to promulgate lists, accept aid of unofficial committees, threaten sellers, and engage in related actions. This was interpreted by the prosecuting attorney as an indirect endorsement of his efforts at unofficial censorship. A rehearing appeal by Bantam was refused by the Supreme Court of the State of New Jersey and the case came to a close, leaving a confusing decision: Bantam had won a victory, but so had extralegal attempts at censorship in New Jersey.

A more decisive court decision was won in 1957 when John O'Hara's 'Ten North Frederick' was banned in Detroit by action of Police Commissioner Edward S. Piggins, who prohibited the sale of this book which had won the 1956 National Book Award for fiction. The original ban against the paperback edition was followed by a similar action against the hardcover edition published by Random House. Bantam and Random brought suit against Piggins, contending that the police department lacked jurisdiction to decide on the obscenity of a book. Inspite of a temporary injunction against the police ban, Piggins issued a statement to the press that anyone selling the book in Detroit would still be liable to prosecution. Both publishers consequently instigated proceedings against him charging him with contempt. Piggins then indicated his willingness to comply with the court's injunction, which had upheld "the fundamental doctrine that where a book ban is effected outside the courts, due process has been violated." [13] Compliance with the injunction terminated the policy of prescreening paperbacks and magazines by the Detroit police department prior to sale by wholesalers.

Ballantine Books, Inc. [14]

Ian Ballantine was an American student at the London School of Economics during the 1930's and wrote his master's thesis on publishing, with special attention to paperbound publications. Sir Allen Lane heard of this thesis, became acquainted with the young man, employed him and later put him in charge of the American branch of Penguin Books, where he worked from August, 1939, to June, 1945. When this organization was absorbed by the New American Library of World Literature, he moved to the newly formed firm of Bantam Books, Inc., where he acted as director from July, 1945, to February, 1952. At this time he left Bantam, feeling that his editorial policies could best be worked out in a firm of his own, and founded Ballantine Books, Inc., in the spring of 1952. Stanley Kauffmann, an author and former employee of Bantam Books, Inc., joined the new firm as editor.

Ballantine's plan was new and commanded the publishing industry's attention, though it actually was the outgrowth of a trend which had started in 1949 when paper shortages had disappeared. He proposed the simultaneous publication of original titles in hard covers and paperbacks. "Gold Medal" had started releasing originals in paperbacks in 1949 and during 1951 and 1952 this practice gained momentum; not only anthologies and translations appeared as original paperback releases, but several of the publishers such as Avon, Lion, and Popular Library, followed the "Gold Medal" example by bringing out original novels. Most of these were Westerns and mysteries and their great attraction was their comparatively low production cost. As more paperback publishers came into the field and released an increasing number of titles, the prices for reprint rights were driven upward through competitive bidding and authors were anxious to increase their earnings. After the end of the war they felt that they were providing publishers with the means of expanding their business through paperback production without receiving commensurate financial returns. Ian Ballantine was well aware of this when he launched his plan, which increased substantially the rate of return both to general publisher and author. This meant that the trade publisher would temporarily foot the bill for the paperbound edition but would benefit by the increase in sales of mass distributed books. Ballantine would get the advantage of a stronger line of books because he could draw on the best authors of established publishing houses. Actually, only two publishers, Houghton Mifflin Company and Farrar, Straus and Young joined the Ballantine plan outright. Two representatives of Houghton Mifflin and one of Farrar, Straus and Young are on the Ballantine Board of Directors. Authors, who were offered 8 percent royalties, which was almost twice as much as they usually received from reprinters, welcomed the idea. An additional advantage for Ballantine and the hardcover publishers lies in the possibility of using the same plates for both editions. This was tried at first and it was found that the hardcover price could be reduced to $1.50 because of the savings involved. However, the small format was apparently not attractive and the price was raised to two dollars in May, 1953, for a larger book produced from stereo plates. Heavier paper permitted bulking and the hardcover editions sold satisfactorily at the higher price. The increased royalty costs were balanced by setting the price of the paperback edition at thirty-five cents.

One of the first four titles published in November, 1952, was Cameron Hawley's 'Executive Suite,' one of the firm's outstanding best-sellers, which was made into a successful movie. The hardcover edition was released by Houghton Mifflin at three dollars. The other three titles were 'Saddle by Starlight' by Luke Short, a Western which appeared in a Houghton Mifflin hardcover edition at $1.50, 'The Golden Spike,' by Hal Ellson, and 'All My Enemies,' by Stanley Baron; the two latter books were released in hardcovers by Ballantine Books, Inc.

By 1957 approximately 230 titles had been released, about evenly divided between originals and reprints. Until 1956, science fiction had been the firm's special field with Ray Bradbury's 'Fahrenheit 451' as a significant contribution. In 1957 scientific fiction titles decreased and the firm concentrated on books about the Second World War such as 'The Bridge at Remagen' by Ken Hechler and 'Panzer Leader' by Heinz Guderian. Other interesting titles include 'The Mad Reader,' edited by Harvey Kurtzman, and its three sequels, 'Childhood's

End' by Arthur C. Clarke, two anthologies 'New Poems by American Poets,' edited by Rolfe Humphries, and two volumes of 'Best Television Plays,' one edited by Gore Vidal and one by Florence Britton.

After decreasing the number of hardcover editions of its paperback originals, Ballantine returned in fall of 1955 to the practice of bringing out low-priced clothbounds printed from the same plates. In spring, 1958, a series of exclusive hardcover books were released. Ballantine paperbacks are priced at thirty-five and fifty cents and are distributed through the Capitol Distributing Company.

[1] "Book Publication Statistics for 1957," 'Publishers' Weekly,' CLXXIII:3 (January 20, 1957), pp. 33-34.

[2] Information for both Penguin branches obtained by personal interviews with Sir Allen Lane and Harry Paroissien, November, 1954; correspondence with Sir Allen Lane and Harry Paroissien, 1954, 1955 and 1957.

[3] "Penguins Reach America," 'Publishers' Weekly,' CXXXVI: 7 (August 12, 1939), p. 445.

[4] "Penguin Books," 'Publishers' Weekly,' CXLII:4 (July 25, 1942), p. 243.

[5] Personal interviews with Kurt Enoch and Victor Weybright, 1954 and 1955; Kurt Enoch, "The Paperbound Book: Twentieth-Century Publishing Phenomenon," 'Library Quarterly,' XXIV:3 (July, 1954), pp. 211-25; 'The Complete and Unabridged Statement to the Gathings Committee by the New American Library of World Literature, Inc.' [New York: New American Library of World Literature, Inc., 1953 (?)]

[6] For additional information on Kurt Enoch see Chapter II, "Albatross Modern Continental Library."

[7] 'Complete and Unabridged Statement to the Gathings Committee by the New American Library of World Literature, Inc.,' p. 10.

[8] "FTC Complaint Cites NAL Abridgement Notices," 'Publishers' Weekly,' CLVIII:17 (October 21, 1950), pp. 1856-1857.

[9] Personal interviews with Ian Ballantine and Walter Pitkins, 1954 and 1955; correspondence with Sidney B. Kramer, 1957; questionnaire, 1957; "Bantam Books Celebrates Its Tenth Anniversary," 'Publishers' Weekly,' CLXIX:7 (February 18, 1956), pp. 1064-68.

[10] *still members of the board in 1957.

[11] Letter from Leonard Leone, June 7, 1957.

[12] N. J. Prosecutor Restrained in 'Extra-Legal' Book Ban, 'Publishers' Weekly,' CLXIII:15 (April 11, 1953), p. 1608.

[13] "Censorship Trends During 1957," 'Publishers' Weekly,' CLXXIII:3 (January 20, 1958), pp. 58-60.

[14] Interviews with Ian Ballantine, 1954 and 1955; "Lively Newcomer in a Creaky Industry," 'Business Week,' No. 1218, (January 3, 1953), pp. 42-45; questionnaire, 1957.

CHAPTER 10

MAGAZINE AND PULP PUBLISHERS

Series issued by magazine and pulp publishers, and those brought out by exclusive paperback publishers, are usually referred to as catering to the mass market. To adopt a successful book format and channel it through the magazine distribution system, seemed a logical extension of previous publishing activities. The close association between these series and their editors with magazines, comics and one-shot releases, resulted in a large number of titles in the areas of light fiction, historical romance, detective and mystery stories, Westerns, and, in the field of nonfiction, in many how-to-, cook-and garden books. However, as the series of the magazines and pulp publishers grew and matured, editorial guidance became more "book-minded" and a greater number of worthwhile titles of literary and cultural value came to be included. Crude cover art, which was more extensively used by this group of publishers than by any other, improved in taste and skill of design over the years in many instances.

The seven large firms of the group produced 621 or 42 percent of the 1469 paperback titles which appeared during 1957 (Fawcett 124, Avon 107, Popular Library 101, Dell 85, Pyramid 70, Berkley 67, and Ace 66). The percentage in numbers of copies sold is considerably greater since all these books appear in large editions of at least 100,000 copies.

Avon Publications, Inc. [1]

Avon Publications, Inc., was established late in 1940 by its owner and president Joseph Meyers, who died in the fall of 1957. He had brought out fine editions of classical books at fairly low prices during the 1930's in the Illustrated Editions

Company. Avon Publications issues a number of magazines, such as 'The Cross Word Puzzle Magazine,' comic books, and a series of children's books called "Jolly Books," but its main line is "Avon Books" which appeared first in November, 1941, as the third oldest continuing paperback series, planned to bring out four to five titles monthly in minimum editions of 50,000 copies. Soon after "Avon Books" appeared, the firm was involved in a lengthy court case with Pocket Books, Inc., which charged that Avon issued paperbound reprints similar to their own product. On January 19, 1942, the court decided in favor of Avon because "no ordinarily prudent purchaser would be likely to be deceived or be liable to purchase defendants' books believing that he was purchasing those of the plaintiff."[2] Pocket Books appealed to the Appellate Division of the Supreme Court of the State of New York on October 2, 1942, which decided in their favor because "the evidence sufficiently discloses that the defendants were guilty of unfair competition in intentionally appropriating the style and format of the plaintiff's books . . ."[3] An injunction was issued against the sale of pocket-sized books with red or similar tinged edges and the word "Pocket" appearing on the front cover. Avon, thereafter, stained its edges in contrasting shades and displayed its imprint prominently on the cover, thus obeying the injunction, and continued publication. In January, 1944, Avon was upheld by the Court of Appeals which reversed the previous decision of the Appellate Division in favor of Pocket Books. This cleared the way for the production of competitive lines of pocket-sized paperbound books.

During the first years the firm engaged primarily in reprinting, except for occasional original publications or translations of foreign books which had not yet been made available to the American public. Between 1945 and 1948, the monthly output was stepped up to eight titles and reached a peak with twelve titles in 1950. After that some reduction took place, resulting in an average of eight titles per month in 1954 and about four per month in 1957. By the end of that year, 810 twenty-five cent, 206 thirty-five cent, and thirty fifty-cent titles had appeared.

A substantial percentage of Avon publications are mysteries, suspense and crime, and Western stories of the usual varieties to which science fiction and war novels were added in 1956 and 1957. Higher quality fiction is represented by foreign authors like Vicki Baum, Lion Feuchtwanger, Aldous

Huxley, Émile Zola, Jean Paul Sartre and Guy de Maupassant. Among American authors are Maxwell Bodenheim, Elmer Rice, Philip Wylie, Erskine Caldwell, Ben Hecht, William Faulkner and Sinclair Lewis, as well as psychoanalyists Wilhelm Stekel and Fredric Wertham. Bestsellers, which sold from one to three million copies have been: Jerome Weidman's 'I Can Get It For You Wholesale!,' Irving Shulman's 'The Amboy Dukes' and 'Cry Tough,' Erskine Caldwell's 'Short Story Collection,' and 'Dennis, the Menace' cartoons by Hank Ketcham.

In 1956 a new series was released under the name "Bard Books," of which only four titles have appeared so far. They include the 'Rubaiyat of Omar Khayyam,' translated by E. Fitzgerald, and Wilhelm Stekel's 'Meaning and Psychology of Dreams,' priced at thirty-five and fifty cents respectively, a low price for this type of publication. A fifty-cent "Avon" edition of Dostoyevsky's 'Crime and Punishment' also sold well at newsstands. A short-lived series of twenty-five cent popular nonfiction reprints, "Eton Books," tried out in 1951, did not succeed, possibly due to their similarity to "Signet-Key Books."

In 1954 the top personnel of Avon changed considerably, as Charles R. Byrne, editor-in-chief, and Frederick Klein, vice-president in charge of circulation, left the company to found the Berkley Publishing Corporation, bringing out a new line of paperbacks, "Berkley Books."

Avon's sales promotion is directed primarily at whole-salers and is handled by its circulation department. Advertising in newspapers has been tried occasionally, especially in con-nection with drug store chain advertisements in a given com-munity, as well as radio and television spot announcements, resulting in some increase in sales. 'How to Play Canasta' hit the market just when this game became the fashion and was a bestseller. Most recent effective promotions are reported with movie tie-ins, particularly Jules Verne's 'Around the World in Eighty Days.'

Covers have been toned down and objectionable features removed in the last two to three years, but the colors are still loud and the obviously "pictorial" design aimed at the hurried newsstand purchaser. Distribution is handled by Hearst Inter-national, which works through independent wholesalers. Foreign sales are significant, especially to I.M.G. countries and Canada.

Columbia Art Works, Inc. -- Red Arrow Books [4]

Shortly after "Pocket Books" made their appearance and the American Penguin branch was opened in New York, a new paperback series under the name of "Red Arrow Books" was announced by Columbia Art Works, Inc., a printing, publishing and lithographing concern of thirty-five years' existence, located in Milwaukee, Wisconsin. The format of 4 3/8" x 7 1/16" was identical with that of the Penguin series. Of the first books announced, five were mysteries and crime books in red, five travel and adventure stories in green, and two fiction titles in blue covers. All these were reprints, reset in Baskerville type and printed by offset. They sold for twenty-five cents in book and department stores and were aimed at the magazine market rather than the traditional book buying public, but in spite of a special display rack, "Red Arrow Books" did not succeed and vanished from the scene. The reason for this failure was probably due to the lack of an efficient distribution system.

Western Printing & Lithographing Company [5]

The Western Printing & Lithographing Company was founded in 1907 by Edward H. Wadewitz, who died in January, 1955. During these forty-eight years the firm expanded enormously. As the name indicates, the firm is primarily a printing establishment, but it is actually more than that. Peculiarly enough, the beginnings of the company came about rather by coincidence than by Wadewitz's intent to become a printer. As a young man he worked in a bank in Racine, Wisconsin. One of the bank's customers, the owner of the West Side Printing Company, was forced to close his shop and Edward Wadewitz was sent to investigate the possibilities of liquidation. As a result, he became interested in printing and took over the shop. Together with Roy A. Spencer, a journeyman pressman, he started with a capital of less than $1500. From these humble beginnings the firm rose to a point at which they reached an annual sales volume of approximately eighty million dollars in 1957. Behind these figures stands a physical plant with facilities in Racine, Wisconsin, Poughkeepsie, New York, St. Louis, and Hannibal, Missouri, and Mount Morris, Illinois; sales offices in New York City, Beverly Hills, Atlanta, Detroit,

Boston, Chicago, Minneapolis, Dallas and San Francisco; editorial offices in New York City; and a steady work force of some 4700 employees.

In order to explain the growth of the firm two basic ideas which motivated its founder must be appreciated. They are striking in their simplicity and were highly effective in their execution: (1) In order to realize maximum profits from the investment in plant and equipment, production should proceed at maximum capacity without seasonal fluctuations; (2) To accomplish this aim it is necessary to control demands for printing orders. Mr. Wadewitz, therefore, proceeded to diversify production and embrace related activities in addition to mere job printing to keep his labor force occupied and to create more printing orders by increasing demands from his own publishing firms.

In 1915, the company was manufacturing books for the Lamming-Whitman Company of Chicago, which went bankrupt and left Western, its largest creditor, with many of the finished books. Western sold the books and got in touch with some of Lamming-Whitman's business connections. In the same year Whitman Publishing Company was formed as a subsidiary and Western entered into the field of publishing children's books.

In 1925, another subsidiary was formed, Western Playing Card Company. The production of playing cards, jig saw puzzles, and other games helped the company to get through the comparatively lean depression years.

Still another subsidiary, Artists & Writers Press, Inc., plans, prepares and produces millions of juvenile books annually for other publishers. Among the most outstanding is Simon and Schuster, for which "Golden Books" are produced. Similar arrangements exist with Harper & Brothers, Little, Brown and Company, Row, Peterson & Company and others. In many instances Artists & Writers Press shares copyright privileges with these publishers, so that their imprint may appear frequently on such books.

From playing cards, Western branched into games and established a box factory. Another activity concerns the production of gift wrapping paper, which is created by gravure and aniline processes. The Racine factory, which houses this department, has complete lithoplate engraving facilities. It produces greeting cards, bridge score pads, tallies, place cards, diaries, memo books, cheaper editions of encyclopedias, dictionaries, testaments and Bibles.

Turning to the more conventional articles produced by job printers, Western does everything from billboard posters to catalogs and circulars for companies such as the Ford Motor Company. Western has also been printing maps for a long time and many of the road maps distributed by various gas companies originate in Western's plants. During World War II the company produced close to one hundred million war maps on paper and cloth for the Army Map Service, in addition to navigation books and charts, training booklets, and millions of Armed Services paperbacks.

Two other Western subsidiaries, the K & K Publications, Inc., and Story Parade, Inc., provide newsstand materials such as comics and "one-shot" publications for the juvenile and adult market. There also exists an arrangement between Western and the American Yearbook Company of Owatonna, Minnesota, whereby Western produces high school yearbooks and annuals.

One of the most fruitful activities in the field of newsstand materials brought Western in contact with the Dell Publishing Company. In 1936 a comic magazine was offered to Dell and Western; Western, by that time, had already entered the market as purchaser of copyrights. The two presidents of Western and Dell came to a friendly understanding whereby Western would print comics only for Dell, and Dell would purchase comics only from Western. This agreement created somewhat complicated conditions from the editorial point of view, but apparently these two independent companies were able to solve all problems to their mutual satisfaction.

Actually, most of the editorial decisions are made by Dell and Western in close cooperation, with Western concentrating on what to publish and Dell on how much to publish of each title; Western decides details on acquiring and producing manuscripts and their layout, Dell decides on sales and distribution. But, significantly, if a title is agreed upon, Dell purchases the whole edition on a cash basis and unsold copies are their, not Western's, responsibility. As a result, Western creates and manufactures comic magazines for Dell at a rate of about 25 million per month.

Since the arrangement with comic books worked so well, the two firms decided to enter the paperback field in 1943 with

"Dell Books," which ranks as the fourth oldest of current paperback series.

Dell Publishing Company, Inc.

Dell is owned by George T. Delacorte, Jr. According to trade information, Dell is the largest publisher of newsstand material in the United States, and distributed during 1957 an average of thirty-five million items a month, of which approximately twenty-five million are comic books.

Most of the magazines published are of the true love, true confession and true crime type; others are screen and puzzle magazines and "one shot" publications. Current monthly publications are: 'Modern Romances,' 'Modern Screen,' 'Screen Stories,' 'Front Page Detective,' 'Inside Detective,' 'Horoscope.' Bimonthly publications are: 'Dell Crossword Puzzles,' 'Official Crossword Puzzles,' and 'Pocket Crossword Puzzles.' Quarterly publications are 'Screen Album,' '1000 Jokes' and the "Hints Series," devoted to matters of cookery, diet and beauty. Every month there also appear an average of thirty-five "Dell Comics," and ten titles of the three paperback series, "Dell Books," "Dell First Editions," and "Dell Laurel Editions." The total output of the three paperback series amounts to about ten percent of the items published.

Dell Publishing Company, Inc., was founded in 1922. There exists no official history of the firm as publicity was never sought. Dell at first specialized in pulp paper magazines, later became interested in screen magazines and bought 'Talking Screen.' Titles were dropped and new magazines started with great facility.

An early success was 'Ballyhoo.' This magazine was brought out by Norman Anthony, who had previously worked for 'Judge Magazine.' About 1933, Dell began to publish comics and was the first firm to issue bi-weekly, tabloid-sized, comics. One of the first titles was 'The Funnies.' This publication contained only original comic strips but sales were not sufficient to warrant continuation of the series. About two years later, the Eastern Color Printing Company of Hartford, Connecticut, which had been printing Sunday supplements for various newspapers, began to bring out tabloid-sized comics and asked Dell to handle newsstand distribution. The publication reached the newsstand under the name 'Famous Funnies' but sold only about 40,000 copies and was discontinued by Dell. In 1935, public demand became more noticeable and Dell re-entered the comics field with 'Funnies.' North American Enterprises held the rights to these strips, which originally appeared in the 'Chicago Tribune.' Since success seemed assured, Dell contracted for a second serial called 'Superior Comics' in 1936. By that time Western not only was printing but also purchasing rights to comics and Dell's contract was cancelled and offered to Western. Delacorte and Wadewitz then entered into their mutual agreement. The advantage for Western was to be connected with an organization with wide distribution facilities offering a complete range of newsstand materials and a steady printing assignment, while Dell was assured of reliable printing services.

The production and printing of "Dell Books" is actually handled by Western through their Dell Book Division. Editorial work is under the supervision of Frank E. Taylor, who is executive editor of Dell Books Division but an employee of Western. "Dell First Editions" are edited by Knox Burger, though Frank Taylor is in charge of most of the nonfiction and special projects. Sales, distribution and circulation are arranged by Dell Publishing Company. "Dell Books" were first published in 1943. Since then 1244 titles have appeared in the three series, with an average of ten titles per month appearing during 1957, selling for twenty-five, thirty-five and fifty cents.

Many of the "Dell Books" titles are reprints of popular Westerns and murder mysteries, but a considerable number of serious novels and excellent nonfiction have been brought out as well. Fiction titles include special editions of such classics as Tolstoy's 'War and Peace' and Dostoyevsky's 'The Brothers Karamazov' and modern novels include 'Raintree County' by Ross Lockridge, Jr., 'Bonjour Tristesse' by Françoise Sagan, 'Peyton Place' by Grace Metalious, and books by William Faulkner, Ernest Hemingway, F. Scott Fitzgerald, Henry James and Oscar Wilde. Among the nonfiction reprints are 'Child Behavior' by members of the Gesell Institute, Papini's 'Life of Christ,' and Thomas Merton's 'Seeds of Contemplation' and 'No Man Is an Island.'

The "Dell Great Mystery Library" issues one title in the field of crime and suspense each month.

"Dell First Editions" include original fiction (novels, mysteries and Westerns) and some nonfiction. The first titles appeared in September, 1953. Noteworthy among the nonfiction titles are several anthologies of short stories, poetry and plays, as well as 'Modern French Painting,' 'New Worlds of Modern Science,' 'Our Friend the Atom,' and 'From Medicine Man to Freud.'

In May, 1957, Dell introduced its third series, "Laurel Editions." Laurel includes anthologies of the world's most distinguished literature, such as 'Four Plays by George Bernard Shaw,' 'Great English Short Stories' edited by Christopher Isherwood, and 'Great American Short Stories' edited by Wallace and Mary Stegner. The first of the reference and guide books to become a part of the new series is the 'Modern American Dictionary,' a 640-page giant based on the 'American College Dictionary.' Original nonfiction, included 'Common Wild Animals and Their Young' photographed by William and written by Rita Vandivert, and 'A Short History of the United States' by William Miller. The editors and authors for this series are selected on the basis of academic and professional experience and originality of viewpoint, so that the books are suitable for high school and college classroom use as well as for the general reading public.

Pines Publications, Inc. -- Popular Library[6]

Ned L. Pines, the founder of Pines Publications, Inc., is a man of action rather than contemplation, who manages to remain personally in the background while spending a great deal of effort on advertising his publications. No history of the firm is in existence and very little information about its development has appeared in print. Norman Hill, the promotion manager of the firm, has made some basic data available for this study.

Ned Pines has been interested in publishing since his high school days when he produced a newspaper on a hand press. His first adult publishing occurred in the early 1920's when he launched 'The Brooklyn Post,' a local paper which he sold in 1929 to devote his time to the production of magazines. His first periodical, 'College Life,' published in 1927, was sold by part-time student representatives directly to their campus colleagues and reached a peak circulation of about 200,000 copies.

In 1930, Street & Smith, one of the best customers of the American News Company, left that organization to have its publications independently distributed. Ned Pines was asked to fill the gap created by this withdrawal. He launched a number of fiction magazines and added new periodicals rapidly, including categories such as humor, crossword puzzles, astrology, fiction, detective, Western, and sport magazines. reaching a total of sixty titles. Some of these came out irregularly or were of the "one-shot" type. In 1939 the Pines comic magazine line was started, which includes 'Dennis the Menace,' 'Supermouse,' and many others. In 1942, a picture magazine, 'See,' was begun, and Pines Publications entered the paperback field during the same year with "Popular Library Books." In 1952, 'Real,' a slick magazine for men, was launched, and in 1953 the company purchased 'Silver Screen' and 'Screenland' and added a new magazine for women, 'True Life Stories.' Since 1954, a special projects department has been working on new magazine ideas and titles to supply an expanding publishing empire. The range of publications of the Pines' organization undoubtedly places the firm in a leading position among paperback, magazine, pulp and "one-shot" publishers. According to Norman Hill, 6,500,000 Pines Publications were bought at newsstands every month in the spring of 1955.

The organizational network to carry out these far-flung publishing activities is by necessity complex. The top organization is named Pines Publications, Inc., but several companies within the organization are devoted to magazine publications, while the paperback field is run by Popular Library, Inc. This is under the editorial direction of Charles N. Heckelmann, a vice president of the parent company. All Pines' products were distributed by the American News Company until June, 1957, when they were transferred to the International Circulation Division of Hearst. To adjust to the change-over, book production had to be temporarily curtailed and a number of employees from the book and distribution departments had to be dropped.

By the end of 1957 almost 1100 titles had been issued by Popular Library. Most of the books published are reprints although some of the Western and suspense stories are originals. If possible every month's fare includes a variety of titles-- novels, suspense, Westerns, adventure stories, and some nonfiction. The size of editions varies according to the sales estimates and has at times reached 500,000 copies. According to Mr. Heckelmann, more than half of all the titles published by

Popular Library require additional printings after the initial distribution.

One of the firm's best selling novels, Niven Busch's 'Duel in the Sun,' sold over three million copies. In this instance, promotion in connection with the movie was considered very successful. Other best sellers were 'A House is Not a Home,' by Polly Adler, which sold better than one and one-half million copies, 'Facts of Life and Love for Teen-Agers' by Evelyn M. Duvall, 1,100,000 copies, 'Duke,' by Hal Ellson, 1,540,000 copies, and 'The Parents' Manual' by Anna N. M. Wolf, 'Island in the Sky' by Ernest K. Gann, 'Ramrod,' by Luke Short, 'Three Comrades,' by Erich Maria Remarque, 'Rawhide Range,' an original anthology of stories by Ernest Haycox, 'Bedelia,' by Vera Caspary, all of which had sold around one million copies by 1954. Best selling translations have been 'The Loving and the Daring,' by Francoise Mallet and 'Strange Lovers' by Armando Meoni. One of the best known titles and a 1955 best seller for Popular Library is 'The Adventures of Augie March,' the novel by Saul Bellow, which had won the 1954 National Book Award for fiction as the outstanding book of the year. Some other well-known authors published by the firm include Fulton J. Sheen, John Steinbeck, Fannie Hurst, William Saroyan, Dale Carnegie, Gayelord Hauser, Irving Shulman, George Orwell, and Philip Wylie.

Popular titles in 1957 include Lillian Roth's 'I'll Cry Tomorrow' and Patrick Dennis' 'Auntie Mame,' which in its seventh printing brought the paperback editions to two million copies, while a movie tie-in in 1958 promises additional sales. The edition of 'Webster's New World Dictionary of the American Language' at seventy-five cents, for which a $100,000 advance was paid to the World Publishing Company, is expected to justify the vast full-page advertising campaign aimed to reach eighteen million readers in 1958 through Pines magazines.

Graphic Publishing Company, Inc. [7]

The Graphic Publishing Company was founded in 1948 and is owned by the two founders, Samuel Tankel and Zane Bouregy, who went to school and later into business together, sold their business to join the Civil Air Patrol during World War II, and after the war went jointly into publishing. They brought out a series of paperbacks confined mainly to detective, Western and historical fiction, with only an occasional general or cartoon book.

"Graphic Books" had cover pictures which were technically superior to many of their competitors. The reason for the good press work of the covers may be found in the owners' experience and interest. Tankel and Bouregy wrote a book on color values in two-color reproductions and Tankel was president of the Collier Photo Engraving Company. The books are priced at twenty-five cents for the regular series and thirty-five cents for the "Graphic Giants." Outstanding titles mentioned by Tankel include 'Tex' by Clarence Milford, 'Tough Cop' by John Roeburt, and 'Captain for Elizabeth,' by Jan Westcott, all of which went back to press several times. The firm produced fifty-six titles between 1955 and 1957, but suspended operations in the Fall of 1957.

Checkerbooks, Inc. [8]

This firm was founded by Lyle Kenyon Engel in 1949. The first four titles of the "Checkerbook" series appeared in October and it was planned to produce a maximum of sixteen titles per year, mostly reprints, to be priced at fifteen cents a copy. Actually, only twelve titles were released and publication was suspended in November, 1950. The causes for failure, according to Engel, are simple enough; the series, with its low price and literary fare comparable to the average paperback publication, was attractive to readers, but its price did not allow for a sufficiently high profit margin to the distributors. The first titles included Maxwell Bodenheim's 'Duke Herring' and Ben Hecht's 'The Florentine Dagger.'

Mr. Engel has been in the music publishing field since 1936, was a music consultant to 'Woman's Home Companion' for which he wrote a column, "Records of the Month," and has been active in procuring music scores for many movies.

Almat Publishing Company -- Pyramid Books [9]

The Almat Publishing Company was founded in 1949, and is owned by Alfred R. Plaine and Matthew Huttner. The firm was incorporated for the purpose of publishing "Pyramid Books" but in order to broaden its scope and make full use of its editorial staff, it also published 'Men's Magazine,' "Challenge' and 'Mechanics Today.' In 1956, a new series, "Pyramid Royals," was introduced.

Until 1952 all "Pyramid Books" were reprints, but since then a few original titles also have been released. A total of 295 titles had appeared by the end of 1957, seventeen of which were "Royals." Production at first averaged about four titles per month, except for a slow-down period in 1954 to free the market of oversupplies. During 1956 and 1957 production was considerably increased. Most authors are American, with about 5 to 6 percent of total production given to translations. The books sell at thirty-five and fifty cents, with a few titles still selling at twenty-five cents. Distribution is handled by the Kable News Company and average editions run about 150,000 to 200,000 copies.

The majority of "Pyramid Books" are Westerns, mysteries and romantic novels, with a good deal of sex and violence on and between the covers. However, some serious books and authors of reputation are included in the list, such as 'A Lesson in Love,' by Émile Zola; 'Cellini,' by Benvenuto Cellini; 'The Sea Tyrant,' by Peter Freuchen; 'Two Years Before the Mast,' by Richard H. Dana. There is a short story anthology by famous authors, published under a seductive title with an alluring cover, 'Women on the Wall,' edited by Marshall McClintock with contributions by Wallace Stegner, Ernest Hemingway, Thomas Wolfe, Katherine Mansfield, D. H. Lawrence, Kay Boyle and Dorothy Canfield Fisher. The skyline of the volume reads: "Desires and frustrations of women without men." This pattern of presenting great literature by outstanding authors but making it more palatable to the average reader by sensational misbranding can be found frequently. It was repeated with striking similarity in the "Lion Books" anthology 'Strange Desires,' edited by Vernon Shea and containing contributions by Mark Van Doren. William Faulkner and Thomas Mann. Here the skyline reads: "We all possess within us . . . the germ of atrocities -- Havelock Ellis."

In the past two years the overall quality of titles, authors and covers from this imprint have been improved. "Pyramid Royals" include 'Death Be Not Proud' by John Gunther, which was selected by the U. S. Information Agency for overseas distribution through "Student Editions,' 'A Woman without Love' by André Maurois, and 'The House of Madame Tellier' by Guy de Maupassant.

Lion Books, Inc. [10]

Until 1957 Lion Books, Inc., was owned by Martin Goodman, who also owns the Magazine Management Company, a firm which published in 1955 almost sixty serial publications, among them ten cent picture, movie and confession magazines and various comic and "cheese" periodicals.

Lion Books started publication in November, 1949, and published about 250 titles in five years, at first averaging four to five titles per month, with production stepped up to six in 1953 and 1954. In the beginning, all "Lion Books" sold at twenty-five cents, but after the increase in production costs, four titles of the monthly releases sold for twenty-five cents and two for thirty-five cents. Generally, the publication program followed this pattern: one Western novel, two suspense, crime or detective novels, two straight novels, stressing an emotional or sex problem, one publication of an entirely different type which might be nonfiction, science fiction, religion or an anthology.

Lion Books at times brought out originals, but most titles were reprints and some translations. Editorial policy was often to decide on a type of story, or even on a plot, and then to look for an author to write it. Some well-known authors like Dave Karp and Tom Thompson wrote several books for the firm after Arnold Hano, the former editor, had given them a synopsis of the desired story. The firm's bestseller was 'Joy Street,' by Clifton Cuthbert. In 1955 a regional anthology series was started which showed a great deal of imagination and individuality. 'Strange Barriers,' edited by J. Vernon Shea, presents stories by Lillian Smith, Langston Hughes, Thomas Wolfe and others about Negro-White relationships. Other titles in the series are 'Great Tales of the Deep South' and 'Great Tales of City Dwellers.' More recent novels by individual authors also aimed at a higher literary quality and included such works as 'All Quiet on the Western Front' by Erich Maria Remarque.

Title production dropped from sixty-one in 1954 to forty-three in 1956 and twenty-one in 1957. In the summer of 1957 New American Library absorbed a substantial part of the publishing rights of "Lion Books" and bought the title to the imprint and trade mark of Lion Books, Inc. Unpublished books under contract and reprints of previous titles appear under the

"Signet" imprint. "Lion Books" were previously distributed by Atlas Magazines, Inc., a company also owned by Goodman, which handles all other products of his enterprises. Most of the books were sold in drug stores and chain stores, with small towns providing a good market.

Fawcett Publications, Inc. [11]

Fawcett Publications developed through the success of the first Fawcett magazine which appeared more by coincidence than by design in September, 1919. Wilford H. Fawcett had left home at the age of sixteen to join the Army during the Philippine Insurrection. After his return, he became a railway mail clerk and worked part-time at the night copy desk of the 'Minneapolis Tribune.' He was promoted to reporter, and eventually to the position of city editor of the 'Winnipeg Free Press.' After another stint in the Army in World War I, he decided to publish a bulletin for his disabled veteran friends in Army hospitals. Since this publication was an immediate success, he brought out a pocket-size magazine of jokes selling for twenty-five cents, called 'Whiz-Bang'. To everyone's surprise, this little magazine sold 500,000 copies within a few months. Wilford Fawcett's brother, Roscoe, joined him in his rapidly growing publishing activities. An office building was purchased in Robbinsdale, Minnesota, to accommodate the firm, and with Roscoe Fawcett as editorial director, 'True Confessions,' 'Mechanix Illustrated,' and the first motion picture magazine were added.

The firm continued to grow rapidly and moved to Minneapolis in 1930 and to Greenwich, Connecticut, five years later, with editorial and advertising offices in New York City. Ralph Daigh became editorial director in the early 30's after the death of Roscoe Fawcett. By 1942 Fawcett was issuing more than sixty serial publications, had established offices in San Francisco, Los Angeles, Boston and Detroit, and had purchased a twenty-one story office building in New York City.

'True -- the Man's Magazine,' 'Motion Picture and Television Magazine,' 'Mechanix Illustrated,' 'True Confessions,' 'True Police Cases,' 'Startling Detective' are among the better-known Fawcett magazines. In addition to these, the company releases other publications, "one-shots," yearbooks, annuals and handbooks; "Gold Medal Books," "Fawcett Books."

"Crest Books" and "Premier Books" all paperback series. The firm's circulation department in Greenwich is the distributing outlet for Fawcett releases and serves in this capacity also for other paperback publishers.

The C. T. Dearing Company of Louisville, Kentucky, has supplied the bulk of the printing work for Fawcett since 1926. In 1943, Fawcett acquired the controlling interest and absorbed the firm as a subsidiary in 1944. In 1953, the name of the printing firm was changed to Fawcett-Dearing Printing Company. The capacity of this plant amounts to thirty million magazine copies per month or close to 215 million magazine pages every twenty-four hours.

Gold Medal Books

"Gold Medal Books," first published in 1950, were started with the policy of bringing out exclusively original publications in paperback format, an idea which was unique at that time. Ralph Daigh, Fawcett editorial director, moved the executive editor, William C. Lengel, from his magazine assignments to launch "Gold Medal" originals. A year later Richard Carroll joined the staff.

The choice of fiction materials falls preponderantly in the field of mystery and suspense novels and Western adventure stories. If there is a choice between a good story, crudely told, and a poor story, expertly done, the editors seem to prefer the former. Some nonfiction items also have been published, notably a biography of Henry Ford entitled 'They Never Called Him Henry,' which sold over 300,000 copies.

Minimum first editions ran to 200,000 copies in 1955, while they were more likely to be 250,000 copies in 1952 and 1953. However, several "Gold Medal Books" have been given first printings of 500,000 or more, including 'The Damned' and 'Dead Low Tide,' both by John D. MacDonald.

Average sales of Gold Medal titles are about 350,000 copies; reprint orders average 100,000 to 200,000 copies, but may be as low as 50,000 and as high as 500,000. 'Women's Barracks,' by Tereska Torres, first published in 1950, was still selling well in the fall of 1957, with total sales approaching the three million mark.

One author, Richard S. Prather, a Gold Medal discovery,

has had fourteen titles published with a combined sale of approximately 12,000,000 copies.

The editors are proud of the royalties paid to their authors who receive a minimum guarantee of $2,000. (Author's earnings are usually considerably higher. Richard Prather's books have earned him over $150,000.) Royalties are paid on print orders and not on sales.

In several instances, "Gold Medal Books" and "Crest Books" have placed original manuscripts with hard cover houses, at terms approved by authors and agents for future reprints in soft covers by Crest or Premier.

In the spring of 1955 Gold Medal Books appeared in three series: "Gold Medal Books" at twenty-five cents, "Gold Medal Specials" at thirty-five cents, and "Gold Medal Giants" at fifty cents. There is no essential difference in the type of materials contained in these series; the price merely reflects varying production costs determined by the length and original cost of the manuscript. In 1952, the firm tried a new series, "Red Seal Books," which had a slightly different make-up and sold at thirty-five cents. The series was discontinued because the publishers felt that it was competing primarily with "Gold Medal Books" and that the make-up was less attractive than that of the original series.

Crest Books and Premier Books

In the Fall of 1955 "Crest Books" and "Premier Books," were started. William C. Lengel headed the new venture, and Richard Carroll succeeded him as editor-in-chief of "Gold Medal Books."

"Crest Books," are mostly reprints of novels previously published in hard covers, with a sprinkling of original Western and suspense novels. Guarantees on originals are comparable to those of "Gold Medal."

"Crest Books" published among others 'The Black Obelisk, by Erich Maria Remarque; 'The Blue Camellia,' by Frances Parkinson Keyes; 'Off Limits,' by Hans Habe; 'The Dangerous Games,' by Tereska Torres. In October, 1957 the memoirs of the Duchess of Windsor, 'The Heart Has Its Reasons,' was published as a Crest Giant at seventy-five cents.

The Premier line of nonfiction (priced at fifty cents) presents books in the fields of science, religion, history, literature, philosophy, and psychology. Among them are 'Shakespeare Without Tears' by Margaret Webster, 'Understanding Human Nature' by Alfred Adler, 'The World's Ten Greatest Novels' by Somerset Maugham.

Initial minimum print orders of Premier Books are 85,000. Several titles have gone back for reissue, among them, 'The Art of Thinking' by Ernest Dimnet, 'A Book About American History' by George Stimpson, 'The Home Book of Italian Cooking' by Angela Catanzaro, 'According to Hoyle,' by Richard Frey. The two latter originally published as "Premiers," were reissued as "Crest Books" because of greater distribution facilities.

"Premier" reprints designed also for high school and college students, include 'Mirror for Man' by Clyde Kluckhohn, Professor of Anthropology at Harvard University, and 'The Living Thoughts of Thomas Jefferson' by John Dewey, the first book in the series 'Living Thoughts Library' which presents the essence of the thinking of great men of the past as interpreted by contemporary writers and philosophers.

Fawcett places house advertisements in its own and various other magazines like 'Time' and trade magazines. Whenever a book is made into a film, there is extensive concurrent display and promotion. Examples of successful movie tie-ins are 'Hondo' (John Wayne) by Louis L'Amour; 'Bad Day at Black Rock' (Spencer Tracy) by Howard Breslin; and 'Many Rivers to Cross' (Robert Taylor) by Steve Frazee.

Al Allard, Fawcett's art director, has introduced some innovations in paperback covers with the use of bright colors, eye-catching bands and designs. While many of the covers are quite attractive and in good taste, they have a tendency to resemble magazines rather than books. This style is suitable for Westerns and mysteries, but one regrets that some of the serious and truly worthwhile titles in the "Premier" and "Crest" series are not handled with a different approach.

Fawcett Books

One of Fawcett's first publications was 'Mechanix Illustrated' which presents technical, semi-technical and scientific problems of popular interest to the average reader by discussing them in easily understandable form. The magazine also aims at hobbyists, the outdoor sportsman, and the "do-ityourself" group of home repairmen and gardeners. By 1930, the editors felt that they had sufficient knowhow and materials to put out individual publications dealing with specific topics of special interest to their readers. A flying manual, 'The Handyman's Home Manual,' 'The Home-Builder's Manual,' and 'How to Build Boats' were "one-shot" publications of this type which were distributed with other Fawcett magazines. They sold for fifty cents, but as the number of photographic reproductions, all in rotogravure, increased, the price was raised to sixty cents in 1939. 'The Handyman's Home Manual' enjoyed continuous sales and came out in several new and completely revised editions. Books on photography like the 'Photography Handbook' and 'Good Photography' were added.

During the war, the "one-shot" publications of 'Mechanix Illustrated' were discontinued because of the paper shortage and the lack of leisure and available materials to engage in hobbies and home improvement. Soon after the end of the war, the interest in "how-to" books increased and took on the aspects of a national movement. Fawcett helped this trend along by sponsoring the first National Crafts and Science Show held at Madison Square Garden in 1946, which was followed by similar exhibits in other parts of the country. In 1950 a department of "Fawcett Library Books" was established, and a regular publishing program decided on. The series was started with Number 101, the publishing schedule calling for two titles a month. This was increased to three in December, 1951. Editorial policies remained much the same as for the "one-shot" publications, but appeal to female audiences was made from 1951 on by stressing various cook books and other titles of interest to homemakers. In December, 1954, the name of the series was changed from "Fawcett Library Books" to "Fawcett How To Books" and later to "Fawcett Books." In 1956 the name was again changed to "Science and Mechanics Handbook Annual." The individual volumes, selling for fifty and seventy-five cents, are published and copyrighted by the Science and Mechanics Publishing Company of Chicago, Illinois.

They differ from other paperbacks, as they are not "perfect bound" and are 6 5/8" x 9 3/8" in size, which is the format of the 'Mechanix Illustrated' magazine. The main reason for the adoption of this size was the difficulty in presenting all photographs and illustrations in small-sized books. Since many of the mats from 'Mechanix Illustrated' are used, production on the same machines is more economical. Publications are not listed in 'Publishers' Weekly' and other sources as paperbacks, and the series has actually reverted to a "one-shot" operation in format, distribution and method of release.

Ace Books, Inc. [12]

Ace Books, Inc., is owned by A. A. Wyn and his family, who also own A. A. Wyn, Inc., which publishes magazines of the "confessions" and "secrets" type. A. A. Wyn is president and editor-in-chief of both firms, which are located on the same premises. Editorial policy, selection of titles, author contracts and day-to-day operations are handled by Donald A. Wollheim, editor of "Ace Books." Ace began its activities in September, 1952, and published 263 items between that time and December, 1957. Two series are published, "Ace Double Novels," which consist of two complete novels in one cover, and "Ace Books." The latter series was started in February, 1954.

The double novel plan is unique to the extent that each novel has its own cover picture and title page, beginning at each end of the book; they are bound back to back. At first, the firm published two double novels a month, one containing two Westerns, the other two detective stories. The output was increased to three double novels in January, 1953, and to four in September, 1953. Adventure stories, science fiction and romances were added. Some of the titles are originals, some reprints, and approximately half of the company's output is now single titles, half "Double Novels." Copies sell at twenty-five and thirty-five cents and average editions run 150,000 copies. With the exception of a few titles, all publications are fiction. Nonfiction, includes a cookbook, autobiographical material of a narcotic agent, a description of the white slave trade in the United States and a handbook on vocabulary self-improvement.

For the last two years the firm has specialized in science fiction, but the two 1957 best sellers dealt with science facts: 'Earth Satellites and the Race for Space Superiority' by G. Harry Stine, and 'Report on Unidentified Flying Objects' by Edward J. Ruppelt.

Berkley Publishing Corporation [13]

The Berkley Publishing Corporation was founded in September, 1954, by Frederick Klein, president, and Charles R. Byrne, executive vice president and editor-in-chief, who, together with a third party not engaged in publishing, own the corporation. Both worked for many years with the Avon Publishing Company, where Klein was vice-president in charge of circulation and Byrne vice-president, editor-in-chief, and director of "Avon Books." The new firm started with two pocket-sized magazines, 'Chic,' a monthly woman's magazine, and 'News,' a weekly news magazine, both of which were suspended. In 1956, a reorganization took place and Byrne became president, Stephen Conland, executive vice-president, and Frederick Klein left the firm.

Berkley began a line of paperback books in the spring of 1955, known as "Berkley Books." The series was advertised as a "solid, readable list with mass appeal" priced at twenty-five, thirty-five and forty cents. Distribution was originally handled by the American News Company but was shifted to the Kable News Company early in 1956.

Initial printings were set at 150,000 copies and the first titles included two anthologies, one nonfiction title, eight modern novels, two Westerns, one mystery, three suspense thrillers and one cartoon book. One-hundred and seventeen titles had been produced by Fall, 1957, and an attempt has been made to include some titles of definite literary interest. 'Eleven Blue Men,' by Berton Roueche, a collection of stories dealing with medical detection won the Lasker Foundation award for medical reporting and has been adopted for classroom use by a number of colleges. It was also released in a special edition for sale in the Far and Middle East under the auspices of the U. S. Information Agency. Other significant titles include 'Night Rider' by Robert Penn Warren, 'Sweetie Pie' by Nadine Seltzer, which was adopted by the Teen Age Book Club and became one of their all-time bestsellers, 'S. S. San Pedro' by James Gould Cozzens and 'Salammbo' by Gustave Flaubert. 'Modern Writing #3,' a paperback magazine compiled by the editors of 'Partisan Review,' also appeared under the Berkley imprint. The first two issues had been released by Avon Publications.

[1]Personal interview with Charles R. Byrne, 1954; questionnaire, 1957.

[2] "First Class Mail," 'Publishers'Weekly,' CXLII:1 (July 4, 1942), p. 20, quoting decision of Judge Peter Schmuck of the New York Supreme Court, rendered January 19, 1942.

[3] "Pocket Books Wins Unfair Competition Appeal," 'Publishers' Weekly,' CXLII:19 (November 7, 1942), p. 1951.

[4] "Among the Publishers," 'Publishers' Weekly,' CXXXVI:15 (October 7, 1939), 1439.

[5]Personal interviews with Frank Taylor, Knox Burger, Helen Meyer and William F. Callahan, 1954 and 1955; correspondence, 1957; Don H. Black, "The Story of 'Western'; A Brief History of Western Printing & Lithographing Co." (Racine, Wisconsin: Western Printing & Lithographing Co., 1954).

[6]Personal interviews with Charles Heckelman and Norman Hill, 1955; correspondence with Norman Hill 1955 and 1957, including a specially prepared history of the firm.

[7]Correspondence with Samuel Tankel, 1955; "The Case for Two-Color Printing," 'The American Printer' (July, 1948), pp. 24-27; "What Makes Graphic Books Sell So Well?" 'American News Trade Journal,' XXXVII:1 (February, 1955), pp. 14-15.

[8]Telephone conversation with Lyle Kenyon Engle, 1955; "Fifteen-cent Checkerbooks Now on Newsstands," 'Publishers' Weekly,' CLVI:26 (December 24, 1949), p. 2499.

[9]Personal interview with Alfred R. Plaine, 1955; questionnaire, 1957.

[10] Personal interview with Arnold Hano, 1954. "NAL Buying Rights to Some Lion Books," 'Publishers' Weekly,' CLXXII:6 (August 5, 1957), pp. 32-33.

[11]Personal interviews with Larry Eisinger, editor, Fawcett Books and Richard Carroll, editor, Gold Medal Books, 1955; correspondence with William C. Lengel, editor, Crest and Premier Books, 1957; William C. Lengel, "Today's Trend in Publishing Good Books in Paper Covers," (New York: Fawcett Publications, mimeographed release, 1952).

[12]Personal interview with Donald Wollheim, 1954; questionnaire, 1957.

[13]Personal interview with Charles R. Byrne, 1955. "Berkley Publishing Corporation," 'Publishers' Weekly,' CLXVI:25 (December 18, 1954), p. 2347; "Berkley Books," 'Publishers' Weekly,' CLXVII:25 (June 18, 1955), p. 2801; questionnaire, 1957.

[14]"Bartholomew House Launches Regular Book Program," 'Publishers' Weekly,' CLXXII:13 (September 23, 1957), p. 42.

CHAPTER 11

TRADE PUBLISHERS

When the average American refers to "books" he usually thinks of adult trade books. Trade publishing, broadly defined as the issuing of books for general retail bookstore sale, typifies American publishing, though it is by no means its largest segment in terms of sales figures or production of copies. Its economic structure is somewhat chaotic because its market potential is inadequately known and even less adequately realized. The basis for business decisions ranges from analysis to intuition as publishers deal with a commodity whose value is judged by the least reliable of all possible yardsticks -- the public's fickle taste.[1]

General trade books in America are usually expected to be hardbound volumes. The entry of trade publishers into the soft cover field during the contemporary phase of paperback publishing was made rather tentatively by Simon and Schuster who at first issued occasional papercovered titles, then expanded them into a series, "Readers' Editions", in 1950. Neither format nor general conception was of significance to the overall trend. The establishment of "Permabooks" by Doubleday in 1948 was a large publishers' excursion into the mass market. The books were not significantly different from NAL or Pocket Books and were eventually merged with the latter. The actual beginning of a new type of trade publication was the release of Doubleday's "Anchor Books" in 1953 which alerted trade publishers to the unrealized potentials of reprinting their own or other publishers' titles of general interest in an inexpensive format; the success of serious titles paved the way for paperback lines of university presses and educational and scholarly publishers.

Since the histories of most of the firms in this chapter are well known and covered in trade literature, they are offered here only in briefest outline. While the general format of arranging the firms according to the date of establishment of their paperback series is followed, the operations of several specialized publishers are combined in the concluding paragraphs.

Doubleday & Company, Inc. [2]

Today the firm of Doubleday & Company still carries the name of its founder but has gone far beyond its original scope. Together with its subsidiaries, it is the largest book publisher in America and probably the largest in the world.

Frank Nelson Doubleday was attracted early to books and printing. Born in 1862, he set up as a young man a printing establishment in his parents' home in Brooklyn. Later he worked for Charles Scribner's Sons, where he rose to the position of business manager for 'Scribner's Magazine.' He remained with this company until 1897 when he founded, together with Samuel Sidney McClure, the Doubleday & McClure Company. McClure withdrew in 1899 to form McClure, Phillips and Company.

Doubleday & McClure published authors like O. Henry, Kipling and Stevenson. When McClure left, the firm's imprint changed to Doubleday, Page & Company, as Doubleday joined forces with Walter Hines Page. Five years later, McClure's organization was absorbed by Doubleday. The successful firm established its own printing facilities for a daily production of 5000 books, The Country Life Press, in Garden City, Long Island.

In 1910, Doubleday moved to Garden City, Long Island, and kept only a small office in New York. In 1920, Doubleday, Page & Company took over a large part of the shares of the British firm of William Heinemann. However, these shares were returned to British stockholders in 1933. In 1920, the Garden City Publishing Company, a subsidiary handling the manufacture of low priced books, was established. Reprint possibilities were explored successfully and various series like the "Star Dollar Books," "The Sundial Series," and the "Deluxe Series," and cheaper ones featuring original works like the "Crime Club" and "The Dollar Mystery Club" were developed. A juvenile department was also added to the firm.

In 1927 Arthur Page, son of W. H. Page, withdrew and George H. Doran entered into partnership with Doubleday. The imprint changed to Doubleday, Doran & Company. In the

1930's, Nelson Doubleday took over the firm's leadership from his father and continued the use of the Doran name until 1946. George H. Doran died in 1956.

The book club idea had its beginning in the U.S.A. in 1921. Five years later, in 1926, the two largest, the "Book-of-the-Month Club" and the "Literary Guild" were started, followed by some fifty others, some successful, some not. Nelson Doubleday held a part interest in "The Literary Guild" from its begin ning and purchased it outright in 1934. In 1955, Doubleday owned fourteen book clubs, including "The Dollar Book Club," "Family Reading Club," "Fireside Theatre," "Science Fiction Book Club," and "Junior Literary Guild."

In 1944 the Blakiston Company, a medical and scientific publisher established in 1843, was purchased by Doubleday. It was run as a subsidiary, maintaining its own imprint and independent publishing program, but its officers were the same as those of the parent organization. In 1955, Blakiston was sold to McGraw-Hill Co. Doubleday maintains two separate educational divisions, the College Textbook and Catholic Textbook Division.

The first Doubleday book store was established in 1910 in the Main Arcade of New York's Pennsylvania Station. Since then, the chain has increased to over thirty. These stores sell books, records, and, in some instances, greeting cards and toys. Doubleday has also taken over several book departments in large department stores.

Country Life Press closed operations in June, 1956 to make room for 2100 clerical employees engaged in book club and other activities. Printing and binding were shifted to Hanover, Pennsylvania, which had been engaged in book production since 1948, and to a plant in Smithsburg, Maryland. The firm's main editorial office is in New York City. The largest distributor of books and book club subscriptions in Canada is Doubleday, Canada, Ltd., located in Toronto, Ontario. Doubleday also has offices in London and Paris.

Since 1946 Douglas M. Black, formerly legal adviser of Doubleday & Company, Inc., has been president, following the retirement of Nelson Doubleday.

Doubleday's authors comprise a distinguished list, including Rudyard Kipling, Christopher Morley, Theodore Dreiser, W. Somerset Maugham, Noel Coward and Edna Ferber. Outstanding recent best sellers of the firm have been Dwight D.

Eisenhower's 'Crusade in Europe' and Herman Wouk's 'The Caine Mutiny.'

Permabooks

Doubleday's first paperbacks were "Permabooks," established in 1948 as a subsidiary of Garden City Books, Inc. Until 1954, when "Permabooks" was sold to Pocket Books, Inc., George de Kay was editor of the series. During that period all Doubleday paperback lines were part of the Newsstand Division, under the general supervisory direction of Mel Evans. After the sale of "Permabooks," the Newsstand Division was dissolved; the promotion and sales of "Image Books" was transferred to the Catholic Textbook Division and "Anchor Books" are handled by the trade book department.

During the Second World War, Garden City had been successful with its "Triangle Books," a hardcover reprint series that sold for thirty-nine, forty-nine and fifty-nine cents in chain, department and some drugstores. After the end of the war, sales dropped because store managers who had used the books to fill their shelves when other merchandise was hard to obtain, now found more profitable items competing for space, and the regular pocket-sized paperbacks, which were just beginning to flood the market, required less space and were easier to handle. As a result, "Triangle Books" were discontinued and Doubleday entered the inexpensive market with "Permabooks" which were published in small format with hard covers. This series concentrated at first on nonfiction. Towards the end of 1950, the hard glossy covers were replaced by soft covers and "perfect binding" was introduced. From 1951 on, both fiction and nonfiction, almost exclusively as reprints, were offered at thirty-five cents; in 1953, two other lines, "Perma Stars" at twenty-five cents, and "Perma Specials" at fifty cents made their appearance. "Perma Specials" offered material of quality like Louis Untermeyer, 'Concise Treasury of Great Poems,' Dwight D. Eisenhower, 'Crusade in Europe,' Sigmund Freud, 'Introduction to Psychoanalysis,' Hendrik W. van Loon, 'Story of the Bible' and 'Bartlett's Familiar Quotations.'

The thirty-five cent "Permabooks" include a comparatively large number of nonfiction titles like Alfred Adler, 'Understanding of Human Nature' and Morris Fishbein, 'Handy Home Medical Advisor.' There are also dictionaries, anthologies, books of poetry and some good fiction by authors like Irving Stone, Vicki Baum and W. Somerset Maugham. Some of the dictionaries sold between one and three million copies. "Permabooks" rather consistently kept away from the sex and sadism type of book.

Covers were done by Country Life Press in Garden City, books were printed on special presses in Hanover, Pennsylvania; occasional volumes were done by commercial printers. "Permabooks" were distributed by McFadden until fall, 1953; after that, distribution was handled by the Doubleday sales staff.

In 1954, "Permabooks" and "Pocket Books" were merged and the operations were taken over by Pocket Books, Inc.[3]

Anchor Books

"Anchor Books," were first published in April, 1953. Jason Epstein, a scholarly young man of twenty-five, had conceived the idea of a reprint line of serious fiction and nonfiction and wrote a long report on its possibilities which he submitted to Doubleday. Based on his observations of the market trends for "Penguin," "Pelican" and "Mentor" titles, to which "Anchor Books" have an "intrinsic, but not generic relationship" (to quote Epstein) his study consisted of a general statement and an evaluation of the book market; he discussed the growing college population, and the possibility of considering 10-15 percent of that population, and a smaller percentage of the general public, as potential buyers. He took into account manufacturing problems, the cover layout and price of the series, the size of editions and distribution, which he recommended to be through book stores rather than news dealers.

As a result, he was retained by Doubleday as editor of "Anchor Books," a paperback line which had several significant characteristics. The paper is of heavier stock than that of the cheaper lines, the covers are of more durable, non-glossy quality, covers use modernistic designs instead of portrait illustrations and prices, originally ranging from sixty-five to ninety-five cents, are now from seventy-five cents to $1.95. Original plans were for editions of 20,000 copies but past sales successes have justified editions of as many as 37,500. Reissues are made on runs as low as 12,500.

By 1957, 119 "Anchor" titles had been released, and it is

the publisher's intention to keep them in print, as the series is intended for the permanent collection of the serious reader. "Anchor Books" sold 1,350,000 copies in the first twenty-two months; bookstores account for roughly 44 percent of the sales, wholesalers for 46 percent and 10 percent go to direct accounts, some of which are selected drugstores and other outlets in neighborhoods catering to readers of heavier literary fare. Approximately 10 percent of the series are exported through the Export Division of Doubleday. Printing and binding are done by the high-speed printing presses in the Doubleday plant at Hanover, Pennsylvania.

Suggestions for titles are received from all parts of the country and from various groups, particularly university communities. Outstanding titles have been David Riesman's 'The Lonely Crowd,' which made the 'Time' cover story as a reprint four years after it had appeared in the original hardcover edition; Jacques Barzun, 'Teacher in America,' Edmund Wilson, 'To the Finland Station,' Joseph Conrad, 'The Secret Agent,' William H. Whyte, Jr., 'The Organization Man.' Over two dozen publications are "Anchor Originals," consisting of new titles or new translations or anthologies. The series also includes a literary periodical 'The Anchor Review,' edited by Melvin J. Lasky.

"Anchor Books" won the 1954 Carey-Thomas Award for a distinguished book publishing project, the only paperbound publisher to have received this honor. (Plate 16)

Simon and Schuster, Inc. [4]

Founded in 1924 Simon and Schuster was already very successful by 1939 when Richard L. Simon and Max Lincoln Schuster took an active part in the launching of Pocket Books, Inc., in which they owned half of the shares, but carried no editorial responsibility. In 1942, they established a Juvenile Book Department which created "The Little Golden Books" through the cooperation of the Artists and Writers Guild of America, a subsidiary of Western Printing & Lithographing Company, and the Sandpiper Press, a subsidiary of Simon and Schuster. In 1944, both Simon and Schuster and Pocket Books, Inc. became part of Field Enterprises, Inc., but each of the firms maintained separate editorial boards, editorial policies, and individual existence.

The success of Simon and Schuster as a firm is largely due to the personalities of its founders: Richard Simon had a thorough understanding of the market possibilities of manuscripts dealing in lighter literary fare, while Max L. Schuster developed an appreciation for scholarly works.

The firm's list of outstanding authors of every type is large and varied, and its approach to publishing was referred to by Sam Myerson, assistant treasurer, as "creative publishing," the willingness to experiment with authors, formats, titles and advertising, as well as the concerted effort to find an author and a topic to fill an existing demand. Over the years, there has been no hesitation on the part of the two founders and their staff to try new ideas and to drop old ones if they do not succeed. This adaptability explains some of the firm's outstanding successes.

Richard L. Simon, born in 1899 in New York, went to Ethical Culture School and was graduated from Columbia University in 1920. As a salesman for a piano company he met his future partner, Max Lincoln Schuster, in 1921. He worked for two years as a salesman for Boni & Liveright. Schuster, born in 1897, also went to Columbia University and developed an early interest in journalism, working after graduation from high school as a part time correspondent for the 'New York Evening World.' By 1924, he had saved four thousand dollars and, together with an equal amount contributed by Simon, the firm was established and brought out a crossword puzzle book upon the demand of a relative as its first publication, which helped to start a fad in the 1920's and 1930's. Paperbound crossword puzzle books are still successfully sold today. A similar request for a book to give to a sick friend resulted in 'Fun in Bed,' (1932), edited by Frank Scully, which sold many editions over the years. Schuster's interest in philosophy was instrumental in the publication of Will Durant's 'The Story of Philosophy' as a full-length book, after he had first come across it as a Haldemann-Julius "Little Blue Book." Other titles which won wide acclaim were started in the same casual manner. Simon, concerned about writing his will, discovered that no popular book on this topic was available and encouraged his lawyer, René Worsmer, to write 'Your Will and What Not to Do About It.' A Dale Carnegie course attended by one of the firm's business managers resulted in 'How to Win Friends and Influence People.' Simon's interest in music led to the 'Victor

Book of the Symphony.' In similar ways, Schuster sponsored many books and found time to compile two himself: 'A Treasury of the World's Great Letters,' and 'Eyes on the World,' the latter a photographic record of history in the making. The sure hand in choosing books with mass appeal in a light and serious vein is shown by the publication of cartoon books like David Low, 'A Cartoon History of Our Time'; George Baker, 'Sad Sack'; and Walt Kelly, 'Pogo,' as well as most of the books of Hendrik W. Van Loon.

"Little Golden Books" were conceived when one of the firm's editors brought his ailing daughter some children's books and she tore up ten dollars' worth in eight minutes. In this fashion, good children's books at a low price were brought on the market and proved phenomenally successful. Between 1942 and 1955 over 400 million copies were sold and since 1944 the sales of "Little," "Big" and "Giant Golden Books" amount to approximately three times the dollar volume of the adult publications. There are also Golden Records, and "Golden Nature Guides." Minimum printing orders of "Little Golden Books" are 150,000 copies; some titles sell up to one million copies, averaging around 250,000. Approximately forty-eight titles are added to "Little Golden Books" every year. In order to satisfy the demands of libraries and schools for permanent bindings, Goldencraft cloth bindings were introduced for library editions of the otherwise paper over board releases.

In April 1957, following Marshall Field's death in November, 1956, Leon Shimkin, president of Simon and Schuster, and James Jacobson, executive vice president in charge of sales, purchased Pocket Books, Inc. Included in the sales was the transfer of Affiliated Publishers, Inc., the Pocket Books distribution division which also handles the firm's other mass market items like "Little Golden Books." In October 1957, Schuster and Shimkin purchased Simon and Schuster from Field Enterprises and Simon ended his association with the publishing house which continues to bear his name.

Readers' Editions

Many titles were originally issued in soft covers like J. K. Lasser's 'Income Tax Guide'; others were released simultaneously in hardcover and paper editions. Due to the close connection between the firm and Pocket Books, Inc., it can be assumed that the pamphlet format of Simon and Schuster paperbacks is motivated by the attempt to reduce competition, yet cater to a wider market. Popular editions selling at one dollar were released to bookstores at strategic moments and found wide reader acceptance. The first pamphlet of this kind was Wendell Willkie's 'One World' in 1943. Others were 'Report from Tokyo,' by Joseph C. Grew and 'I Never Left Home,' by Bob Hope.

In 1950, the firm formalized this policy of issuing paperbound editions of some of its hardcover titles by establishing its "Readers' Editions." The announcement on each book stated that it is a "new book, and unabridged. It is made available at the low price of one dollar because of: (1) thinner paper; (2) a huge printing; (3) soft cover binding. We would appreciate your reactions to this experiment in publishing. This book is also published at $2.50 in a more permanent cloth-bound edition on better paper."

"Readers' Editions" were of regular library size format. The first title was 'The Cardinal,' by Henry Morton Robinson. Others are: Robert Smith, 'One Winter in Boston'; Joshua Loth Liebman, 'Peace of Mind'; Langston Hughes, 'Simple Speaks His Mind'; William T. Tilden, 'How to Play Better Tennis.' While the books were successful, the idea of publishing them as a series was discontinued. Yet, the policy of publishing titles of interest to a wide segment of the population in two formats has been maintained. Recent works released in this manner include: Edward R. Murrow's 'This I Believe,' Ernest Havemann's 'The Age of Psychology' and Smiley Blanton's 'Love or Perish.'

Scientific American Books

In late 1955 Simon and Schuster announced a new paperback series, of similar format to "Readers' Editions," called "Scientific American Books," consisting of titles in specific areas of science, compiled by the editors of 'Scientific American.' A statement by the publishers explains that

these are areas in which work in progress is pushing out the frontiers of human knowledge at a rapid rate, and finds new and troubling questions. The books are based on contemporary articles from the magazine. Each is written by a leading scientist and newly edited

to give the reader -- whether he is a specialist or a
non-specialist in each field -- an understanding of what
is exciting and important in modern research.

Titles, priced at $1.45, include 'Atomic Power,' 'The New
Astronomy,' 'Automatic Control,' 'The Physics and Chemistry
of Life.'

Alfred A. Knopf, Inc. -- *Vintage Books* [5]

In studying modern American publishers and their products,
one realizes that, in spite of the leveling influences of similar
production methods and the modern merchandising approach,
the choice of titles and the format reflect the publisher's or
editor's personal taste and views. This holds particularly true
for Alfred A. Knopf, who is responsible for the revival of the
colophon in contemporary books and has consistently maintained
high typographical standards for trade books with the attempt to
blend content, type and outer garment. He was the first to
recognize the talents of the great typographer, W. A. Dwiggins,
and of many budding European, American and Russian authors,
nine of whom were later awarded Nobel prizes. His list includes
names like Willa Cather, Henry L. Mencken, Joseph Herge-
sheimer, Max Beerbohm, Robert Bridges, Thomas Mann,
André Gide, Nikolai Gogol, Maxim Gorky, Leo Tolstoy, Sigrid
Undset and many others.
   Alfred Knopf studied at Columbia University, entered the
firm of Doubleday, Page and Company in 1912 and opened his
own publishing firm in 1915. The firm has remained a family
enterprise, Mrs. Knopf serving as vice president and Alfred
A. Knopf, Jr., as secretary and director of the trade department, and now also editor of "Vintage Books." In March, 1957,
Mrs. Knopf became president, Alfred Knopf, Jr., vice president
in charge of sales, and Alfred A. Knopf, chairman of the board.
Knopf is devoted to serious and high quality literature, with
occasional excursions into the fields of social science. Many
titles are chosen according to the Knopfs' tastes. They both
have intimate personal contacts with many of the great
twentieth-century authors here and abroad. Their list is
strong in titles which keep selling year after year, and it was
from them that the company decided to establish a line of
paperback reprints, called "Vintage Books." Knopf is the first

publisher in the serious book field to reissue his own titles in such a way.

Vintage Books, Inc. was organized in 1954 as a separate corporation but is owned by Alfred A. Knopf, Inc., and managed by Alfred Knopf, Jr. The choice of the first ten titles was based on a canvass of ten college and university faculties. Vintage pays 10 percent royalties and the size of editions was originally planned to be around 20,000. In April, 1954, Knopf, Jr., believed that about 50 to 60 percent of the Knopf imprints would make suitable Vintage choices. "Vintage Books" sell usually for $1.25 and book-dealers receive full trade discounts; distribution to regular book outlets is handled by Knopf salesmen.

Of the first nine titles published in September, 1954, five were non-fiction: Gilbert Highet, 'The Art of Teaching;' Alfred Einstein, 'A Short History of Music'; Alexis de Tocqueville, 'Democracy in America' (2 volumes); Eric Bentley, 'In Search of Theater'; Richard Hofstadter, 'The American Political Tradition.' Fiction titles were: Albert Camus, 'The Stranger'; Thomas Mann, 'Death in Venice and Seven Other Stories'; E. M. Forster, 'Howards End'; Andre Gide, 'The Immoralist.' The titles which followed showed the same high quality but leaned more in the direction of nonfiction, with strong emphasis on literary criticism and psychiatry. Occasional originals, like 'The Economic Basis of Politics and Other Essays' by Charles A. Beard, are included.

The Viking Press, Inc.[6]

The Viking Press, as well as Alfred A. Knopf, Inc., has long realized "the value of careful and attractive book design, not only of individual volumes, but of their entire list."[7] The publications of both firms are similar in many respects -- they have stressed a large number of outstanding European writers, and a good number of America's best. These include in Viking's case Graham Greene, James Joyce, Gerhart Hauptmann, Franz Werfel, Stefan and Arnold Zweig, Lion Feuchtwanger, Rebecca West, D. H. Lawrence, Thorstein Veblen, Van Wyck Brooks, Carl Van Doren, Ludwig Bemelmans, Rex Stout, John Steinbeck, Gene Fowler, Upton Sinclair, Sherwood Anderson, and many others. The similarity of the two firms extends, to a limited extent, even to their respective presidents.

Viking was founded in March, 1925, by Harold Guinzburg

who had been graduated from Harvard in 1921. He studied law for two years at Columbia and then did newspaper work for a few months. While Knopf began his publishing career at Doubleday, Guinzburg joined for a year the new firm of Simon and Schuster, after which he felt ready to start his own organization with the financial assistance of George Oppenheimer, who had previously worked for Alfred A. Knopf. Rockwell Kent designed as printer's mark a viking ship which Guinzburg liked so well that he adopted it for his firm's name. Before the first book was published, Harold Guinzburg combined with Benjamin W. Huebsch, who brought a small, but strong backlist, his experience and his assistant, Marshall A. Best, into the business. Huebsch became vice president, and Best, general manager, until 1956 when the latter became vice president.

Harold Guinzburg conceived the idea of the "Literary Guild" on one of his frequent European trips. During the depression in 1934, when the "Literary Guild" needed financial support for expansion, it was sold to Doubleday, Doran, which had previously acquired some financial interest in it.

In 1933, the Viking Junior Books Department was founded under the editorship of May Massee, who is responsible for a large list of distinguished children's books which have sold exceedingly well. 'The Story about Ping' by Marjorie Flack sold 150,000 copies over a period of nineteen years, and Munro Leaf's 'Ferdinand the Bull' had sold over 350,000 copies by 1956.

Viking publishes an average of about fifty adult and twenty-five children's books yearly. In 1937 Pascal Covici, who had brought out books under the imprints of Covici-McGee, Covici and Covici-Friede, joined the Viking Press as editor. He brought, among others, the Steinbeck titles to Viking.

Viking Paperbound Portables

The story of "Viking Paperbound Portables" begins with the "Viking Portable Library" which started in 1943 as a lucky accident of wartime with the publication of Alexander Woollcott's anthology 'As You Were,' a compendium of American prose and poetry prepared for the members of the Armed Forces. The aim was to produce an attractive volume of maximum content, durability and reliability that could be carried in the pocket.

So enthusiastically received was the little book that it was decided to extend the 'portable' format to other books. [8]

This series now includes over sixty titles -- from Plato to Dorothy Parker. It sold at first at two dollars, but the price was later raised to $2.50. The examples of "Mentor," "Anchor" and "Vintage" books were sufficiently encouraging to suggest that the series would enjoy additional sales in paper covers, especially as the hardbound edition had been a great success. All of the original titles, except the Hemingway and Thomas Wolfe volumes, whose reprint rights expired and were not renewed by the original publishers, are still in print and have sold from 10,000 to 100,000 copies each, averaging about 40,000 to 50,000.

Fifteen "Paperbound Portables" were released in 1955 and sixteen during 1956 and 1957. The books are printed from the same plates as the clothbound editions, average 700 pages and feature specially designed non-glossy covers. Editions run an average of 20,000 copies. The books sell for $1.25 and $1.45 and measure 4 1/4" x 7 3/16".

Two types of reading material are covered by the series: comprehensive anthologies of special subjects like 'The Portable Medieval Reader,' edited by James B. Ross and Mary Martin McLaughlin, and 'The Portable Greek Reader,' edited by W. H. Auden, and representative works of single authors like 'The Portable Whitman,' with a biography and critical introduction by Mark Van Doren and 'The Portable Voltaire,' edited by Ben Ray Redman. The bestseller of the group is the Mark Twain volume, edited by Bernard de Voto.

Compass Books

The second series of Viking paperbacks, "Compass Books," was started in March 1956 and by 1957 eighteen titles of reprints from Viking's and other publishers' backlists had appeared. The books, priced ad ninety-five cents to $1.45 have most attractive covers, designed by Bill English, Raphael Boguslav and Robert Hallock. They are primarily individual works of significant modern authors. The bestselling title to date is James Joyce's 'A Portrait of the Artist as a Young Man.' Others include Malcolm Cowley's 'Exile's Return,'

Stefan Zweig's 'Erasmus of Rotterdam,' John Steinbeck's 'The Long Valley.'

Grove Press -- Evergreen Books [9]

The Grove Press was started in 1949 by Robert Phelps and John Balcomb "to publish the kind of books that other publishers publish books about -- those unexpected masterpieces of the past and present that have been more read about than read, simply because they have been hitherto inaccessible to the general reader.[10] This statement shows a certain idealism and optimism towards publishing, as well as the courage to "walk where angels fear to tread," the angels being more cautious publishers. The first three titles, published in 1949 and 1950, followed this editorial policy; they were 'The Confidence Man,' by Herman Melville; 'Selected Writings of the Ingenious Mrs. Aphra Behn'; and 'Verse in English of Richard Crashaw.' These books were brought out in hardcover as well as paperback editions, the latter selling from $1.25 to $1.50. The firm was forced to close down after these first three titles. At that time, the market may not have been acclimated to this type of publication in paperback, the price was comparatively high and the distribution system inadequate. The makeup was unattractive, with undistinguished typography on plain white background.

In November, 1952, Barney Rosset took over the assets of Grove Press, maintained the original editorial policy, but limited the output to hardcover editions. He brought out fifty-eight titles, some originals, some new editions of older works, including numerous translations from the French (Simone de Beauvoir, Gerard de Nerval, Valery Larbaud, Arthur Rimbaud, Stendhal, Émile Zola). Other authors published were Samuel Beckett, Wallace Fowlie, Henry James, Ashley Montagu and Gertrude Stein. Grove Press also became the American publisher of "The International Library of Sociology and Social Reconstruction," founded by the late sociologist, Dr. Karl Mannheim. It releases for the American market art books from the National Gallery of London, the "Zodiac Library," a series of well designed reprints of the works of Jane Austen, the Brontës, Charles Dickens, William M. Thackeray, and others, as well as the publications of the University of Liverpool, entitled "Liverpool English Texts and Studies."

In 1954, the firm sold one of its publications to Anchor Books. Barney Rosset knew that most of his readers bought their books in college and regular bookstores in close proximity to campuses throughout the country. As the books are well made, attractively bound and published in editions usually not exceeding 5000, their price was comparatively high (around five dollars). It was felt that the potential market could be better exploited by publishing a new series of paperbacks, to be distributed by the same outlets as well as by strategically located drugstores. The series appears under the name of "Evergreen Books" and titles are also available in hardcover editions.

A few "Evergreen Books" were distributed for testing purposes in selected bookstores in fall, 1954, and general distribution began early in 1955. Twenty titles appeared during the first year and by the end of 1957 the series consisted of seventy-nine titles, ranging in price from $1.00 to $2.45. Initial editions usually do not exceed 5000 copies. The list consists of reprints of fiction and nonfiction works appealing to a college audience and of originals of literary value, with a decided avant-garde slant, which is also expressed in the modernistic abstract cover designs, most of which are done by Roy Kuhlman.

"Evergreen Books" of original poetry, like 'True and False Unicorn' by James Broughton and 'Meditations in an Emergency' by Frank O'Hara are unique in paperbound series. The works of Samuel Beckett ('Malone Dies,' 'Proust') are the first American editions of this writer and the 'Evergreen Review' introduces new authors and styles to the public. Bestsellers, of which over 20,000 copies have been sold, include Robert M. Lindner's 'Rebel without a Cause' and Herman Melville's 'The Confidence Man.'

Meridian Books, Inc.[11]

"Meridian Books" first appeared as the paperback series of Noonday Press in 1955. In March 1956 a separation was effected whereby the managing director of the series, Arthur Cohen, took the name "Meridian" when he started a new firm which began to issue a religious series in August 1956, "Living Age Books."[12] The "Meridian Library," a general paperback series, took over the titles formerly produced by Noonday

Press and brought out thirty-two titles in 1956 and thirty-five in 1957. Cecil Henley, formerly editor of "Meridian Books" together with Arthur Cohen, inaugurated another series, "Noonday Paperbacks," with the original firm. "Greenwich Editions," a hardcover series, was begun by Meridian Books in September 1957.

The series was originally designed by the late Alvin Lustig; covers are of dull finish, heavy paper, with sometimes striking abstract designs and colors; the books are Smythsewn, of good paperstock and are priced at $1.25 to $1.95. Titles are reprints and originals, stressing philosphy, psychology, the social sciences and literary criticism. Bestsellers have been Jacques Maritain's 'Creative Intuition in Art and Poetry,' 'Existentialism from Dostoevsky to Sartre,' edited by Walter Kaufman, and Herbert Read's 'The Philosophy of Modern Art,' all of which had sold between 30,000 and 40,000 copies by the end of 1957.

Noonday Press [13]

The Noonday Press was founded in 1951 with the editorial policy of publishing fiction and nonfiction of a high literary and scholarly level. The range of publications is rather varied, including jurisprudence, physics, history, psychology, literary criticism, poetry, and some fiction, among which there are translations of South American and Portuguese authors. Prices range from $1.25 to $100 (the latter for 'Elegy of Ihpetonga,' by Iwan Goll, with four original lithographs by Pablo Picasso), but the average book sells for three to four dollars.

The firm also was the American distributor of Schocken Books, Inc., the publishers of books on Jewish religion, philosophy, history, the Bible, literature and art; over the last forty years, Schocken Books has published about 300 titles in German and Hebrew, and since 1946 some seventy titles, primarily in English.

After the separation of "Meridian Books," "Noonday Paperbacks," were started in fall, 1955 with Machado de Assis, 'Epitaph for a Small Winner,' which had been the first successful hardcover release of the firm in 1952. By the end of 1957 twenty titles, mostly reprints of the firm's own list, had appeared, priced at $1.25 to $1.95. Essentially, make-up and editorial policy begun with "Meridian Books" have remained unchanged.

Harcourt, Brace & Company -- Harvest Books [14]

One of the most successful and widely respected American publishers today, Harcourt, Brace & Company, was started in 1919 by Alfred Harcourt and Donald Brace together with Will D. Howe. Howe transferred after one year to Scribners. Both Harcourt and Brace had worked for many years for Henry Holt and, after an unsuccessful attempt to buy that firm's general trade department, decided to found their own firm. Harcourt resigned in 1942, Brace in 1948, when Harcourt, Brace and Reynal & Hitchcock were merged.

Harcourt, Brace's paperbound series "Harvest Books" presents a distinguished list of reprints, well designed, well bound volumes with striking covers, priced at ninety-five cents to $1.45, which are sold in regular book stores. Bestselling titles have been Carl Gustav Jung, 'Modern Man in Search of a Soul,' T. S. Eliot, 'The Waste Land and other Poems,' and 'The Oedipus Cycle of Sophocles' in the English version by Dudley Fitts and Robert Fitzgerald.

New Directions -- New Directions Paperbooks [15]

James Laughlin, a Harvard graduate, started the New Directions Press in a reconverted stable in 1936 at Norfolk, Connecticut. His interest in publishing developed early in his life. He started the publication of an annual, 'New Directions Anthology,' which has continued to appear through the years. In the fall of 1955, 'New Directions 15' appeared at $3.50 in hardcovers while "Meridian Books" distributed the paperback edition at $1.35. 'New Directions 16' came out in the fall of 1957 as a "New Directions Paperbook." The firm has a list of over two hundred titles, all of literary character and promoting many new and experimental writers, and offers many significant translations of European authors.

The paperback series started in January 1956 and brought out twenty-two titles in two years, all reprints. Covers are done in black and white, using a clever and artistic arrangement of photographs which gives them a distinctive look. Prices are from ninety-five cents to $1.55. Best-selling titles have been Dylan Thomas, 'Portrait of the Artist as a Young Dog' and Federico Garcia Lorca, 'Three Tragedies.'

Grosset & Dunlap -- Universal Library [16]

Grosset & Dunlap was founded in 1898 by Alexander Grosset and George T. Dunlap and was incorporated under its present name in 1900. The firm specialized in its beginnings in "rebinds," a process which consisted in the purchase of papercover books and rebinding them in cloth. As these were a success, the firm began to reprint books from publishers' original plates and binding them in the same way and later developed its own publications, particularly in the juvenile field. In 1944 Grosset & Dunlap was sold to a group of publishers consisting of Random House, Harper, Little, Brown, Scribner and the Book-of-the-Month Club.

"Universal Library" was created in September 1956 with the intent to cover the in-between area of the inexpensive mass market titles and the more expensive series catering to specialized groups of readers. In order to reduce costs original plates, when available, are used, resulting in rather large volumes of 5 3/8" x 8" trim size. Covers are fittingly designed to distinguish them from the slick inexpensive paperbacks as well as from the austere or modernistic covers of the more sophisticated lines. They combine pictorial representations with graphic ornamentations, usually in two or three colors. The most appealing ones were designed by Cliff Condak, Irv Docktor and Edward S. Gorey. The sixteen titles released during 1956 and 1957 in editions of 10,000 copies are priced at ninety-five cents to $1.45 and include John P. Marquand, 'The Late George Apley,' Thomas Wolfe, 'You Can't Go Home Again,' Margaret Leech, 'Reveille in Washington,' 'The Shock of Recognition,' a two-volume American literary anthology edited by Edmund Wilson.

Oxford University Press -- Galaxy Books [17]

In spite of its name, Oxford University Press is a trade publisher established in New York since 1896, though it also operates as the American branch of Oxford University Press, the oldest publisher of its type in existence. Books have been published directly from New York since 1909 ('The Scofield

Reference Bible') in the fields of general serious nonfiction, college texts, children's religious, medical and reference books. These are supplemented by British imports. In 1955, Oxford University Press, Inc. organized a subsidiary, Essential Books, Inc., which publishes British books from various firms in the United States and acts as wholesaler of various British and American imprints.

"Galaxy Books," began in September 1956 to bring out reprints of titles, primarily from Oxford's backlist, which are no longer available in other editions or difficult to obtain but for which a definite demand seems to exist. First editions run from 7500 to 15,000 copies and prices are from $1.50 to $2.95. Covers are of simple, modernistic design and the series' primary markets are urban bookstores and campus communities. Ten titles had appeared by the end of 1957: the top seller was C. Wright Mills, 'White Collar.' 'English Men and Manners in the Eighteenth Century' by A. S. Turberville has nearly three hundred illustrations.

E. P. Dutton & Co. , Inc. -- Dutton Everyman Paperbacks [18]

E. P. Dutton was established in 1852 in Boston as Ide & Dutton, sellers of schoolbooks and supplies. The following year emphasis was shifted to religious items when the firm bought Charles S. Stimpson's Church Bookstore and provided books for the Episcopal Church. The first title published by Ide and Dutton was 'Lectures on Education' by Horace Mann in 1855. In 1858, Edward P. Dutton bought out Lemuel Ide and the name was changed to E. P. Dutton & Co. The concern continued to grow, and Dutton bought the Old Corner Book Store in 1865. Three years later a swap with James R. Osgood & Co. resulted in the move to New York. Dutton remained in charge until his death in 1923. The trend of publications shifted from religion to education and general literature and in 1906 the American editions of J. M. Dent's "Everyman's Library" began to be distributed by the firm.

In September 1957 the first ten titles of "Dutton Everyman Paperbacks" appeared. The books are reprints of substantial fiction and nonfiction works along the same line as Grosset & Dunlap's "Universal Library," but smaller in format and more attractively designed. Prices are from ninety-five cents to $1.95. Titles include Axel Munthe, 'The Story of San Michele,'

Marchette Chute, 'Shakespeare of London,' Van Wyck Brooks,
'The Flowering of New England,' P. A. Sorokin, 'The Crisis of
Our Age.'

Sagamore Press, Inc. -- American Century Series [19]

Sagamore Press was organized in 1956 by Russell G.
D'Oench, Jr., former California newspaper publisher, and
Robert Smith, author and founder of the Author's Book Company, as well as president of a correspondence school for
writers. The firm entered trade publishing with three titles
bound in boards: 'The Price of Courage' by Curt Anders, 'The
Seven Lively Arts,' by Gilbert Seldes, and 'The Clowns of Com-
merce' by Walter Goodman. "The American Century Series" of
paperbacks consists of twenty-six reprints of American titles of
literary or social significance, including works by Lincoln
Steffens, Booth Tarkington, Mark Twain, Oliver Wendell
Holmes, Herman Melville, Theodore Dreiser, Louisa May Alcott. Prices range from $1.25 to $1.95. Early in 1958 it was
decided to release the entire series also in clothbound format
for library use, with the bindings done by Hertzberg-New
Method Binding Company. Distribution is handled by A. C.
McClurg & Co. of Chicago.

St. Martin's Press [20]

Established in 1952 as the American branch of Macmillan
& Co., Ltd., St. Martin's Press not only imports publications
of the British parent firm but also releases books over its own
imprint. The name of the press as well as of its paperback
series "St. Martin's Library" is derived from the location of
Macmillan on St. Martin Street in London. The series, begun
in 1957, consists of reprints from Macmillan's backlist issued
in editions of 7500. Covers are uniform, representing a modernized version of a nineteenth century British design. Prices are
from ninety-five cents to $1.25 for otherwise hard to obtain
titles like 'The Savoy Operas' by Sir W. S. Gilbert, 'Rogue
Herries,' a novel by Sir Hugh Walpole, 'Far from the Madding
Crowd' by Thomas Hardy.

Paperbacks of Specialized Trade Publishers [21]

Trade book publishing encompasses so many firms that

some who also have brought out paperbacks will by necessity have been omitted. The few firms mentioned here can be considered representative of other similar ones.

Caxton Printers Ltd. in Caldwell, Idaho, was founded in 1903 and incorporated in 1907. Pamphlets were first issued in 1926. By 1957 nineteen paperback titles had been produced at irregular intervals, most of them originals. These were also issued in hard cover editions of the firm's "Libertarian Library." Three titles by Garet Garrett, 'Ex America,' 'The Revolution Was' and 'Rise of Empire,' according to the publishers "alerted our people to the dangers of the Socialist Illfare State." Stress is put on Western Americana and political titles. Prices range from twenty-five cents to $1.25.

In 1944 Wittenborn & Company, booksellers, started publishing two paperback series: "The Documents of Modern Art," edited by Robert Motherwell, and "Problems of Contemporary Art," in order to offer the art student at reasonable prices translations and domestic texts, which are either very expensive or hard to find. Original texts considered of importance by the publishers are also produced.

In 1947, the publishing activities were separated from the store and the firm became Wittenborn, Schultz, Inc. During 1953, George and Joyce Wittenborn became sole owners of the publishing organization and changed the name to George Wittenborn, Inc. Fifteen titles have appeared in both series. The format is approximately 8" x 11", covers are sophisticated in design. All books are heavily illustrated, appear in first printings of 5000 copies, and are priced from $1.75 to $6.00. Best sellers have been 'The New Vision' by Laszlo Moholy-Nagy (20,000 copies), 'Plastic Art and Pure Plastic Art' by Piet Mondrian (15,000 copies) and Herbert Read's 'The Grass Roots of Art.' While the financial returns have been small, the publishers feel that they have filled a very definite need for their limited and well informed public.

Boxwood Press was established in July 1953 and began to issue paperbacks a few months later. The firm is owned by Dr. Ralph Buchsbaum, a zoology professor at the University of Pittsburgh, who, together with Mildred Buchsbaum is the author of one of the titles, 'Basic Ecology.' Editions usually run from 500 to 2500 copies, prices from $1.50 to $2.35. All titles are originals, are scholarly in character, and are useful as college texts. While privately owned, Boxwood Press performs like a small university press.

City Lights Books was founded in 1953 by a San Francisco bookshop owner, and started its "Pocket Poets Series" in 1954. Looking more like pamphlets than regular paperbacks, they sell for seventy-five cents and offer original poetry and, as of 1958, prose, such as Kenneth Patchen's 'Memoirs of a Shy Pornographer.' Bestseller to date has been Allen Ginsberg's "Howl and Other Poems."

The Charles E. Tuttle Company traces its history to 1832 when George Albert Tuttle worked as printer and publisher of a newspaper in Vermont. After several divisions among the family, the current company was established in 1935 as an antiquarian book firm with minor publishing activities. The present owner inherited the business in 1943 and established a branch in Tokyo in 1948 which brought out publications for sale only in the Far East. Forty American and British titles were reprinted in paperback form between 1952 and 1957, among them Ruth Benedict, 'The Chrysanthemum and the Sword' and James Michener, 'Sayonara.' Since 1954 Tuttle also produces paperbacks for the American market designed to acquaint the American public with interesting aspects of Japanese life. Of the fifty-seven titles published, eleven are part of the "Library of Japanese Art," which covers important artists from the earliest times to the modern period in excellently illustrated volumes. These sell at $1.25. Other titles include such varied topics as religion, cookery, the use and theory of the abacus, Mah Jong instructions and sightseeing guides. The covers of the books are Japanese in design and especially those of the art series are outstandingly lovely and attractive. Tuttle's paperback program is unique in being devoted to the simple cause of building a bridge between two countries through books. One can only hope for its success and imitation in other parts of the world.

Hill & Wang was established in February 1956 and began to release "Dramabooks," a paperback series devoted exclusively to books on and about the theatre, including collections of plays, criticism, biographies of playwrights, and techniques of teaching dramatics. Twenty-three titles had appeared by Fall, 1957, most of them reprints, some of them, like 'Papers on Playmaking,' edited by Brander Matthews, especially prepared for the series. The titles appear in editions of 10,000 and are priced from ninety-five cents to $1.45. Some are also issued in hardbacks. Covers are attractively designed in two-color prints.

The Philosophical Library, founded in 1941 by Dagobert D. Runes, established a reputation for publishing a variety of books. During 1956 a paperback series of originals and reprints, the "Wisdom Library," was established which grew in two years to nineteen titles selling for ninety-five cents to $1.65. They offer works of the world's great thinkers, with a definite slant towards philosophy. The bestselling title to-date has been Jean-Paul Sartre's 'Existentialism and Human Emotion.' Others include Albert Einstein, 'Out of My Later Years,' Bertrand Russell, 'Understanding History,' and Leonardo da Vinci, 'The Art of Painting.'

[1] Chandler B. Grannis, ed., 'What Happens in Book Publishing' (New York: Columbia University Press, 1957).

[2] Personal interviews with George de Kay and Jason Epstein, 1954 and 1955; firm history supplied by Louise Thomas, director of promotion; correspondence and questionnaire, 1957.

[3] See Chapter 8, pp. 125-37, supra.

[4] Interviews with Richard L. Simon, Max L. Schuster and Sam Myerson, April, 1955; Lehmann-Haupt, Wroth and Silver, op.cit., pp. 343-44; "Simon, Richard L. and Schuster, Max L." in 'Current Biography,' 1941, edited by Maxine Block (New York: H. W. Wilson Co., 1941), pp. 794-97; questionnaire, 1957.

[5] Personal interview with Alfred A. Knopf, Jr., April, 1954; Geoffrey T. Hellman, "Alfred A. Knopf, Publisher," 'The New Yorker,' XXIV (November 20, 1948), pp. 44-56; (November 27, 1948), pp. 36-52; (December 4, 1948), pp. 40-52; questionnaire, 1957.

[6] Personal interview with Keith Jennison, promotion manager, March, 1955; questionnaire, 1957.

[7] Lehmann-Haupt, Wroth and Silver, op. cit., p. 300.

[8] News and Notes of Books and Bookmen,' Viking Press, company release, December 11, 1953.

[9] Personal interview with Barney Rosset, December, 1954; questionnaire, 1957.

[10] Stated by Barney Rosset, publisher and editor of Grove Press, in an interview in December, 1954.

[11] Personal interviews with Arthur Cohen and Cecil Henley, December, 1954; questionnaire, 1957.

[12] See Chapter 14, p. 241, infra.

[13] "Noonday Press, Meridian Books Separate Their Operations," 'Publishers' Weekly,' CLXIX:5 (February 4, 1956), p. 751; questionnaire, 1957.

[14] Correspondence with Edward A. Hodge, sales manager, April, 1955; Questionnaire, 1957.

[15] Questionnaire, 1957.

[16] Questionnaire, 1957.

[17] Questionnaire, 1957.

[18] Questionnaire, 1957.

[19] Promotional material.

[20] Questionnaire, 1957.

[21] Questionnaires, 1957.

CHAPTER 12

TEXTBOOK PUBLISHERS

The paperback series covered in this chapter are geared to the needs of college students, teachers and adults wanting to learn more about specific subjects. Scholarly paperbacks are generally distinguished from the mass-produced series by their physical appearance and price, and from the higher-priced, quality paperbacks of the trade publishers by the topics covered and the larger percentage of new titles. They are by and large less avant-garde and experimental than those issued by university presses. They are usually printed on good paper, frequently sewn or stapled, use non-glossy covers with rather sedate typographical designs, and appear in editions of 5,000 to 10,000 copies. Contentwise, they are fairly strong in the areas of the humanities, biography and history, but branch out into the social and occasionally the pure sciences and technology. In the latter field, they embrace a wide area ranging from occupational interests to hobbies. Titles dealing with literature are almost with exception related to class use and here reprints dominate, but introductions, explanatory notes and glossaries are usually original contributions. They are extensively used for purposes of collateral reading.

Barnes & Noble, Inc. [1]

Barnes & Noble is an organization concerned with various phases of the educational book business. The combination bookstore-publisher, which was a dominant pattern in American publishing during the eighteenth and nineteenth centuries, has almost disappeared. Barnes & Noble has continued this pattern for the last eighty years, with a fine tradition which one can sense throughout the establishment, but it has also adapted its working procedures to present-day conditions and modern technological advances, so that one is impressed with the healthy fusion of the old and the new and with the unique integration of the firm's activities. The publishing program has been worked out and is constantly being revised through the close and active cooperation of the various divisions with the responsible executives, John W. Barnes, president; Dr. Samuel Smith, editor; Mrs. Louise Hinds, production manager; and Warren Clymer, sales manager.

The First Barnes Firm

During the Civil War, Charles Montgomery Barnes, the founder of the firm whose grandson, John W. Barnes, is now president, served as a chaplain in the army of General Sherman. After the war, he continued in the ministry, but contracted an illness which affected his voice, and, unable to preach, was compelled to sell books from his very extensive personal library. This experience convinced him that the distribution of used books could be developed into a successful enterprise. In 1873, he started a jobbing business in second-hand books in Wheaton, Illinois, beginning with wholesale purchase and sale of textbooks. This venture was perhaps one of the earliest of its kind in the United States.

Charles Barnes moved from Wheaton to Chicago where he expanded by including new books and stationery. In 1894, the firm was reorganized under the name of C. M. Barnes Company to deal exclusively in schoolbooks. William R. Barnes, the founder's son, had joined the company in 1884 and soon after, his father-in-law, John W. Wilcox, also entered the business. Upon the death of the founder in 1907, the name of the firm was changed to C. M. Barnes-Wilcox Company.

The Second Barnes Firm

In 1917, William R. Barnes sold his interest in the C. M. Barnes-Wilcox Company and came to New York City where he bought a partnership in Hinds and Noble, a firm engaged in publishing and operating a book store dealing with educational books. This firm had been founded in 1883 by Arthur Hinds; C. Clifford Noble entered it in 1887 and in 1904 the firm consolidated with Eldredge & Brothers of Philadelphia. When

Barnes was taken into the partnership, Hinds left and the company's name was changed to Barnes & Noble.

In 1929, Noble sold his interest in the store to Barnes' son, John W., who had joined the firm in 1924. Thereafter, the company was under the sole direction of William R. Barnes, who died in 1945 after sixty-one years as an active bookseller. John W. Barnes has been president of the firm since 1942.

In addition to its retail business, the company specialized in providing schools, colleges and libraries with scholarly books at wholesale prices and, at the same time, developed an extensive market in second-hand books. In 1932 and again in 1941 the firm moved to larger quarters to expand its growing retail trade. The organization now consists of the following divisions:

Wholesale Division, the oldest part of the business, which buys and sells used textbooks.

Retail Division, greatly expanded in recent years, which consists of eight retail stores: five in metropolitan New York, two in Chicago, and one in Cambridge, Massachusetts.

Scholarly and Out-of-Print Books Division, which deals in current new, used, and out-of-print books.

Publishing Division, which releases educational books for students, scholars, and laymen.

Of the total operations, publishing accounts for approximately one-third of the business volume. Within the publishing division, the paperback program amounts to about 80 percent of the total turn-over.

The Publishing Division -- College Outline Series
and Everyday Handbook Series

For some years, the staff of Barnes & Noble, in close touch with the needs and buying habits of students through the retail stores, noted a brisk demand for paperbound high school review books provided in the 1930's by local New York publishers. In 1931, A. W. Littlefield, a department head of Barnes & Noble, developed the idea of a series of review books, to be written by educators, which would summarize salient points in the elementary courses of instruction offered by colleges throughout the country. At about the same time Dr. Samuel Smith, who was then a graduate student at New York University, was impressed by the notes on small cards from which one of his professors lectured. He suggested that these notes be

published as a paperbound outline of the course and assisted in
the preparation of the manuscript which was released as a
syllabus by the university. Dr. Smith proposed that similar
outlines be developed for other college courses. He attempted
to interest several publishers, but they rejected the idea.
Only Barnes & Noble decided in favor of this type of publication and later invited Smith to help Littlefield to develop
several titles for the series which soon became known as the
"College Outline Series."

By 1938 it was felt that certain subjects, if treated in a
popular style, might appeal to a wider audience of students and
laymen. This conviction led to the beginning of the "Everyday
Handbook Series" on a variety of educational topics, such as
religion, history, literature, sports, hobbies and skills. The
series cover academic, how-to- and recreational subjects.
Three types of books are included: originals, revised paperbound editions of clothbound books, and straight reprints of
hardcover editions of out-of-print titles of regular trade
publishers. The titles are issued at irregular intervals, depending on the availability of suitable materials, and range
in price from seventy-five cents to $1.95. The covers have
outline drawings appropriate to the contents.

The majority of the books in the "College Outline Series"
are designed to give the reader a survey of a subject. The
main points, as presented in the most widely used college
textbooks, are briefly summarized. Each book is an original
publication which is revised frequently and is reprinted according to demand. Two-thirds of the authors on the present
list of eighty-eight titles are full professors; twenty of them
are department heads in leading colleges or universities. Two
volumes in this series were written by Dr. John Krout, vice
president and provost of Columbia University. One of the outstanding titles is Frederic M. Wheelock's 'Latin' which introduces a new emphasis on the teaching of Latin. The best seller
of both series is 'The Atlas of Human Anatomy' by Franz
Frohse et al. which had sold over 450,000 copies by the end of
1957. The colors of the "College Outline Series" distinguish the
contents of the book and, for the past two years, have adopted
very attractive designs to replace the former plain covers.
The company credits the new style with having been instrumental in sales increases at home and particularly abroad.
Prices range from fifty cents to $2.50.

Since the beginning of both series, one hundred and fifty titles were released of which one hundred and thirty-five were in print in 1957. In addition to the paperback series, Barnes & Noble publishes clothbound books, either alone or in conjunction with British publishers. There the emphasis is on history and literature. Some of the paperbound titles are also brought out in hard covers for school and library use.

Barron's Educational Series, Inc. [2]

Manuel H. and Gloria M. Barron established in 1939 Barron's Textbook Exchange in Brooklyn, N. Y. and in January 1945 began to publish guide books, handbooks and other educational material on the secondary, high school and college level. The store was sold in 1956 and the owners continue in the publishing field where they release several paperbound series, some in pamphlet, some in paperback format. "College Reviews" is a series designed to clarify literary works for study or general reading. Each volume contains summaries, interpretations, criticisms and historical and biographical data. Representative volumes are: 'Essentials of English Literature', (2 volumes), by Bernard D. N. Grebanier, covering English literature from the beginning to the present times; 'Essentials of Contemporary Literature,' by Donald W. Heiney; 'Essentials of Greek and Roman Classics, by Meyer Reinhold. The volumes in this series sell for $1.50 to $1.85.

Barron publishes also classics of literature in translation at ninety-five cents to $1.50. Among these are Geoffrey Chaucer's 'Canterbury Tales.' 'Selected Interlinear Translation,' edited by Dr. Vincent F. Hopper of New York University, Friedrich Schiller's 'Kabale und Liebe' and 'Wilhelm Tell,' Pierre Corneille's 'Le Cid,' Miguel de Cervantes' 'Don Quijote,' and Anatole France's 'Le Livre de Mon Ami.'

The "Regents Exams and Answer Series" consists of twenty-five paperbound titles based on recent New York State Regents Examinations questions and answers, and are designed to help students in their preparation for these tests. They cover a variety of high school subjects and sell for sixty cents. The "Exam Refresher Series", which sells at seventy-five cents, consists of twenty-six titles.

'How to Prepare for College,' by Samuel Brownstein and Mitchell Weiner offers complete reviews of basic high school courses required for college entrance examinations, numerous questions and problems, and a list of American colleges and their entrance requirements. The work was originally published in cloth in 1954, later offered in paper, and has had several reprintings.

Appleton-Century-Crofts, Inc. [3]

The current publishing house of Appleton-Century-Crofts is the result of several mergers and reorganizations of a firm which had its beginnings in a small drygoods store established by Daniel Appleton in 1825 in New York City. There are no records to indicate why Appleton should have given so much space to the book section in his store, but apparently they were his main interest as he began to sell books exclusively after he moved to larger quarters in 1830. In 1831 he began to publish books of a religious nature, then added general works, particularly by British authors. In 1835, he sent his son Henry abroad to strengthen the firm's European connections and at that time arrangements were made with the great German reprinter Baron von Tauchnitz for the translation of certain German works. Tauchnitz acted as Appleton's agent in Germany. In the 1840's publication of Spanish books for South American countries was begun. This venture was very successful, with the main emphasis given to primary and secondary school texts and titles in technology and science. By mid-century, Appleton had become one of the world's largest publishers. A printing and binding plant had been added which was the first to use David McConnell Smyth's sewing machine for bookbinding purposes.

Textbook publishing had a large share in the firm's production, particularly after 1855 when Noah Webster's 'Elementary Spelling Book' was acquired. It had sold more than thirty-five million copies over the Appleton imprint by 1890. Reference works included 'Appletons' Cyclopedia of Biography.' 'The New American Cyclopedia,' and 'The American Annual Cyclopedia,' conceived as a supplement to the basic set, which appeared from 1883 to 1902.

Inclusion of works on science brought authors such as Charles Darwin, Thomas H. Huxley and Herbert Spencer under contract, and interest in the Civil War was reflected by the memoirs of General William T. Sherman and 'The Rise and

Fall of the Confederate Government' by Jefferson Davis. In spite of accomplishments in many subjects, among them successful children's books like Joel Chandler Harris' 'Uncle Remus' and Lewis Carroll's 'Alice's Adventures in Wonderland,' financial difficulties made reorganizations necessary in 1900 and 1917. In 1933 a merger with the Century Company took place. This company, originally a magazine publishing firm ('The Century Illustrated Monthly Magazine') branched out, publishing reprints of serialized novels in book form at the end of the nineteenth century and later expanding into the field of reference works and textbooks.

Early in 1948 D. Appleton-Century Company purchased the stock of F. S. Crofts, Inc. Frederick S. Crofts had been manager of the Educational Department of Century Company from 1910 to 1918, later worked for Harper and established his own company in 1924. His firm specialized in college texts, with emphasis on the teaching of English and foreign languages. Later series in American history, literature, speech, philosophy, political science and music were issued and the list further expanded by the purchase of A. A. Knopf's college texts.

"Crofts Classics" and "Current Problems in Education"

At various times Appleton engaged in inexpensive paperback publishing. The "New Handy Volume Series" appeared in the 1870's, "Appleton's Town and Country Library" began to appear monthly in 1888 in paper bindings at fifty cents and in cloth at one dollar. This series of fiction, mostly reprinted from more expensive editions, brought out a total of 312 titles which introduced a large segment of the American reading public to writers like Justin McCarthy and Joseph Conrad.

Currently, two scholarly paperback series are published. "Crofts Classics" originated in 1946 with F. S. Crofts, Inc. and offer, at a price of forty-five cents, masterpieces of world literature, each title edited by distinguished authorities, some titles newly translated. By 1947 forty-nine titles had appeared, to which only six have been added in the last ten years. The books are smaller than average (4 1/4" x 6 3/4"), covers are plain and of uniform design. They are printed on good paper and produced in editions of 7500 to 15,000 copies. Fourteen titles are Shakespearean plays and two are Bible anthologies. The others include works by Milton, Dante, Goethe, Voltaire,

Molière and Keats. The second series "Current Problems in Education" consists of originals, selling at ninety-five cents. Four titles have appeared so far.

Oceana Publications, Inc. [4]

Oceana Publications, Inc., founded in 1947 by Philip Cohen, specialized since its inception in publications for the law profession, law school teachers and students, and interested layman. The "Legal Almanac Series," started in 1947 and the "Docket Series" in 1955; both appear in paperbound format at $1.00 and clothbound at $2.00 and $3.50 respectively.

Over the last decade, the "Legal Almanac Series" brought out forty-six volumes offering information on a wide variety of legal subjects covering the following areas: Everyday Living ('How to Make a Will' and 'Law of Real Estate' by Parnell Callahan, 'Law of Insurance' by J. M. Taylor), 'Citizenship and Social Welfare ('Labor Law' by Carl Rachlin, 'How to Become a Citizen of the U. S.' by Margaret E. Hall, 'Election Laws' by Bertram M. Bernard, 'Insanity Laws' by W. R. Dittmar), and Business Law ('Debtor and Creditor' by Lawrence G. Greene, 'Law of Selling' by J. H. Hoehlein). Of this series, Irving Mandell's 'Law of Marriage and Divorce' is the best seller with over 250,000 copies.

The "Docket Series" consisted of twelve titles by December 1957. The books are anthologies of the writings of famous men on one subject or compilations of the writings of one author. They all deal with the fields of political science and law and interpret landmarks of Anglo-American legal concepts to a popular audience. Edited and compiled by experts in their respective fields, they combine primary source material with interpretative comments. The books have been widely adopted for classroom use and several titles were distributed by the U. S. Information Agency abroad. Representative titles are 'The Freedom Reader,' edited by Edwin S. Newman, a collection of materials on civil rights and civil liberties in America, 'The Medico-Legal Reader,' compiled by Samuel Polsky, the director of the Philadelphia Medico-Legal Institute and professor of law at Temple University, and "readers" on individual jurists like Holmes, Marshall, Brandeis.

Oceana publications are predominantly originals and published in editions of 10,000 copies. About six new titles are added every year. Oceana also publishes individual titles which appear in paper and hard covers, like 'The Problem Boy' by Ben Solomon, prepared for Youthleaders, Inc. and 'A United Nations Peace Force' by William R. Frye, prepared for the Carnegie Endowment of International Peace, "Docket Classics," an extension of the "Docket Series," selling at $1.25 brought out three volumes entitled 'Traditions of Freedom,' anthologies of democratic philosophers, edited by Milton Mayer for the Fund for the Republic.

Baker & Taylor handle wholesale distribution. Oceana titles make a valuable contribution to paperback publishing, particularly in the field of law.

Rinehart & Company, Inc. -- Rinehart Editions [5]

Stanley Rinehart, the president of Rinehart & Company, has had a long and distinguished publishing career. Married to the daughter of George H. Doran, he was taken into his father-in-law's firm after the end of World War I and joined the new organization formed by the merger of Doubleday and Doran in 1927. Two years later he left to establish Farrar & Rinehart with John Farrar. In 1931, they purchased the Cosmopolitan Book Corporation from the Hearst interests and in 1933 acquired the college textbook properties of Long & Smith. In 1943 the publications of Ghirardi's Radio and Technical Publishing Company were added. In this way Farrar & Rinehart became a diversified firm engaged in regular trade publishing as well as in the production and distribution of college texts and technical books.

In September, 1944, John Farrar resigned from the company and, in January, 1946, formed his own firm. In order to distinguish the two firms, Stanley Rinehart changed the name of his organization to Rinehart & Company. To the publication of two extensive series, the "Dollar Juvenile Reprints" and the "Rivers of America" series was added in 1948 a new technical line, the "Murray Hill Series on Applied Electricity." Increased attention to college texts was given through the purchase of a substantial interest in the A. S. Barnes Company in 1951. Barnes college textbooks have from then on been represented by the Rinehart college sales staff. In 1954, textbooks amounted to about one-half of the firm's business.

In the fiction field, the firm's outstanding best seller

was Hervey Allen's 'Anthony Adverse' which sold between 1933 and 1954, 1,795,987 copies in all editions and in all languages. The three volume Dell paperback edition sold 500,000 copies at seventy-five cents a set. Other best sellers include Charles Jackson, 'The Lost Weekend,' Frederic Wakeman, 'The Hucksters,' and Norman Mailer, 'The Naked and the Dead.' During 1953, the firm produced 160 new titles and more than 200 reprints.

Since 1948 the paperback series, "Rinehart Editions," has made a notable contribution to serious paperbacks for college use. In 1957 of eighty-nine titles in the field of literature, ranging in price from fifty cents to $1.65 had been widely adopted by American colleges. Each book is published with an introduction by an expert in the field and the various series are distinguished by uniformly colored paper covers: green for works of the English language, yellow for translations, and lavender for anthologies. The series is designed by Stefan Salter and its popularity undoubtedly inspired the interest of other firms in this area. Several titles were selected for American Institute of Graphic Arts awards.

Representative titles are: Herman Melville, 'Benjamin Franklin's Autobiography,' Mark Twain, 'The Adventures of Huckleberry Finn'; Walt Whitman, 'Leaves of Grass'; James Fenimore Cooper, 'The Prairie'. Many of the translations were done specifically for "Rinehart Editions" and translators receive advance payments and royalties depending on sales, giving them an arrangement similar to authors. All other titles are reprints with the exception of 'Fifteen Modern American Poets,' a collection of authors born after 1906, giving twenty pages to each poet. This volume is edited by George P. Elliott. Among best sellers are 'Moby Dick,' 'Gulliver's Travels,' 'The Rinehart Book of Verse' edited by Alan Swallow, and the two volume 'Anthology of Greek Drama,' edited by C. A. Robinson, Jr. Some of these have sold over 100,000 copies. Distribution is mainly to college and regular book stores.

Liberal Arts Press, Inc. [6]

The hallmark of the Liberal Arts Press is scholarship in titles and editorial work, simplicity and austerity of binding, and quiet efficiency of office routines. Oskar Piest, the president and sole owner of the firm, is a former accountant who has always been interested in history, philosophy, political science, comparative religion and serious literature. He publishes the books he likes to read and edit. His publishing program is based on the idea that college and university faculties are moving from the textbook method of teaching the use of original source material, that they and their students cannot afford to spend much money but appreciate good paper and expert editorial work in inexpensive bindings as well as reliable translations.

Piest had developed all these ideas, except the paperback format, by 1938 when he started to publish under the imprint Veritas Press, which operated from 1938-40. From 1940 to 1941 he brought out books under the imprint of Oskar Piest. The paper shortage and the dwindling college population during the war years forced him to abandon publishing, but he re-entered the field in 1947, when he became editor-in-chief of the "Hafner Library of Classics," a series of books published simultaneously in cloth and paper covers. By 1948, he had decided that he would like to be his own publisher, that he wanted to do not only full size but also smaller works of substantial content which he thought would be used by college faculties. He established the Liberal Arts Press in 1948, incorporated his firm in 1950 and appointed a distinguished editorial advisory board consisting of Curt J. Ducase, Clarence H. Faust, Robert M. MacIver, Roscoe Pound and Herbert W. Schneider.

The Liberal Arts Press has published one hundred and thirty titles in four series: "The Library of Liberal Arts," "The American Heritage Series," "The Library of Religion," and, ·since 1956, "Forum Books." The first three series are inexpensive paperbound student texts, designed to provide source material for use in classwork and collateral reading. "Forum Books" are reprints of political and literary classics, mostly by American authors on American themes, designed for sales in foreign countries. Seventeen books were released in this series during 1956 and 1957, which include: Thomas Paine, 'Common Sense and other Political Writings,' Benjamin Franklin, 'The Autobiography and Selections from his other Writings,' Hamilton, Madison and Jay, 'On the Constitution. Selections from the Federalist Papers' and Thomas Jefferson, 'The Political Writings."

"The American Heritage Series" is designed to show the development of American thought and the shaping of American tradition. Twenty-one titles had been published by the end of 1957. The series contains works like 'Literary Criticism in America,' edited by Albert D. Van Nostrand, Henry D. Thoreau, 'Selected Writings on Nature and Liberty,' and anthologies of short stories and various aspects of political theory. 'Alexander Hamilton. Selections Representing his Life, his Thought and his Style,' edited by Bower Aly, received an award from the Alexander Hamilton Bicentennial Commission.

"The Library of Liberal Art," contains nearly one hundred shorter classics in the fields of philosophy, religion, political science, education and literature. The books have introductions by college teachers and experts in the respective subjects. Sales possibilities are evaluated and, if minimum print orders of 5000 seem justified, the title will be adopted. Maximum first print orders go as high as 15,000. Plato's "Euthyphro, Apology, Crito, and the Death Scene from Phaedo,' Rene Descartes' 'Discourses on Method' and 'Meditations'. Immanuel Kant's 'Fundamental Principles of the Metaphysics of Morals' have sold together about 160,000 copies. The Plato title is the firm's overall bestseller.

Titles of smaller size are priced from forty to sixty cents and book-sized, Smyth-sewn editions from seventy-five cents to $1.75. Liberal Arts Press sales are primarily to college and university book stores. The four series are now established in almost eight hundred colleges and universities, without the assistance of a traveling salesman. Regular trade book stores buy copies only occasionally.

Littlefield, Adams & Company [7]

Littlefield, Adams & Company was founded in the spring of 1949 by Arthur W. Littlefield. Until then, he had been vice-president and general manager of Barnes & Noble, where he had worked for twenty-two years and had been instrumental in establishing with Dr. Samuel Smith the "College Outline Series." Littlefield was joined in the new firm by Chev Adams, president of the Collegiate Manufacturing Company, producers of specialty items for college stores, and John Korinda, former sales manager of Barnes & Noble.

About a year after Littlefield had established his firm,

the first seven titles of his "New College Outlines" had been distributed to college and university book stores and other outlets serving serious readers. The first titles were devoted to the field of business administration and accounting and also appealed to beginning businessmen. Later titles covered college freshman courses, with emphasis on the social sciences, though subjects like chemistry and mathematics were included. By 1957, the series consisted of nearly sixty titles, with twelve releases planned for 1958.

In 1952, the Company also acquired the "Students Outline Series," abbreviated to "S.O.S.", which was first published by Longmans, Green & Company in 1932. This series consists of twenty-one titles, with fifteen additional ones planned for 1958. The average retail price for both series is $1.50. All authors are specialists in their subject fields and actively engaged in teaching. Outlines are frequently revised and usually permanently retained in print. Most major college courses are now covered by the outlines.

Random House -- Modern Library, Inc. [8]

The firm of Boni & Liveright was established in 1917. One of the founders' projects was the "Modern Library," a reprint series of masterpieces of contemporary world literature, including, however, certain older works which the publishers considered of vital importance to the present generation. [9]

In 1918, Albert Boni and Horace Liveright separated, but the firm kept the name until 1928 and the "Modern Library" remained with it until 1925 when it was bought by Bennett Cerf and Donald Klopfer who did not change its plan but amplified it greatly. Of the original one-hundred and nine titles fifty-five were dropped, but by 1957 the list contained almost four-hundred. About 80 percent of these are of regular size, selling at $1.45; the rest are "Giants," averaging about 1000 pages in length and selling at $2.45.

In 1927, Cerf and Klopfer established Random House, deriving the firm's name from their intention to publish anything they liked at random. In line with these ideas Random House became the exclusive American agent for the Nonesuch Press, the British publisher of beautiful limited editions. During the depression emphasis was given to regular trade publishing which brought the plays of Eugene O'Neill and the poems of Robinson Jeffers under exclusive contract.

In 1936, Harrison Smith and Robert K. Haas, Inc. were merged with Random House and added such authors as William Faulkner, Edgar Snow and Robert Graves to the publication list. Other famous authors of the firm include James Joyce, Truman Capote, Sinclair Lewis, John O'Hara, Gertrude Stein, Adlai Stevenson, Sigmund Freud and Marcel Proust. Children's books and important plays have been continuously added to the growing list. In 1950 a new children's series, "Landmark Books," was introduced which has been distributed since 1952 by Young Readers of America, a children's book club operated by the Book-of-the-Month Club. Since 1947 when the 'American College Dictionary' was published, Random House has expanded in the reference and textbook field. Future plans include the establishment of a series in psychiatry and psychoanalysis. Modern Library, Inc. has still a separate corporate existence but is managed as a department of Random House.

Modern Library College Editions

In addition to regular "Modern Library" books and the Giants, Modern Library publishes a paperback line, "Modern Library College Editions", started in 1950. Jess M. Stein, the editor of the series, is also the head of the College and Reference Department of Random House. The series consisted of approximately sixty titles in 1957, selling for sixty and seventy-five cents. One-third of the titles were edited specifically for the paperback editions and some of these are now also available in cloth bindings.

The selection of books is based on requests from college and university faculties throughout the country. The introductions are written by outstanding teachers and critics, including David Daiches, Cambridge University; Mark Schorer, University of California; Howard Mumford Jones, Harvard University; Henry Steele Commager and Gilbert Highet, Columbia University; Max Lerner, Brandeis University; Harlan Hatcher, University of Michigan; and others of equal prominence. Many of the titles are reprints but a good percentage are collections, anthologies or translations specifically prepared for these editions. The subject areas covered are literature and drama. First printings are usually 10,000 copies.

Distribution in trade channels is handled by the Eastern News Distribution Company. No royalties are paid for college editions. Depending on the length of the book and the sales possibilities, editors receive fees ranging from $150 to $250 per book. All titles are continuously kept in print and printing orders are given for 5000 copies. The books are now "perfect bound," though they were at first sewn, and are of a simple, basically uniform design and small format (4 3/4" x 7 1/4").

Modern Library Paperbacks

A second series, "Modern Library Paperbacks," also edited by Stein, appeared in January, 1955. The titles are
. . .aimed at bringing to a wider audience the most popular titles in the regular "Modern Library" series as well as other titles from the publisher's regular trade list which have gone out of print but are still
in demand.[10]
All books have striking illustrations or attractive typographic designs on their covers, and are uniformly priced at ninety-five cents except W. Somerset Maugham's 'Of Human Bondage' which sells for $1.25. They do not compete with the "Modern Library College Editions," even though some of the titles previously appeared in that series since they are presented without introductions or comments and intended for general rather than classroom use. Titles include Dante, 'The Divine Comedy'; Plato, 'The Republic'; Feodor Dostoyevsky, 'Crime and Punishment'; Jonathan Swift, 'Gulliver's Travels'; William M. Thackeray, 'Vanity Fair'. Reprints of previous Random House titles are Truman Capote, 'Other Voices, Other Rooms'; Gertrude Stein, 'The Autobiography of Alice B. Toklas'. Best-sellers to date are 'The Hamlet and The Sound and the Fury' by William Faulkner, 'The Brothers Karamozov' by Feodor Dostoyevsky, and 'The Great Modern Short Stories,' edited by Random House's versatile president, Bennett Cerf.

Studies in Sociology

In August, 1955, Random House took over the College Textbook Department of Doubleday and incorporated fifty titles which were involved in this transfer into the operations of its own college department. Among the materials acquired were the series of "Short Studies" in sociology, political science and psychology. "Short Studies in Sociology" are now issued in regular paperback format, 4 3/8" x 7 1/4", with attractively designed covers and priced at ninety-five cents.

Doubleday's interest in textbooks dates back to the acquisition of the Blakiston Company in 1944 and seems to have diminished since the sale of that imprint to the McGraw-Hill Book Company in 1955. Frank Egner, who had come to Doubleday with Blakiston, planned a series of short studies in the social sciences. Publication began in 1954 and in 1955 three series had appeared, shortly before they were transferred to Random House. The studies were written for undergraduates and cover material for basic courses with large enrollments. The style of writing is adjusted to that level and footnotes were kept at a minimum. "Doubleday Short Studies in Sociology" included: George Simpson, 'Man in Society'; Ely S. Chinoy, 'Sociological Perspective'; Elizabeth K. Nottingham, 'Religion and Society'; Norman F. Washburne,' Interpreting Social Change in America.' Random House expanded the series to fifteen titles, including Peter M. Blau, 'Bureaucracy in Modern Society' and Gresham M. Sykes, 'Crime and Society.'

The transfer of this series from Doubleday to Random House was significant, as it demonstrated the potential of the paperback over the pamphlet format, and indicated Random House's expanding interest in scholarly publications.

Dover Publications, Inc. [11]

Founded in 1942 by its president, Hayward Cirker, Dover Publications was at first mainly engaged in the sale of books, but began to publish in 1945. From the beginning, its specialty were scientific materials. In November, 1951, Cirker decided to bring out publications in paperbacks. They are side-wire stapled and on free sheet, offering the buyer a better physical product than is usually obtainable at low prices. Cirker believes that his firm is the first American publishing house which offered high quality books for less than two dollars. By 1957, two hundred titles had been released, concentrating on the pure and physical sciences, with occasional philosophical titles, like Ernst Cassirer, 'Substance and Function' and Einstein's 'Theory of Relativity'; René Descartes, 'The Geometry -- complete French text and translation'; Einstein, Lorentz, Miskowski & Weil, 'The Principles of Relativity'; Werner Heisenberg, 'The Physical Principles of the Quantum Theory'. Even the more popular books on this list are serious, i.e., Royal V. Heath, 'Mathemagic: Magic Puzzles and Games with Numbers'. During the last two years publications in the field of the humanities and fine arts have become more numerous. Titles include George Santayana, 'The Sense of Beauty,' Franz Boas, 'Primitive Art,' Amedée Ozenfant, 'Foundations of Modern Art,' H. S. Butcher, 'Aristotle's Theory of Poetry and Fine Art.' The majority of Dover titles are issued both in cloth and paper covers, although some can be obtained only in one format or the other.

Dover also publishes the "Dover-Foyle Craft and Hobby Series" of regular pocket-sized paperbacks, priced at sixty-five cents. They contain advice on all kinds of crafts and hobbies, from bee-keeping and fencing to puppetry, the care of goldfish and parakeets, and pigeon racing and are written by leading authorities in the field, each illustrated with fifty to one hundred line drawings and photographs.

The "Say It" series, smaller than the usual paperbacks and selling for fifty or sixty cents, contains basic language instructions (approximately 1000 phrases), with each entry given in English, the foreign language and in a phonetic transcription. The series includes the following languages: French, Russian, Italian, Japanese, Spanish, German, Hebrew, Swedish and English (the latter for Spanish-speaking people). "Pronounce It Correctly" records, to be used in conjunction with the books, are also produced by the company and sell for seventy-five cents.

Dover's hardcover editions average 1500 to 3000 copies, the paperbacks 2000 to 4000, with maximum printings of 10,000. Whenever sales warrant, editions are released. Only 10 percent of the firm's output are original publications. Best sellers have sold around 20,000 copies, except for the "Say It" series, where over half a million sales were realized for some titles.

Abelard-Schuman, Ltd. -- Schuman's College Paperbacks [12]

In 1953, when the term "paperbacks" was not as widely

accepted as in 1957, and the attempt to publish paperbound books for the college market and sophisticated readers with special interests had barely started, Henry Schuman, Inc. brought out such a series at one dollar. Printed on good paper with heavy covers in black and white lettering, and stapled, the series of historical studies was announced as "being developed through the collaboration of leading British and American scholars . . ., designed to show how the history of civilization, of the arts and institutions of mankind, can help in the under-standing and solution of contemporary problems." [13] The first five titles, all about 100 pages long and containing black and white illustrations, seemed exceedingly worthwhile. They included: V. Goron Childe, 'What Is History?' Grahame Clark, 'From Savagery to Civilization'; Frank W. Walbank, 'The Decline of the Roman Empire in the West.'

During the fall of 1954, the assets of Henry Schuman, Inc. were acquired by Abelard Press, which later changed its name to Abelard-Schuman, Ltd. All titles of the "College Paperbacks" were still available in 1957 from the firm; 'Social Evolution' by V. Gordon Childe however, only in a clothbound edition. One title has been added by the new firm, 'Adlai's Almanac. The Wit and Wisdom of Stevenson of Illinois.' The books sell for $1.00 and distribution in the British Isles is handled by the British branch of the same name.

Academic Reprints [14]

Academic Reprints was organized in February, 1953, by Richard B. Fisher, who has a Ph.D. in history and taught at San Francisco State College and Stanford University, and Frank S. Morsman, Jr., with the aim of providing reissues of out-of-print books, articles and translations of foreign works in demand in colleges and universities by faculties and students. The first four publications came out in April, 1953, and were produced by photo-offset from the original editions. They included Auguste Comte, 'A General View of Positivism,' translated by J. H. Bridges (1908 ed.), $5.50; Bartolomé de las Casas, 'The Tears of the Indians,' as translated by John Phillips in 1656, $6.50; Thomas T. Meadows, 'The Chinese and Their Rebellions,' (1856 ed.), $11.00.

Starting with a capital of less than $10,000 the firm expanded considerably. Libraries, college as well as public, were its main customers, although many of their books were sold to faculty members and students as well as non-academic readers throughout the country. Business was transacted solely by mail. The board of directors consisted of five members, and had an advisory council of two librarians and eight faculty members of Stanford University. However, no official connection between the University and the firm existed.

Sixteen hardcover titles were available in the fall of 1955, mostly in the social sciences and philosophy. Paperbound volumes were first issued in November, 1953. They were designed to help Academic Reprints in the expansion of its list through publication of less expensive reprints and to make available lesser known monographs and articles to a new audience, particularly students. In May, 1955, ten pamphlets of one hundred pages or less were in print, issued in two series: "Social Science Papers" and "Natural Science Papers." They sold at seventy-five cents, were not issued in hard covers and editions were limited to three hundred copies. Henri Pirenne's 'Stages in the Social History of Capitalism' was the best seller. 'Iphigenia in Tauris,' by Johann Wolfgang von Goethe, in an English verse translation by Bayard Quincy Morgan of Stanford University, was the first of a series of translations of famous German classics which was continued under Professor Morgan's editorship by the "College Translations" of the Frederick Ungar Publishing Company.

In spring, 1955, Richard B. Fisher organized the Paper Editions Book Club as a separate business. The Club mailed out catalogs every three months, containing forty selections. Prepaid orders were sent free of handling and postage charges. Bonus books varying in price from twenty-five cents to $1.25 were given for orders from two dollars up. All titles were good selections of fiction and non-fiction issued by a variety of publishers. This seemed an interesting experiment which could have brought more quality titles to a wider group of readers and yet one could not help wondering if the combination of the paperback, an inexpensive book to be bought on the spur of the moment, and the book club idea, to select carefully from a chosen list, were not in conflict.

In March, 1956, Lewis Lengfeld, owner of several California book stores, purchased the capital stock of the Paper Editions Book Club and began to concentrate on wholesale distribution. The book club became inactive. By November,

1956, the Paper Editions Corporation, distributor of paper-backs, had established warehouses in St. Louis and New York. Fisher, the founder of Academic Reprints and the Paper Editions Book Club, gave up his enterprises to become an editor at Dell Publications.

Made Simple Books, Inc.[14]

Established in July, 1954, by Max Shapiro, its president, the series aims to provide comprehensive introductions to the standard academic subjects for the general reader without previous preparation. The first titles covered academic subjects presented by professional teachers, 'Mathematics Made Simple' by Abraham Sperling and Monroe Stuart, 'English Made Simple' by Arthur Waldhorn and Arthur Zeiger, 'Chemistry Made Simple' by Fred C. Hess. Later subjects include hobbies and topics of general interest such as chess, contract bridge, business letter writing, everyday law and well-rounded selection of academic subjects. To date twenty-five titles have appeared.

The pamphlets, size $8\frac{1}{2}$" x 11", sell for $1.00 and are also available in hard covers. Wholesale distribution is handled by Garden City Books, Inc. Covers have no drawings, are all of similar design, and give a short description of the contents.

D. Van Nostrand Co., Inc. -- Anvil Books[16]

In November, 1954, the D. Van Nostrand Company announced a new paperback series, released in January, 1955. The firm was founded 108 years ago by David Van Nostrand, a Long Islander who showed in his youth an interest in scholarly subjects. He obtained a good education and in 1826 entered the establishment of John P. Haven, bookseller and publisher. After a short and unsuccessful independent publishing experience, he moved to New Orleans where he resided until 1848. During these years he pursued studies in engineering and became closely associated with U. S. Army Engineers.

In 1848 he again opened a book selling and publishing business in New York, specializing in military, technical and scientific books; some were imported from Europe and others published by him. During and after the Civil War the demand for these books increased. Slowly the military titles were replaced by the growing demands of industry and educational institutions. The firm passed into the hands of Edward N. Crane, president from 1888 to 1911, and Charles E. Speirs, vice president from 1888 to 1928. After Edward Crane's death his younger brother, Arthur M. followed him as president until 1926, and Edward M. Crane, son of the first has been president of the company since. Family ties between the Cranes and the Du Ponts have kept the company on the alert for publications needed for industrial research. The separation of the book store from the publishing firm was delayed until 1947.

In 1937, Van Nostrand began to publish books in the social sciences, going back to the tradition originated by David Van Nostrand. At the end of World War II the firm expanded into the field of high school texts by absorbing the list of two smaller companies and also added a sports book department.

"Anvil Books," are designed as collateral reading material for college courses in history and the social sciences, in somewhat the same fashion as "Rinehart Editions" are used for English and humanities courses. All titles are uniformly priced at $1.25, have one-color, non-glossy covers without pictures and are of standard pocket-sized format. The series is edited by Louis L. Snyder, professor of history at the City College of New York, who selects the titles and wrote three of the first six published in early 1955. Professor Snyder is the author of: 'The World in the 20th Century,' 'Fifty Major Documents of the 20th Century,' and 'The Age of Reason.' Others are: 'The Making of the Modern French Mind,' by Hans Kohn, professor of history at City College of New York, and 'The Late Victorians, a Short History,' by Herman Ausuble, of Columbia. By the end of 1957 twenty-eight titles had been released. All texts are original manuscripts containing extensive bibliographies and collateral reading lists, an index and large selections of basic documents supporting the texts, the latter a novel feature which contributes to the value of this series.

Production cost is reduced by the fact that a group of six titles is printed simultaneously. Minimum runs are 15,000 copies. Distribution is handled only through trade channels to regular trade and college book outlets. The trade sales force carries "Anvil Books" along with their hardcover titles. Best-sellers to date are: Walter A. Agard, 'The Greek Mind,' Sidney Hook, 'Marx and the Marxists' and Richard B. Morris, 'The American Revolution.'

Henry Regnery Company -- Gateway Editions [17]

Henry Regnery Company, which originally produced the "Great Books" series in cooperation with the Great Books Foundation, entered the paperback field in the summer of 1955, with "Gateway Editions." The books consisted at first of reprints of the most popular titles of the "Great Books," with added introductions by well-known scholars. During 1955 twenty-three titles appeared and in the following two years eleven more were added, dealing with a variety of serious and scholarly topics, frequently in translations. Prices range from sixty-five cents to $1.35 and books are distributed through regular and college bookstores. The first eleven titles, released in August, 1955, included the following: Edmund Burke, 'Reflections on the Revolution in France'; Sigmund Freud, 'The Origin and Development of Psychoanalysis,' Thomas Hobbes, 'Leviathan' (with an introduction by Russell Kirk); Niccolo Machiavelli, "The Ruler: A Modern Translation of Il Principe'; Karl Marx, 'Communist Manifesto'; Friedrich W. Nietzsche, 'Beyond Good and Evil' (translated and with an introduction by Marianne Cowan).

Frederick Ungar Publishing Co. -- College Translations [18]

This New York publishing firm, which specializes in reprints of foreign books and translations, started a paperback series, "College Translations," in 1955. Titles issued were translations of German works, including: Gotthold E. Lessing, 'Nathan, the Wise,' Johann W. von Goethe, 'The Sufferings of Young Werther,' Erich Kästner, 'A Salzburg Comedy.' The series is under the general editorship of Bayard Quincy Morgan of Stanford University.

Houghton Mifflin Company -- Riverside Editions [19]

The annals of Houghton Mifflin form an integral part of America's nineteenth century publishing history. The first beginnings trace back to the Old Corner Bookshop in Boston, owned by John Allen and William B. Ticknor in 1832. Actual publishing was started in 1852 when Henry Oscar Houghton founded H. O. Houghton & Co. and the Riverside Press in

Cambridge, Massachusetts. In 1864 Houghton went into partnership with M. M. Hurd (Hurd & Houghton); they were joined in 1872 by George H. Mifflin. A merger with James R. Osgood & Co. resulted in a change of name to Houghton, Osgood & Co. and upon Osgood's retirement in 1880, to Houghton, Mifflin & Co.

To describe the literary and educational accomplishments of a company over the years would require the writing of a cultural history of American publishing. The firm publishes a long list of distinguished titles in general literature, fiction, biography, juvenile and textbooks. Books are produced by the Riverside Press.

The firm has issued paperbounds in the past, among them "Riverside Literature Series." Their current "Riverside Editions," was inaugurated in March 1956 and by the end of 1957 consisted of nineteen titles. Publishing plans call for ten to twelve new titles annually, appearing in average first printings of 10,000 copies. The series is under the general editorship of Gordon N. Ray, of the University of Illinois, and presents American, British and Continental classics, edited and annotated by scholars and critics primarily for college use. Prices run from sixty-five cents to $1.45, and the books are sold chiefly through college books stores. The simple one-color typographical series cover design is maintained for all books with varying colors. Typical works are Jane Austen, 'Pride and Prejudice,' edited by Mark Schorer, Henry James, 'The Portrait of a Lady,' edited by Leon Edel, 'Poems of Robert Browning,' edited by Donald Smalley, Thomas Hardy, 'Far from the Madding Crowd,' edited by Richard L. Purdy.

Charles Scribner's Sons [20]

Charles Scribner's began operations in the basement of the Old Brick Church in New York City in 1846 when Charles Scribner joined Isaac Baker in the establishment of a publishing house. Baker died in 1850 and except for a temporary association with Andrew C. Armstrong and Edward Seymour the firm remained primarily a family enterprise. It was incorporated in 1904. Importation and sale of books was handled by a separate organization, Scribner, Welford & Co. In addition to book publishing the firm also brought out magazines. Scribner's Magazine enjoyed great popularity from 1886 to 1939.

Scribner's long history has produced many outstanding works in various fields of publishing and the author list includes Robert Louis Stevenson, John Galsworthy, F. Scott Fitzgerald and Ernest Hemingway.

Scribner's has released paperbound books occasionally, in the past. The current group of paperbacks which has no series name but is referred to on the cover as "Student's Edition" is intended primarily for the textbook market. They are published whenever a demand exists and are distributed exclusively to colleges and college book stores. By the end of 1957 thirteen titles had been released which were predominantly reissues or new editions of hardcover releases of the firm. Prices range from ninety-five cents to $3.00, nearly half of the titles being priced at $2.00 or higher. The basic cover design is a textured pattern of grey with a two color label for author and title. The colored panel on which the title appears changes from book to book. Titles include original novels, such as Ernest Hemingway 'The Sun also Rises,' anthologies, texts and guides.

[1] Personal interviews with John W. Barnes, Samuel Smith and J. Warren Clymer, March, 1955; correspondence with Samuel Smith, 1955 and 1957.

[2] Correspondence with Gloria Barron, 1955; questionnaire, 1957.

[3] Questionnaire, 1957; Samuel C. Chew, ed., 'Fruit Among the Leaves' (New York: Appleton-Century-Crofts, Inc., 1950).

[4] Questionnaire, 1957.

[5] Personal interview with Ronald Hobbs, April 1955; correspondence, 1957; John T. Winterich, "Rinehart Celebrates on September 3 Its 25th Anniversary," 'Publishers' Weekly,' CLXVI:10 (September 4, 1954), p. 829.

[6] Personal interview with Oskar Piest, spring, 1955; correspondence, 1957.

[7] Correspondence with John Korinda, April, 1955, and A. W. Littlefield, December, 1957.

[8] Personal interview with Jess Stein, April, 1954; correspondence with Jess Stein, 1955 and 1957.

[9] Lehmann-Haupt, Wroth and Silver, op. cit., p. 339.

[10] "Random House Launches Modern Library Paperbacks," 'Publishers' Weekly,' CLXVII:8 (February 19, 1955), p. 1204.

[11] Personal interview with Hayward Cirker, May, 1955; "This Month in Book Making," 'Publishers' Weekly,' CLXII:18 (November 1, 1952), p. 1899; correspondence with Hayward Cirker, 1955 and 1957.

[12] Telephone conversation with Florence Barber, May, 1955. Correspondence, 1957.

[13] Quoted from back cover of "Schuman's College Paperbacks."

[14] Correspondence with Richard B. Fisher, 1955; "Available Reprints," 'Newsweek,' XLII (July 27, 1953), p. 74; Ben R. Redman, "A Quartet of Revivals," 'Saturday Review,' XXXVI (November 21, 1953), p. 55; "Lengfeld Buys Interest in Paper Editions Book Club," 'Publishers' Weekly,' CLXIX: 11 (March 17, 1956), pp. 1406-07.

[15] Questionnaire, 1957.

[16] Personal interview with Edward M. Crane, Jr., January, 1955; 'A Century of Book Publishing, 1848-1948' (New York: D. Van Nostrand Co., 1948); questionnaire, 1957.

[17] "Gateway Editions," 'Publishers' Weekly,' CLXVII:25 (June 18, 1955), pp. 2800-01; questionnaire, 1957.

[18] Frederick Ungar's "Paperback Series for College Market," 'Publishers' Weekly,' CLXIX:7 (February 18, 1956), pp. 1041-42. No additional information received.

[19] Questionnaire, 1957.

[20] Questionnaire, 1957; Roger Burlingame, 'Of Making Many Books' (New York: Charles Scribner's Sons, 1946).

CHAPTER 13

PAPERBACKS OF UNIVERSITY PRESSES

American University Presses

Great Britain served as an example in America in a field of publishing which has no parallel outside the Anglo-Saxon world. University presses, originally established in 1478 in Oxford and in 1521 in Cambridge, have maintained a continuous record of religious, scholarly, and later serious popular publishing since the 1580's. American university press publishing did not come into existence until the end of the nineteenth century. The first beginnings at Cornell (1869) and the University of Pennsylvania (1870) were of short duration.

Harvard University Press started operations as a printing office which was created in 1871, but no general publishing was accomplished before 1896. Johns Hopkins University Press, founded in 1878, issued its first book in 1887 and is generally considered the oldest American establishment of its kind. During 1878-79 it began the successful release of two scholarly journals. The University of Chicago Press entered its career in 1892 through a private corporation owned jointly with the D. C. Heath Company; two years later it became a division of the University. Columbia University Press dates back to 1893.

The influences which led to these expanding publishing activities on university campuses were "the secularization of American education, the university extension movement . . . and the Americanization of letters and of scientific inquiry." [1] Over the last seventy years, the number of presses has increased to over forty, which are presently producing from eight to nine hundred titles a year. [2] They are engaged in nonprofit publishing, a function which they perform as a division of their parent institution. They produce scholarly books, journals, pamphlets, and, since 1955, paperbacks for scholars and serious readers. Occasionally, they bring out trade, reference and textbooks for the college community and books of regional interest. The latter materials are usually bypassed by commercial publishers, most of whom are segregated in and around New York City, Boston and Chicago. Outwardly, books of university presses do not differ greatly from general trade books except that they were, until recently, somewhat duller in appearance. During the last decade significant strides have been made in improving typography, book design and layout.

University Presses in the Paperback Field [3]

When confronted with shorter manuscripts and doctoral dissertations university presses have always used paperbound editions which they released in academic monograph series. Covered in drab colored papers without illustrations, sewn or sidestapled and usually measuring 6" x 9" or $5\frac{1}{2}$" x 8", they were actually pamphlets or brochures rather than books. The interest of university presses in paperbacks was undoubtedly aroused by the higher-priced commercially produced series which found widespread acceptance on university campuses. As many commercial publishers acquired reprint rights for their paperback series from university presses, the thought to participate in this newly found source of revenue became obvious. University presses are now making greater strides than ever to increase their sales because income derived from this source decreased between 1948 and 1955 from 84.1 percent to 70.7 percent due to greater costs of manufacture, shipping and related items in spite of the growth of the dollar sales volume by 73 percent or nearly three million dollars. [4]

Conditions of the foreign market also indicated additional possibilities for paperbacks of American university presses. The '1956 Annual Survey of the General Book Publishing Industry' shows that all U. S. books sold abroad amounted to 4.6 percent of total gross sales but 11.1 percent of university press sales in 1954. By 1956 this percentage had increased to 12.2 [5] Shortage of our currency eliminates the lighter works of fiction but the serious and scholarly book at a lower price is becoming increasingly attractive abroad. 'The Saturday Review' summarized this situation in the editorial introduction of its 1957 University Press issue, with the comment that university presses ". . . through paperback editions . . . are making the fruits of scholarship available at popular prices."[6]

The distribution, pricing and size of these editions is somewhat different from the higher-priced commercially produced series like "Anchor" and "Vintage" books and from other scholarly paperbacks. Since the sales force and advertising budget are usually small and the potential audience as well as the outlets carrying the presses' products restricted, editions are smaller than those of the other series, reaching usually less than 5000 copies. Prices are accordingly somewhat higher, running on the average from $1.25 to $2.00. Mail order distribution and advertising by means of circulars is more common than with other publishers.

Since paperbacks were introduced in 1955, their sales have increased at a faster rate than the presses' total sales. By the fall of 1957, six university presses were publishing paperbacks which showed the following characteristics: scholarly materials, appearing under a series name, offering full length books in attractive format at cheaper than clothbound prices. They are nearly always sewn and usually have colorful, attractive, and rather sophisticated covers. As to content, they seem to reflect the general trend of their presses: 78 percent in the humanities and social sciences, only 15 percent in the biological and physical sciences, less than 6 percent textbooks and about 2 percent fiction, verse and drama. [7] The lack of titles in science is also apparent in trade released paperbacks and an extension into this area may open up new possibilities of sales at home and abroad.

In addition to the six established series described below, Yale University and the Bureau of Publications of Teachers College, Columbia University, are experimenting with the paperback format. Yale issued during 1957 twelve titles of the "Yale Shakespeare" at seventy-five cents, in printings of 10,000 copies. The Bureau of Publications released the first volume of a projected series "Classics in Education." This collection of extracts from the annual reports of the Horace Mann School was compiled and edited by Lawrence A. Cremin, the general editor of the series, and is entitled 'The Republic and The School: Horace Mann on the Education of Free Men' ($1.50). Future titles will deal with various aspects of education and for the most part authors will be faculty members of Teachers College.[8]

The University of Pittsburgh Press released two titles in a series of "Critical Essays in English and American Literature." The manuscripts will be original scholarly criticisms. The size of the books is 6" x 9"; they are priced at $1.50 and $1.80. During the 1957 meeting of the Association of American University Presses the University of Oklahoma and Princeton University announced their interest in entering the paperback field but had not definitely decided on a publishing program.

If the paperbacks of university presses establish themselves successfully on the competitive market, these institutions may eventually no longer fit Chester Kerr's castigating characterization that they are "this foolhardy branch of publishing which produces the smallest editions at the greatest cost and sells them at the highest prices to people who can least afford them."[9]

Cornell University Press -- Great Seal Books

Cornell, one of the pioneers of university press publishing, was also the first to bring out a paperback series in 1955. "Great Seal Books" originated through the demand of faculty members who suggested the reissue of a number of out-of-print titles. The first one, Henry Adams' 'The United States in 1800,' was released in September 1955 and had sold over 9000 copies by June 1957. To date, thirteen titles have come off the press and production schedules call for from two to six additional titles per year. Editions are usually 5000 copies and best-sellers include Edward S. Corwin's 'The "Higher Law" Background of American Constitutional Law' and Karl Von Frisch's 'Bees: Their Vision, Chemical Senses, and Language.' The books sell at prices from 95 cents to $1.75, are somewhat larger than "Anchor" and smaller than "Beacon" books, and very conservative in make-up.

Indiana University Press -- Midland Books

Established in 1951, Indiana University Press was the first to release a paperbound edition with an attractive cover design, 'Ovid's Metamorphoses' in an outstanding translation by Rolfe Humphries, which was published in 1955. The success of this book stimulated the establishment of a paperback series, "Midland Books," in spring, 1957. To date, six titles have been produced, ranging in price from $1.25 to $1.75. Plans call for eight titles a year, selected on the basis of their suitability as supplementary texts for college courses. Subject areas are mainly literature, history and the arts; so far they include 'Ovid's The Art of Love,' also translated by Rolfe Humphries, and Mark Spilka's 'The Love Ethic of D. H. Lawrence.' The covers are attractively designed and the books widely advertised and reviewed. Most titles are also available in hard covers. Overseas distribution is carried out by W. S. Hall in Europe and different agents in Great Britain and Canada.

The University of Chicago Press -- Phoenix Books

The University of Chicago Press is one of the oldest and largest in the country. It produced fifty-nine titles in 1956 (ranging fourth after Harvard, Columbia and California) and operates in many ways more like a trade publisher than a university press. In 1956, "Phoenix Books" were started as a paperback reprint series of the press's own publications, on the assumption that the paperback market for a scholarly book is about five times that of its hardcover edition. The choice of titles, cover designs and promotion was so successful that twenty-two titles in editions running from 5000 to 7500 copies had been brought out by fall, 1957. Several titles are in their second and third printing. (Plate 13)

Ranging in price from $1.00 to $1.95 "Phoenix Books", designed by the press' typographer Greer Allen and his wife, Sue, have the most striking covers of any of the university press series. Their format is 5 1/4" x 8". They are printed on good paper, sewn, and have fairly heavy, flexible covers, and good illustrations. Exports are handled through Cambridge University Press, W. S. Hall, Feffer & Simons and the University of Toronto Press. Bestsellers are Edward Chiera's 'They Wrote on Clay,' John A. Wilson's 'The Culture of Ancient Egypt' and Gilbert Murray's 'The Literature of Ancient Greece,' all of which had sold over 10,000 copies by fall, 1957. The series includes Friedrich A. Hayek's 'The Road to Serfdom,' four volumes of selections from the writings of philosophers from ancient Greece to Kant, edited by T. V. Smith and Marjorie Green, 'Man and the State' by Jacques Maritain and other important works in the humanities and social sciences. Most of them are still available in hard covers.

The University of Chicago also publishes two other paperback series: "Complete Greek Tragedies," of which seven titles are in print, and the "Chicago History of American Civilization" with six titles. Neither of these series compare in scope or physical appearance with "Phoenix Books."

University of Michigan Press -- Ann Arbor Paperbacks

Operating since 1931, Michigan has been devoted to the production of significant scholarly publications. During the last few years the dynamic directorship of Fred Wieck saw a rapid expansion of titles. The creation of "Ann Arbor Paperbacks" was motivated by the desire "to solve a special and acute problem -- how to make the bookstores aware of Michigan's trade books."[10]

Books sell from $1.25 to $1.95 and a discount of 40 percent is granted but the press refuses to fill orders for fewer than ten copies. Initial printings range from 5,000 to 10,000 copies. All titles are reprints and more than half of the first thirteen are English copyrights and not for sale in the British Commonwealth. Titles include Alfred North Whitehead, 'The Concept of Nature,' George Santayana, "Dialogues in Limbo,' Allen Tate, 'Stonewall Jackson,' George Frisbie Whicher, 'This Was a Poet: Emily Dickinson.'

The format is comparable to "Phoenix Books." The art work of George Lenox and Ron Stachoviak is rather attractive but somewhat loud and does not compare to the work done at California and Chicago. The Press's self-imposed limitations to sales at home and partly abroad may encounter difficulties particularly for larger editions.

University of California Press

The press has been in existence since 1893 though publishing had been started through a printing office in 1877. A paperback series, which was not given a special name, was started in September 1956 because "it seemed that publishers of quality paperbacks had jumped right into the university press market . . ."[11] It was also felt that paperbacks would help its other trade books in bookstore sales. The first group published consisted of five titles, the second, released in September 1957, of six. Initial printings were for 4000 to 6000 copies and reprints had to be made after six months. Of the eleven titles released and the six planned for spring, of 1958, eight are originals, nine reprints. Noteworthy books include 'Two Novels of Mexico: The Flies and The Bosses' by Mariano Azuela, translated by Lesley Bird Simpson, 'Rilke: Selected Poems,' with English translations by C. F. MacIntyre, 'Culture, Language and Personality,' selected essays by Edward Sapir.

California does not intend to reprint originals of other presses but plans to re-issue suitable materials of its own imprint as well as new books. Prices are from $1.25 to $1.50 and the size is 4 5/6" x 7 1/4", identical with Knopf's "Vintage Books." To keep the price low they are, whenever possible, produced by photo offset; the books are Smyth-sewn. The art work, done by the staff, is simple and attractive, generally using two and three colors for typographical ornamentation and some design. Overseas distribution is handled by the same firms as those employed by the University of Chicago. Paper Editions Corporation handles the wholesale distribution.

Wayne State University Press -- Wayne State University Studies

Established in 1941 the press released over seventy titles in fifteen years; nearly half of these appeared in brochure or pamphlet format. Due to increased financial support from the university and an enlarged staff, since 1956 the press has engaged in an expanding publications program which includes in addition to books and pamphlets three new quarterlies and a scholarly paperback series, "Wayne State University Studies." Begun in March, 1957 the series will present publications of original research in various disciplines, scholarly in content but sufficiently broad in scope to attract the interest of students, teachers and general readers. The first two titles were 'Ballot Position and Voter's Choice' by Henry M. Bain and Donald S. Hecock and 'Political Party Patterns in Michigan' by Stephen B. and Vera H. Sarasohn, selling at $1.95 and $1.75. They are produced by IBM composition, sewn, and have attractively designed three-color print covers. They are distributed abroad by W. S. Hall and Feffer & Simons. Spring

1958 releases will include 'Reviews in Library Book Selection' by LeRoy C. Merritt, Martha T. Boaz and Kenneth S. Tisdel, with a foreword by Maurice F. Tauber, which was compiled by the author of this study.

[1] Chester Kerr, 'A Report on American University Presses' (The Association of American University Presses, 1949), p. 16.

[2] Leon E. Seltzer, "University Presses," in Chandler B. Grannis, ed. 'What Happens in Book Publishing' (New York: Columbia University Press, 1957), pp. 359-60.

[3] Questionnaires, 1957.

[4] "Chester Kerr Reports on University Press Publishing 1955," 'Publishers' Weekly,' CLIX:25 (June 25, 1956), p. 2734.

[5] '1956 Annual Survey of the General Book Publishing Industry' (New York: American Book Publishers Council, Inc., 1957), Table 1, p. 3.

[6] Herbert S. Bailey, Jr., "How to be Literate in a Scientific Age," 'The Saturday Review,' XL:18 (May 4, 1957), p. 13.

[7] Chester Kerr, "A Seven-Year Look," 'Saturday Review,' XXXIX:20 (May 19, 1956), p. 23.

[8] Letter from M. E. Brunstetter, Bureau of Publications, September 17, 1957.

[9] Seltzer, op. cit., p. 369, quoting Chester Kerr.

[10] "University Press Aims and Methods Examined at Annual Meeting," 'Publishers' Weekly,' CLXXI:22 (June 3, 1957), p. 22.

[11] Ibid.

CHAPTER 14

RELIGIOUS PAPERBACKS

In 1957, one out of every thirteen titles published in the United States dealt with some aspect of religion. The wide-spread interest in this topic, its pervasiveness into all phases of human life, the traditional non-interference by the state, and the great variety of faiths and sects give religious publishing a more heterogenous pattern than any other segment of the industry.

Among earliest American publications religious titles played a dominant role. In order to reach the largest possible group of readers, to keep established congregations unified and to recruit new members, churches have always made use of inexpensive formats. Religious tracts and pamphlets are still in use (i.e. "Pendle Hill Pamphlets") but since 1950 the new paperback format has been increasingly adopted by parochial publishers of various denominations and commercial publishers. Among the latter three groups can be distinguished: those who publish religious materials exclusively, such as P. J. Kenedy & Sons and Jewish Pocket Books; those who devote a series to religious publications, as Doubleday's "Image" and Harper's "Torchbook" series; and finally those who release occasional religious titles in their otherwise secular series, which is done by many trade and paperback publishers.

New American Library publishes the "Mentor Religious Classics", which offer titles dealing with the non-Judeo-Christian religions such as 'The Meaning of the Glorious Koran' by Marmaduke Pickthall, and 'The Song of God; Bhagavad-Gita' by Christopher Isherwood and Swami Prabhavananda, as well as 'The Holy Bible in Brief,' edited by James Reeves and 'The Papal Encyclicals in Their Historical Context,' edited by Anne Fremantle. The Liberal Arts Press series, "Library of Religion," offers titles on ancient and Eastern religions such as Francis R. Walton, 'Ancient Greek Religions;' Frederick C. Grant, 'Ancient Roman Religions;' and Arthur Jeffery, 'Islam, Muhammad and His Faith,' as well as works on Judaism, Protestantism and Catholicism such as 'Judaism: Postbiblical and Talmudic Period,' Salo W. Baron and Joseph L. Blau, eds.; John Calvin, 'On God and Political Duty;' and St. Thomas Aquinas, 'On the Freedom of Choice.'

The first three exclusively denominational series in modern format, devoted to the Catholic faith, appeared between 1950 and 1954 ("Lumen Books," "Catholic Home Library," and "Image Books.") During 1955 to 1957 several Protestant denominational and non-denominational series and one small Jewish series were added, offering a wide variety of religious topics. The growth of the subject area is best demonstrated by the fact that the selective subject index of 'Paperbound Books in Print' of Summer 1955 lists seventy-two titles under "Religion" while the Fall-Winter 1957 issue offers 174 titles under the same heading.

P. J. Kenedy & Sons [1]

John Kenedy, an Irish immigrant, founded a small book selling business in 1826 and began publishing after his move to New York City in 1836. He served the Irish Catholic population, issuing catechisms, prayer books and devotional works and selling religious goods. The firm's name changed in 1865 to John Kenedy & Sons and was incorporated in 1904 as P. J. Kenedy & Sons. Specializing at first in works of Catholic authors who had difficulties in getting secular houses to publish their work, Kenedy concentrated later more on purely religious topics and today represents the oldest existing firm of its kind in the United States. When the John J. Murphy Co. ceased operations in 1943 its list was taken over by P. J. Kenedy. One of the titles, James Cardinal Gibbons' 'The Faith of Our Fathers,' sold three million copies and is now obtainable in paperbacks at one dollar.

The firm released books in paper covers as early as 1832. The present paperbacks are issued as needed and do not have a series name. Most titles are original publications covering mainly the field of Catholic apologetics, such as John L. Stoddard, 'Rebuilding a Lost Faith,' Fulton J. Sheen, 'Preface to Religion,' Paul Bussard and Felix Kirsch, 'The Meaning of the Mass.' The books are uniformly priced at one dollar and are sold through religious and general stores and distributed through Campbell & Hall, Baker & Taylor and A. C. McClurg & Co. The size of editions is usually 20,000 copies.

J. S. Paluch Co. , Inc. -- Lumen Books [2]

The J. S. Paluch Company was founded in 1923 and since then has been devoted to printing and publishing for the Catholic faith. In addition to its special publications, the company syndicates two church bulletins from coast to coast. One of these, 'Catholic View,' may be obtained under different mastheads as parish bulletins. In a circular to priests about 'Catholic View,' the firm stated:

> We do not believe folk will hold still these days for lengthy, scholarly instruction; but we know from experience that it's possible to teach a great deal of Catholicism pleasantly and painlessly -- without the subject realizing what's going on. We're turning this trick by means of Catholic View, the sprightliest and most entertaining Sunday bulletin.

The combination of Catholicism with mass appeal is carried over into the paperback field. The company issues devotional booklets and other pamphlets and in 1950 came out with "Lumen Books," the first Catholic popular paperback series. Since then, some forty titles have appeared; some were soon out-of-print, others became perennial favorites.

The standard price for "Lumen Books" is fifty cents. The following titles are prominently advertised: 'The Least of the Brethren,' by Harold Heagney; 'In Garments All Red,' by Godfrey Peage; 'Come With Me to Mass,' by James V. Linden, S. J.; 'So Gentle His Hand,' by L. C. Lovasik, S.V.D.; 'Give Me Souls,' by Lady Mary E. Herbert. "Two great books for converts," to quote the advertisement, "are 'On the Way Back Home,' by James V. Linden, and 'From One Convert to Another,' by John M. Ruach, C.S.P." There also exists a series of smaller paperbacks, "Lumen-ettes," which sell for twenty-five cents a copy.

Catechetical Guild Educational Society [3]

The Catechetical Guild is a non-profit educational organization within the Catholic Church recognized as a tax-exempt society by the Department of Internal Revenue. The purpose of the society is explained by Father Robert Edman, vice president of the Guild, in the following manner: "To teach to all ages and to all channels of communication the philosophical and religious implications of man's origin, nature and destiny, to help all ages grow in knowledge and love of God and their fellow man for God's sake and their own salvation." [4] The Guild has been in existence since 1932 and its success has been in adapting the formats used by the secular publishers to the teaching of religion. There are comparatively few full-length books. Materials stressed are children's books, first colorbooks, comics, and a large number of visual aids, flash cards, symbol sets, filmstrips, religious jig-saw puzzles and activity books. The Guild provides pamphlets for adults at ten and twenty cents, and the "Guild Family Readers" at fifteen cents, which contain titles like 'Crisis in History' by Bishop Fulton J. Sheen and 'The Christmas Story' by Fulton Oursler. It is estimated that 500 million items had been distributed by the Guild by 1955, with the number of titles running to about 700.

The paperback series, "Catholic Home Library," is an extension of the Guild's policy. It started in February, 1954, with six titles priced at fifty cents among them 'The Life of Christ' by Abbé Constant Fouard, a reference for study group and class use which has sold over 200,000 copies; 'The Concise Catholic Dictionary,' completely new, 1900 words; 'The New Testament,' authorized translation, 465,000 copies sold by fall, 1957; 'This is the Faith' by Reverend Francis J. Ripley, basic church doctrines, 200,000 copies sold.

Most titles are also available in clothbound editions. Many titles are reprints, others are written on assignment. The books measure 4 1/4" x 6 1/2" and the covers of two recently published anthologies, 'The Church and Its People' and 'The Church in the World,' designed by Kenneth Knack, compare favorably with the more attractive, commercially produced covers. Initial printings are usually around 100,000 copies. Distribution is primarily to established Catholic outlets and church goods dealers, but also to secular book stores and department stores. There is no distribution to newsstands. Exports are handled by Henry M. Snyder Co.

Doubleday & Company -- Image Books [5]

"Image Books," published by a division of Doubleday, is a series of Catholic writings including works on Catholic literature, history and doctrine.

The series was started in the fall, 1954, and is edited by John J. Delaney, who is assisted by the editorial guidance of Etienne Gilson, director of studies in the Pontifical Institute of Medieval Studies in Toronto, and Anton C. Pegis, president of the same institution. The reason for choosing Catholics as the first group to be reached with a paperback line devoted exclusively to titles of interest to them was based on Doubleday's recognition that this defined segment of the population has book needs peculiar to it. Doubleday has not closed the door on a possible expansion of religious series to serve other faiths.

"Image Books" sell from sixty-five cents to $1.25, and are similar in make-up and format to "Anchor Books." They are produced on the same presses as the other Doubleday paperback lines.

The first eight titles consisted of six reprints and two volumes specially edited for the series, such as William Thomas Walsh, 'Our Lady of Fatima;' Karl Adam, 'The Spirit of Catholicism;' John Farrow, 'Damien the Leper;' Philip Hughes, 'Popular History of the Catholic Church.' These were followed by biographies of famous Catholics, stories of miracles, Joyce Kilmer's 'Anthology of Catholic Poets;' Fulton J. Sheen's 'Lift up Your Heart,' and other inspirational messages and novels. By the end of 1957, fifty-nine titles had been published. Bestsellers are Philip Hughes' 'Popular History of the Catholic Church' (150,000 copies) and Henry V. Sattlers' 'Parents, Children and the Facts of Life' (125,000 copies).

Advertising is done on a large scale. Circulars in quantities of about one-quarter million copies are sent out to all important Catholic outlets with each new group of titles. Year-round advertising is carried in Catholic and secular publications.

Beacon Press [6]

The Unitarians have always relied on books and pamphlets to spread their faith, which they often were not allowed to preach or practice. In the United States, the Unitarian Tract and Book Society was founded in 1821 in Charleston, South Carolina, followed by the Baltimore Unitarian Book Society shortly thereafter. In 1825 the American Unitarian Association was formed, which proposed "to publish and distribute books and tracts inculcating correct views of religion in such a form and at such a price as shall afford all an opportunity of becoming acquainted with Christian truth." [7] At first, the Association mainly published tracts, but in 1854, with the organization of the Book Fund Project, the first book bearing officially the imprint of the American Unitarian Association was published, 'Grains of Gold; or Select Thoughts on Sacred Themes,' by the Rev. Cyrus A. Bartol, Jr. In 1902, the new imprint of the Beacon Press came into use.

Since the 1940's, Beacon Press has opened its facilities to authors who are not necessarily Unitarians but who write on topics in which Unitarianism is interested and are proponents of liberal religious and philosophical thought, such as Albert Schweitzer, Arnold J. Toynbee, P. A. Sorokin, and Gilbert Murray. Starr King Press, a subsidiary, specializes in religious publications of more denominational character. The Beacon list contains well over two hundred titles by distinguished authors, including Paul Blanshard's 'American Freedom and Catholic Power,' of which 240,000 copies were sold in the first edition. A revised edition appeared in spring, 1958, ten years after the original publication.

"Beacon's Paperbacks" were started in 1955 and fifty-two titles have been published since then. The books are large (5 3/8" x 8"), printed on heavy paper, sewn, and have stiff paper covers of sophisticated design. They are priced from $1.25 to $1.95 and were the pioneers of full library-size quality paperbacks, influencing other similar series like Grosset & Dunlap's "Universal Library." Twenty titles are to be added annually and original printings are 10,000 copies. Among the first six titles published in April, 1955, were: Albert Schweitzer, 'An Anthology;' William K. C. Guthrie, 'The Greeks and Their Gods;' George Orwell, 'Homage to Catalonia;' Bertram D. Wolfe, 'Three Who Made a Revolution.'

Of these, the Schweitzer anthology sold 34,000 copies and Wolfe 21,000 copies. All titles are reprints of significant works for scholars and serious readers. Other titles include Sigmund Freud, 'Delusion and Dream,' Martin Buber, 'Between Man and

Man,' Ernst Cassirer, 'The Philosophy of Enlightenment,'
and 'Toward Freedom,' the autobiography of Jawaharlal Nehru.

Jewish Pocket Books [8]

From the scant information available on this series,
"Jewish Pocket Books" are published by the Spero Foundation
of New York, Cleveland and Jerusalem, in cooperation with
the Gudath Israel Youth Council of America, and are edited
by Rabbi Joseph Elias.

According to a pamphlet which was received in April, 1955,
as the only response to an inquiry about the firm's history and
operations, the series consists of twelve titles. Each costs
thirty-nine cents, and the entire series can be obtained as a
clothbound volume at $4.50. Five of the titles are by famous
Jewish authors such as Nathan Birnbaum, 'Confessions;' Judah
Halevi, 'The Kuzari' (Selections); Maimonides, 'The Faith of a
Jew.' The remaining titles are treatises on various Jewish
problems, all written or compiled by Rabbi Elias.

Harper & Brothers -- Harper Torchbooks [9]

Founded in 1817 as J. & J. Harper, the firm printed as its
first title Seneca's 'Morals' for Evert Duyckinck and published
in the following year Locke's 'Essay Concerning Human Understanding.' As other brothers joined the firm, the name was
changed to Harper & Brothers in 1833. Over the last one
hundred and fifty years Harper has maintained a high literary
and educational level in publications of classic and contemporary authors.

A number of magazines contributed in spreading the fame
of the publishers; 'Harper's Weekly,' 'Harper's Bazaar,'
'Harper's Young People,' and 'Harper's Magazine,' the latter
having survived successfully and with great distinction to the
present day.

"Harper Torchbooks" are the firm's only paperback series
and the first series of a trade publisher specifically designed
for the religious interdenominational market. Titles are chosen
to represent a broad spectrum of viewpoints and themes. The
series was started in September, 1956, and contained twenty-
four titles by the end of 1957, with three additional groups of
six titles scheduled for publication every year. Prices range

from ninety-five cents to $1.95. Covers are of dull, smooth, fairly thin paperstock and designs are chosen with rare skill and taste. Caroline Harris' cover for Karl Barth's 'The Word of God -- The Word of Man' and Leo Manso's design for George Santayana's, 'Winds of Doctrine and Platonism and the Spiritual Life' are among the most attractive of all higher-priced paperbacks. Some "Torchbooks" are also available in hard covers. Edition size is 10,000 copies. Titles include Johan Huizinga, 'Erasmus and the Age of Reformation,' Auguste Sabatier, 'Outlines of a Philosophy of Religion,' Martin Buber, 'Eclipse of God,' H. Richard Niebuhr, 'Christ and Culture,' Soren Kierkegaard, 'Purity of Heart.'

Meridian Books -- Living Age Books [10]

"Living Age Books" were inaugurated in August, 1956, as a paperback series designed for the intellectual and scholarly market. The books are primarily reprints of works dealing with Protestant philosophy and ethics and in many instances seem to be typical of the progressive, modern, intellectual approach to religion. Nineteen titles were published in the first year and a half, priced from $1.25 to $1.45. Editions run 15,000 copies. Outstanding titles include Reinhold Niebuhr, 'An Interpretation of Christian Ethics,' Paul Tillich, 'The Religious Situation,' Rudolph Bultmann, 'Primitive Christianity in Its Contemporary Setting' (an original publication), Ernest Lefever, 'Ethics and United States Foreign Policy.'

Abingdon Press -- Apex Books [11]

Abingdon Press is the publishing division of the Methodist Publishing House, the successor of the Methodist Book Concern, established in 1789 in a back room of Old St. George's Church in Philadelphia. Its first book was John Wesley's 'Christian Pattern.' In 1804 the Book Concern moved to New' York City. The different publishing organizations of the Methodist Church (the Methodist Protestant Book Concern, established 1828, the Western Book Concern, established 1839, and the Methodist Publishing House of the Methodist Episcopal Church, established 1844) were merged under the present name in 1939, after the unification of the Church. It is the largest Protestant denominational publishing organization in the United States and has an active backlist of over 1500 items. Four and one-half million copies of its books were produced during the fiscal year of 1956/57. The firm's total advertising budget runs over $300,000 annually. The new office building and plant in Nashville, Tennessee, which employs about 1000 persons was completed in the fall of 1957 at the cost of five million dollars. The firm has fifteen retail stores and six salesmen distribute its publications also to regular and religious book stores and other trade channels.

Abingdon Press not only provides Methodist books, pamphlets and magazines but also religious materials for the interdenominational Protestant market and non-sectarian releases such as children's recreational and leisure-time books. The most extensive recent work was the 'Interpreter's Bible,' a twelve-volume work which was compiled by one hundred and forty editors and writers over a period of ten years, and required an investment of more than one million dollars. The successful journal, 'Religion in Life,' is approaching a quarter of a century of existence.

The paperback series "Apex Books" appeared in March, 1957, and fourteen titles were produced during the first year which are to be followed annually by eight additional books, all reprints of Abingdon publications for which a wider readership is sought. Editions average 10,000 copies. The best-seller to date is George A. Buttrick's 'Prayer,' which sold about 5000 copies in four months. Other publications are Ralph W. Sockman, 'The Higher Happiness,' Frederick C. Grant, 'An Introduction to New Testament Thought,' and Edgar J. Goodspeed, 'How Came the Bible?' The books are attractively designed in three colors, measure 5 3/8" x 8 1/4" and are bound in rather strong boards. They sell for $1.00 to $1.50.

Association Press -- Reflection Books[12]

The Young Men's Christian Association began to release pamphlets in 1865 which stressed the advantages to be derived from religious devotion and physical exercise. By 1907 it was decided to start a publishing organization under the name Association Press, which had its beginnings in a small office in the Twenty-Ninth Street "Y" in New York City. During the first year of operation twenty-eight new pamphlets were released, among them 'Jesus the Joyous Comrade,' 'How to

Deal with Temptation' and 'Camping for Boys.'

Frederick M. Harris, director of the Press from 1915 to the late 1920's, put "Y" publishing on a professional basis and enlarged its scope. He encouraged Harry Emerson Fosdick and Dale Carnegie to write their first books which he published, and was responsible for the increased interest in the problem of juvenile delinquency. Dr. Fosdick's first title, 'The Second Mile,' is still selling today and Dale Carnegie's 'Public Speaking' and 'Influencing Men in Business' has gone through fifty printings, three revised editions and sold millions of copies. During the Second World War, Association Press assisted in the preparation of books and pamphlets for the Protestant section of the USO. After the war an increasing number of titles dealing in human relations and marriage problems appeared. Evelyn Millis Duvall's 'Facts of Life and Love for Teenagers' became a national bestseller and sold over one million copies in all editions, including the "Popular Library" paperback. The spring 1958 list includes 'The Art of Dating' by the same author. Association Press is the world's largest non-profit, non-church-owned organization publisher and generally releases between fifty and sixty titles annually.

"Reflection Books" were started in March, 1957, to "provide churchgoers with popular but substantial material dealing with aspects of Christian faith and daily Christian living." A group of six titles is issued twice a year in editions of 15,000 to 25,000 copies. The books, uniformly priced at fifty cents, are small (4½" x 6"), with glossy covers designed by André Ecuyer in two to four color prints. The designs are in good taste but not as sophisticated as the higher-priced lines. Titles include 'What Archeology Says about the Bible' by Albert N. Williams, 'The Promise of Prayer' by John L. Casteel (advertised as "a 'Reflection Book' that is more for doing than for reading"), and 'Sex and the Christian Life' by Seward Hiltner. The books are displayed in 1500 churches to which they are delivered in self-contained pre-packaged expendable display cases holding forty-eight books in sixteen pockets. "Reflection Books" are also sold through religious and denominational book stores, trade outlets and the Religion Book Club.

[1]Questionnaire, 1957. Lehmann-Haupt, op. cit., pp. 235-36.

[2] Correspondence with Quentin M. Phillip, March 1955. "Tips to the Booksellers," 'Publishers' Weekly,' CLIX:11, (March 17, 1951), pp. 1357-58. No information received since 1955.

[3]Correspondence with Father Robert Edman, 1955; questionnaire, 1957.

[4]Letter from Father Edman, January 7, 1955.

[5]Personal interview with John J. Delaney, January, 1955; questionnaire, 1957.

[6] Correspondence with Dorothy Pocinki, 1955; Jeannette Hopkins, 'Books That Will Not Burn' (Boston: The Beacon Press, 1954); questionnaire, 1957.

[7]Hopkins, op. cit., p. 7, citing The American Unitarian Association.

[8]Jewish Pocket Books pamphlet. No additional information received.

[9]Questionnaire, 1957.

[10]Questionnaire, 1957. "Meridian Announces New Paperback Religious Series," 'Publishers' Weekly,' CLXXIX:1 (January 7, 1956), p. 34. For firm history see Noonday Press-Meridian Books.

[11]Questionnaire, 1957.

[12]Questionnaire, 1957.

SELECTED BIBLIOGRAPHY

Books, Pamphlets and Theses

American Books Abroad. A Report of a Conference called by the National Book Committee, Princeton, N. J., September 29-30, 1955. New York: R. R. Bowker Co., [1955.]

American Book Trade Directory. 13th ed. New York: R. R. Bowker Co., 1956.

Andrews, William L. Bibliopegy in the United States and Kindred Subjects. New York: Dodd, Mead and Co., 1902.

Andrews, William L. The Old Booksellers of New York and Other Papers. New York: Privately printed, 1895.

Blanshard, Paul. The Right to Read. Boston: Beacon Press, 1955.

Brun, Robert. Le Livre Francais. Paris: Librairie Larousse, 1948.

Burlingame, Roger. Of Making Many Books. New York: Charles Scribner's, 1946.

Carter, John. ABC for Book Collectors. London: Rupert Hart-Davis, 1952.

A Century of Book Publishing, 1848-1949. New York: D. Van Nostrand Co., 1948.

Chafee, Zechariah, Jr. Government and Mass Communications. 2 vols. Chicago: University of Chicago Press, 1947.

Chew, Samuel C. Fruit among the Leaves, an Anniversary Anthology. New York: Appleton-Century-Crofts, Inc., 1950.

The Complete and Unabridged Statement to the Gathings Committee by the New American Library of World Literature, Inc., New York: New American Library of World Literature, 1953. (?).]

Cowley, Malcolm. The Literary Situation. New York: Viking Press, 1954.

Cowley, Malcolm, and Smith, Bernard. (eds.) Books That Changed Our Minds. New York: Kelmscott Editions, 1939.

Cutler, John L. Gilbert Patten and His Frank Merriwell Stories. University of Maine Studies, Second Series, No. 13. Orono, Maine: University of Maine, 1934.

Diehl, Edith. Bookbinding: Its Background and Technique. 2 vols. New York: Rinehart & Co., 1946.

Downs, Robert B. Books That Changed the World. New York: New American Library of World Literature, 1956.

Eastman, Fred. Books That Have Shaped the World. Chicago: American Library Association, 1937.

Ede, Charles, (ed.) The Art of the Book. London & New York: The Studio Publications, 1951.

Esdaile, Arundell. A Student's Manual of Bibliography. 3d rev. ed. London: G. Allen & Unwin, Ltd., 1954.

Fünfzig Jahre der Verlagsbuchhandlung Bernhard Tauchnitz, Leipzig: Bernhard Tauchnitz Verlag, 1887.

Guinzburg, H. K., Frase, R. W., Waller, T. Books and the Mass Market. Urbana, Illinois: University of Illinois Press, 1953.

Hackett, Alice P. Sixty Years of Best Sellers, 1895-1955. New York: R. R. Bowker Co., 1956.

Haebich, Kathryn A. "High School Students' Use of Paperbounds." Unpublished Master's thesis, University of Chicago, 1956.

Haight, Anne L. Banned Books, 2d ed. New York: R. R. Bowker Co., 1955.

Haldeman-Julius, Emanuel. The First Hundred Million. New York: Simon & Schuster, 1928.

Hart, James D. The Popular Book; a History of America's Literary Taste. New York: Oxford University Press, 1950.

The Harvest: Being the Record of One Hundred Years of Publishing, 1837-1937. Leipzig: Bernhard Tauchnitz, 1937.

The History of the Council on Books in War Time -- 1942-1946. New York: Country Life Press, 1946.

Hopkins, Jeannette. Books that Will not Burn. Boston: Beacon Press 1954.

Jamieson, John A. Books for the Army. New York: Columbia University Press, 1950.

Jeremias, Günther. Das Billige Buch. Entwicklungs- und Erscheinungsformen. Inaugural Dissertation zur Erlangung der Doktorswürde genehmigt von der Philosophischen Fakultät der Friedrich-Wilhelms Universität zu Berlin. Berlin: Triltsch & Huther, 1938.

Johannsen, Albert. The House of Beadle and Adams and its Dime and Nickel Novels. 2 vols. Norman: University of Oklahoma Press, 1950.

Joseph, Michael. The Adventure of Publishing. London: Allan Wingate, 1949.

Kerr, Chester. A Report on American University Presses. Ann Arbor: Edwards Bros., 1949.

Kyriss, Ernst. Verzierte Gotische Einbände im Alten Deutschen Sprachgebiet. 2 vols. Stuttgart: Max Hettler Verlag, 1953.

Lange, Wilhelm H. Das Buch im Wandel der Zeiten. Wiesbaden: F. Steiner, 1951.

Lehmann-Haupt, H., Wroth, L. C., and Silver, R. G., The Book in America. 2d ed. New York: R. R. Bowker Co., 1951.

Lehmann-Haupt, Hellmut (ed.). Bookbinding in America. Portland, Maine: The Southworth-Anthoensen Press, 1941.

The Literary Market Place, 1957-58. New York: R. R. Bowker Co., 1957.

Little, Brown & Co. One Hundred Years of Publishing, 1837-1937. Boston: Little, Brown & Co., 1937.

Mann, Thomas. Hundert Jahre Reclam. Festrede . . . Gehalten bei dem Festakt Anlässlich der Hundert-Jahr-Feier des Verlages Philipp Reclam, jun . . . Leipzig: Verlag von Philipp Reclam jun., 1928.

A Manual on Foreign Trade for University Presses. n.p.: The Association of American University Presses, 1956.

McKeon, R., Merton, R. K., Gellhorn, W. The Freedom to Read. Published for the National Book Committee. New York: R. R. Bowker Co., 1957.

McKerrow, Ronald B. An Introduction to Bibliography for Literary Students. 2d impr. Oxford: Oxford University Press, 1928.

Meiner, Annemarie. Reclam. Eine Geschichte der Universalbibliothek zu ihrem 75 jährigen Bestehen. Leipzig: Reclam Verlag, 1942.

Meynell, Francis. English Printed Books. London: Collins, 1948.

Miller, William. The Book Industry. New York: Columbia University Press, 1949.

Mott, Frank Luther. Golden Multitudes. New York: Macmillan Co., 1947.

Muir, Percy H. Book-Collecting as a Hobby. New York: Alfred A. Knopf, 1947.

Mumby, Frank Arthur. Publishing and Bookselling. New and rev. ed. London: Jonathan Cape, 1949.

1956 Annual Survey of the General Book Publishing Industry. New York: American Book Publishers Council, Inc., 1957.

Paperbound Books in Print. New York: R. R. Bowker Co., 1955-1957.

Penguins, a Retrospect, 1935-1951. Harmondsworth, Middlesex: Penguin Books, Ltd. 1952 (?) .

Plant, Marjorie. The English Book Trade. London: G. Allen & Unwin, Ltd., 1939.

Reynolds, Quentin. The Fiction Factory or From Pulp Row to Quality Street. New York: Random House, 1955.

Sadleir, Michael. Authors and Publishers. London: J. M. Dent & Sons, Ltd., 1939.

Sadleir, Michael. The Evolution of Publishers' Binding Styles, 1770-1900. London: Constable & Co., 1930.

Sheehan, Donald. This Was Publishing. A Chronicle of the Book Trade in the Gilded Age. Bloomington. Indiana University Press, 1952.

Shove, Raymond H. Cheap Book Production in the United States, 1870 to 1891. Urbana: University of Illinois Library, 1937.

Stefferud, Alfred (ed.) The Wonderful World of Books. Boston: Houghton Mifflin Co., 1953.

Steinberg, Sigfrid H. Five Hundred Years of Printing. Harmondsworth, Middlesex: Penguin Books, Ltd., 1955.

Stern, Madeleine B. Imprints on History. Book Publishers and the American Frontiers. Bloomington: Indiana University Press, 1956.

Tews, Johannes. Geistespflege in der Volksgemeinschaft. Berlin: Gesellschaft für Volksbildung, 1932.

Townsend, Atwood H. (ed.). Good Reading. Prepared by the Committee on College Reading. New York: The New American Library, 1954.

U. S. Congress, House of Representatives. Report of the Select Committee on Current Pornographic Materials. House Report No. 2510 pursuant to H.R. 596. 82nd Congress, 2d Session. Washington: Government Printing Office, 1952.

Wallace, Irving. The Fabulous Originals. New York: Alfred A. Knopf, 1955.

Weiss, Harry B. A Book About Chapbooks. Trenton, N.J.: Privately printed, 1942.

Wertham, Fredric. Seduction of the Innocent. New York: Rinehart & Co., 1954.

Widman, Hans. Geschichte des Buchhandels vom Altertum bis zur Gegenwart. Wiesbaden: Otto Harrassowitz, 1952.

Williams, Sir William E. The Penguin Story. Harmondsworth, Middlesex: Penguin Books, Ltd., 1956.

Winship, George P. The Cambridge Press. 1638-1692. Philadelphia: University of Pennsylvania Press, 1945.

Wroth, Lawrence C. The Colonial Printer. 2d ed. Portland, Maine: The Southworth-Anthoensen Press, 1938.

Articles and Chapters in Books and Periodicals

"Annual World Production of Library Materials," Library of Congress Information Bulletin, October 25, 1954, pp. 1-5.

Asheim, Lester. "Afterword to New Problems in Plotting the Future of the Book," Library Quarterly, XXV:4, Oct. 1955, pp. 384-85.

Asheim, Lester and Underbrink, Robert. "A Hard Look at Soft Covers," Library Quarterly, XXVIII:1, pp. 18-26.

Balleny, W., "British Paperback Survey; a Report to the Publishers' Association's Paperback Group," Publishers' Circular and Booksellers' Record, vol. 171, May 18, 1957, pp. 598-99.

"Bigger and Better Book Business," Business Week, No. 1419, Nov. 10, 1956, pp. 72-83.

"Books for the Masses," New Republic, Vol. XCII, Oct. 6, 1937, pp. 229-30.

Borchardt, Georges. "French Publishing in 1955," Publishers' Weekly, CLXVIII:10, Sept. 3, 1955, pp. 867-68.

Borchardt, Georges. "French Publishing in 1956," Publishers' Weekly, CLXX:9, Aug. 25, 1956, pp. 880-81.

Cerf, Bennett, "Trade Winds," Saturday Review, XXXVI:51, Dec. 19, 1953, pp. 5-6.

"Cheap Books," Time, XXXIV:2, July 10, 1939, pp. 63-66.

Cohen, Arthur A., "Oversize Paperbooks; with some Asides on Paperbooks in General," Publishers' Weekly, CLXIX:1, Jan 7, 1956, pp. 24-26.

Cousins, Norman, "Revolution in Cardboards," Saturday Review, XXXVIII:45, Nov. 5, 1955, p. 22.

Deale, H. Vail, "Library Sells Paperbounds," Library Journal, LXXIX:21, Dec. 1, 1954, pp. 2296-97.

DeGraff, Robert F., "Cheap Editions to Widen the Ownership of Books," Publishers' Weekly, CXXX:16, April 22, 1939, p. 1499.

Dempsey, David, "The State of Business (1954) Along Publishers' Row," New York Times Book Review, LX:1, Jan. 2, 1955, p. 23.

"Emanuel Haldeman-Julius," Publishers' Weekly, CLX:6, Aug. 11, 1951, p. 564.

Enoch, Kurt, "The Mass Media: Challenge/Chimera?" Essential Books, I:5, June, 1956, pp. 10-13.

Enoch, Kurt, "Need for Integrity in Paperback Publishing," Publishers' Weekly, CLXVIII:21, Nov. 19, 1955, pp. 2142-45.

Enoch, Kurt, "The Paperbound Book: Twentieth-Century Publishing Phenomenon," Library Quarterly, XXIV:3, July, 1954, pp. 211-25.

Fadiman, Clifton, "Party of One," Holiday, XIX:3, March, 1956, pp. 6-14.

Gaster, Bertha, "Pocket Books: a Coin in the Slot and Out Pops Plato," UNESCO Courier, Feb. 1947, pp. 23-34.

Gelderblom, Gertrude, "Paperbound Books and Public Libraries," UNESCO Bulletin for Libraries, X:2-3, Feb.-March, 1956, pp. 55-59.

Hale, Arthur. "Mass Market Paperbacks," What Happens in Book Publishing, edited by Chandler B. Grannis. New York: Columbia University Press, 1957, pp. 371-79.

Hellman, Geoffrey T., "Alfred A. Knopf, Publisher," The New Yorker, Vol. XXIV, Nov. 20, 1948, pp. 44-56, Nov. 27, 1948, pp. 36-52, Dec. 4, 1948, pp. 40-53.

"Hot Melts Bind a Market," Chemical Week, No. 73, July 18, 1953, p. 68.

Jackson, William A., "Printed Wrappers of the Fifteenth to the Eighteenth Centuries," Harvard Library Bulletin, VI:3, Autumn 1952, pp. 313-21.

Jennison, Peter S., "How American Books Reach Readers Abroad," Library Trends, V:1, July 1956, pp. 5-16.

Kuhns, Elinor C., "Paperback Expendables," Library Journal, LXXIX:19, Nov. 1, 1954, pp. 2059-62.

Lamb, Lynton, "Penguin Books -- Style and Mass Production," The Penrose Annual, 1952, Vol. XLVI. London: Lund-Humphries & Co. Ltd., 1952, pp. 39-42.

Lane, Sir Allen. "Paper-bound Books," The Book World Today, edited by John Hampden. London: G. Allen & Unwin, Ltd., 1957. pp. 101-104.

Lewis, Freeman, "Books and the Mass Market," Publishers' Weekly, CLXVI:16, Oct. 16, 1954, pp. 1664-68.

Lewis, Freeman, "Paper-bound Books in America," Bowker Lectures on Book Publishing. New York: R. R. Bowker Co., 1957, pp. 306-35.

Lewis, Roy, "Paperbacks," The Bowater Papers, No. 3. London: The Bowater Paper Corporation, Ltd., 1954, pp. 54-62.

"Lively Newcomer in a Creaky Industry," Business Week. No. 1218, Jan. 3, 1953, pp. 42-45.

McCarthy, William H. Jr., "An Outline of the History of Bookbinding," The Dolphin, No. 3, A History of the Printed Book. New York: Limited Editions Club, 1938, pp. 447-61.

Melcher, Frederic G., "Paper Books at the Turn of the Century," Publishers' Weekly, CLXVII:17, April 23, 1955, p. 1948.

Melcher, Frederic G., "The Publisher as a Factor in Popular Reading," The Practice of Book Selection. edited by Louis R. Wilson. Chicago: University of Chicago Press, 1940, pp. 272-87.

Pollard, Graham, "Serial Fiction," New Paths in Book Collecting; Essays by Various Hands, edited by John Carter. London: Constable & Co., 1934, pp. 245-277.

Porter, Arabel J. "New American Library Celebrates Tenth Anniversary," Publishers' Weekly, CLXXIII:11, March 17, 1958, pp. 22-24.

"Reading Plan and Cahen's Report on Cold Adhesive are BMI Highlights," Publishers' Weekly, CLXVIII:19, Nov. 5, 1955, pp. 2004-08.

Redman, Ben R., "A Quartet of Revivals," Saturday Review, Vol. XXXVI, Nov. 21, 1953, p. 55.

"Resinous Adhesives for Book Binders," Chemical Age, No. 59, Sept. 12, 1953, pp. 547-48.

Rorty, James, "The Harassed Pocket-Book Publishers," The Antioch Review, XV:3, December 1955, pp. 411-27.

Sadleir, Michael, "Yellow-Backs," New Paths in Book Collecting, Essays by Various Hands, edited by John Carter. London: Constable & Co., 1934, pp. 125-161.

Schick, Frank L., "American Paperbacks -- the Evolution of a Success Story," Publishers' Circular and Booksellers' Record, Vol. 171, May 18, 1957, pp. 602-04.

Schick, Frank L., "Trends in Publications Affecting Binding and Conservation," Library Trends, IV:3, Jan. 1956, pp. 222-38.

Schmoller, Hans, "Reprints; Aldine and After," The Penrose Annual, 1953, Vol. XLVII. London: Lund Humphries & Co., 1953, pp. 35-38.

Smith, Vernon M., "Trials; Paperbound Originals," Law Library Journal, XLIX:8, Aug. 1956, p. 267.

Stone, E.O. and Melvin, M.B., "Paperbounds Go to College," Library Journal, LXXX:14, Aug. 1, 1955, pp. 1644-49.

Strehler, H., "Pocket-books on the Continent," The Penrose Annual 1954, Vol. XLVIII. London: Lund Humphries, 1954, pp. 33-34.

Strout, Donald E., "Paperbound Books -- Boon or Bane," Nature and Development of the Library Collection. Urbana: University of Illinois Library School, 1957, pp. 35-62.

Urgoiti, Jose N., "Spain," Printing in the Twentieth Century, A Survey, London: Times Publishing Co., Ltd., 1930, p. 261.

Whipple, Leon, "Books on Main Street," Survey Graphic, Vol. XXVII, March 1938, pp. 174-75.

Winship, George T., "The Literature of Printing," The Dolphin, No. 3, A History of the Printed Book. New York: Limited Editions Club, 1938, pp. 471-491.

Winterich, John T., "Rinehart Celebrates Its 25th Anniversary," Publishers' Weekly, CLXVI:10, Sept. 4, 1954, pp. 826-32.

INDEX

The index contains references to significant terms, facts, firms and personalities relevant to the development of paperback publishing as treated in the preceding pages. If three or more entries appear under a single heading and one could be identified as most pertinent, it is underlined. No page references are given for authors or titles mentioned throughout the text because these serve merely illustrative purposes.

257